Complex Issues in Child Custody Evaluations

To my parents, Perle and Mort,
who always encouraged me to do my best,
and to my grandmother, Geetcha,
who was always sensitive to the needs of others.

Complex Issues in Child Custody Evaluations

Philip M. Stahl

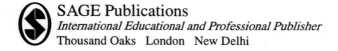

SAGE Publications
International Educational and Professional Publisher
Thousand Oaks   London   New Delhi

For information:

 SAGE Publications, Inc.
2455 Teller Road
Thousand Oaks, California 91320
E-mail: order@sagepub.com

SAGE Publications Ltd.
6 Bonhill Street
London EC2A 4PU
United Kingdom

SAGE Publications India Pvt. Ltd.
M-32 Market
Greater Kailash I
New Delhi 110 048 India

Printed in the United States of America

Library of Congress Cataloging-in-Publication Data

Stahl, Philip Michael.
    Complex issues in child custody evaluations / by Philip M. Stahl.
       p. cm.
    Includes bibliographical references and index.
    ISBN 0-7619-1099-9 (cloth: alk. paper)
    ISBN 0-7619-1277-0 (pbk.: alk. paper)
    1. Custody of children—United States—Evaluation. I. Title.
KF547 .S725 1999
346.7301'73—dc21   98-40245

This book is printed on acid-free paper.

99 00 01 02 03 04 05 7 6 5 4 3 2 1

Acquiring Editor:	Jim Nageotte
Editorial Assistant:	Heidi Van Middlesworth
Production Editor:	Diana E. Axelsen
Editorial Assistant:	Nevair Kabakian
Typesetter/Designer:	Lynn Miyata
Indexer:	Virgil Diodato
Cover Designer:	Michelle Lee

Contents

Acknowledgments

Giving birth to a book requires much love and labor. I want to first thank Ann Milne and Peter Salem of the Association of Family and Conciliation Courts. Without their support, I would not have had the opportunity to be a presenter at conferences and learn as much as I have about child custody and child custody evaluations. Second, I wish to thank Jim Nageotte and Margaret Zusky of Sage Publications for their ongoing encouragement of my writing. I have known Margaret for many years, as she was the editor of my first book, *Children on Consignment,* a book for foster parents about foster children. Margaret helped me with the early editorial tasks associated with this book, while Jim moved the book into print.

I wish to thank Theresa Schuman and Rosemary Vasquez. Terry and I have worked together on various task forces, and she has maintained an expertise in sex abuse evaluations. Without her efforts, I would not have a chapter on sex abuse allegations. Rosemary and I have worked together in our local community, and she has helped raise my awareness of cultural issues in divorce. She contributed the chapter on culture for the book.

I particularly want to thank my many friends and colleagues who read early drafts of this book and whose editorial comments and words of wisdom helped me to clarify my own thinking while suggesting other places to look for important information. This includes evaluators Milton Schaefer and Andrea Jeremey of Bay Tree Psychology Associates; Phil Bushard and Joel Glassman from AFCC; John Osborne, Shary Nunan, Karen Hobbs, and Randi Johnson from the Family Resolution Center; Rhonda Barovsky and Benita Smith of Contra Costa County Family Court Services; and evaluators Lindsay Patton,

Peggie Ward, Beth Clark, Lynne Markam, and Sherrie Bourg Carter. I would like to also thank my friend and attorney colleague Stuart Goldware; my cousin Eryn Kalish, an excellent editor; and attorneys Dee Samuels, Marcia Lassiter, and Dan Harkins.

I also want to thank Terry Czapinski, who typed early drafts of this manuscript, and my brother Stan for helping me with computer and technical assistance. I wish to thank the many children of divorce who continue to teach me about their feelings and show me how divorce affects them.

Finally, I again want to thank my wife, Ruth, whose love and support have inspired me to complete this project. She helped to edit many drafts of this book. I also thank my children, Jason and Rebecca. Jason has provided valuable insight into many of these complex issues along with excellent editorial skills. Rebecca continues to have a keen sense of humor that keeps me focused on enjoying my life, even when I work too hard. Their love and inspiration have helped me stay focused on the needs of all children, no matter what I do.

Introduction

Over the past several years, since completion of *Conducting Child Custody Evaluations: A Comprehensive Guide* (Stahl, 1994a) and the subsequent publishing of two other books on custody evaluations (Ackerman, 1995; Bricklin, 1995), the task of child custody evaluations has become increasingly complicated. There has been evolving research on the effects of divorce on children and on factors that contribute to the success or failure of shared and sole custody.

At conferences around the United States, in local court-affiliated trainings, and from my own experience, I have observed that custody evaluations have grown more complex. In the late 1980s and early 1990s, the typical complex custody evaluation was seen in the area of child sexual abuse. More recently, however, there has been a significant growth in allegations of parental alienation, domestic violence, and high conflict between the parents. In addition, with economic and employment opportunities changing, there has been an increased need for many parents of divorce to consider moving away from the other parent. Courts are increasingly faced with a tough dilemma in this area.

In many states, legislatures have taken to "solving" some of these problems, though some of their solutions have not worked well for children. At other times, courts have made rulings that seem to resolve other problems of divorce. Whatever the legal or judicial decisions, courts are looking more frequently to the child custody evaluator to help in understanding and providing recommendations for families of divorce.

My previous book focused largely on the basic issues in child custody evaluations, the processes involved in interviewing adults and children, and the nuts and bolts of providing information to the court. While touching on some of the professional and ethical issues and focusing a bit on the more complex issues, it was beyond the scope of that book to go into such detail.

In contrast, this book is written for that purpose. By devoting a separate chapter to each of several complex issues facing custody evaluators today, this book is a logical outgrowth from the first one, and it is designed to provide evaluators with the salient information and research on a variety of topics. Each chapter focuses on a different complex task, guiding the evaluator to the important skills necessary for understanding each of them.

The book will be presented in three parts. Part I is about the complex issues. These include the alienation and alignment of children (Chapter 1), domestic violence (Chapter 2), sexual abuse (Chapter 3), and move-away evaluations (Chapter 4). Each of these chapters will initially present the relevant research and focus on the tasks for the evaluator who wants to practically apply that research to a given family. For many of the issues, a range of potential recommendations will also be included.

Part II is on children and report issues. These include the effects of high conflict on children (Chapter 5), child considerations in custody evaluations (Chapter 6), and the components of an evaluator's recommendations (Chapter 7). In these chapters, the primary focus will be on the needs and issues of the children, whose interests custody evaluations are designed to protect.

Part III focuses on advanced professional issues. These topics include the use and misuse of psychological testing (Chapter 8), cultural issues (Chapter 9), testifying in court (Chapter 10), and ethics (Chapter 11). Though some of these issues (e.g., the use and misuse of psychological testing) have been addressed somewhat in other publications, others (e.g., culture) have never been directed to the child custody evaluator.

The focus of this book is on the complexity of child custody evaluations. I believe that many areas need to be explored when doing child custody evaluations. In most custody evaluations, this will include the following:

- ❖ the psychological functioning of each parent;
- ❖ the history of the parents' relationship;
- ❖ the parenting skills and relative strengths and weaknesses of each parent;
- ❖ the quality of the relationships between the child and each parent;
- ❖ the child's relationships with siblings;
- ❖ the degree of family violence or abuse, if any;
- ❖ the intensity of the parents' conflict and the degree to which the child is exposed to the conflict;
- ❖ the temperament, emotional functioning, and needs of the child;

❖ the developmental needs of the child; and

❖ the ability (or inability) of the parents to work together to meet the child's needs.

Depending on the particular evaluation, additional areas that may need to be explored are the following:

❖ the degree of alignment and alienation in the child's relationships and reasons for such alignment,

❖ geographic issues (with move-aways),

❖ sexual abuse issues, and

❖ the impact of a parent's own childhood on the current dynamics.

In all evaluations, the evaluator will focus on many of these components. Depending on the evaluation, a range of issues will be explored and reported on. For every child custody evaluation, the pertinent issues must be addressed and integrated into the "best interests of the child." Each evaluation must be guided by the statutes of the state in which the evaluator lives. The evaluator must know the laws and statutes in his or her state. For example, he or she might need to know if there are rules on relocation or if the statute requires the evaluator to consider domestic violence as more important than frequent and continuing contact. For example, in California, the health, safety, and welfare of the child (in the areas of abuse) take precedence over the need for frequent and continuing contact with each parent.

The material for this book continues to be based on the sum of my experience, gained from meetings, conferences and workshops, readings, participation on task forces related to custody work, and my own custody evaluations. I have been fortunate to teach at National Judicial College, several family courts around the country, and the California Statewide Office of Family Court Services. Wherever I teach, I learn that the task of child custody evaluations is a complex one.

I have also learned that some people do not understand how complex and difficult this task can be. As a result, I have some worries. I worry that legislatures may try to oversimplify the issues, through a presumption that any one issue (e.g., domestic violence) is more important than any other (e.g., the child's developmental needs) for a family. I worry when courts try to oversimplify the issues by either encouraging evaluators to be short and brief or making rulings that tend to polarize the problems. I worry when judges, attorneys, and evaluators do not understand that there are limits to the "truths" one can learn in any given evaluation. This tends to cause evaluators to stretch beyond the data.

I worry when evaluators have little or no training in this complex field, believing that they are qualified to perform child custody evaluations simply because they have read a book or know how to perform family interviews or psychological testing. Novices need experience gained by work in the field, an understanding of the research, and supervision, consultation, or a combination of both. In particular, I have found that evaluations of child alignment and alienation and child sexual abuse require advanced training. For example, issues of alignment are very complex and difficult, as there is a need to focus on each parent and the children individually as well as on the way in which the dynamic surfaces for the family as a whole. Similarly, evaluations of child sexual abuse require familiarity with the research on divorce, sexually abused children, and offenders.

I worry when evaluators oversimplify the issues in a given evaluation by either relying on limited and discrete pieces of data or misinterpreting the data. I especially worry when mental health professionals testify in court, because it is so easy to avoid taking a position when we have one, just as it is too easy to become rigid and dogmatic in the defense of our conclusions. I worry that mental health professionals do not have enough information and direction on ethical issues, as I often hear about practices that include one-sided evaluations, dual roles, and being a hired gun. I worry about experts who are arrogant and try to bully parents into accepting their work.

I worry that licensing boards do not understand the special issues pertaining to child custody evaluations as they investigate licensing complaints. They might either ignore valid complaints against a poorly done custody evaluation or misinterpret or overreact to complaints, not understanding the ways in which child custody evaluations differ from other work in the field. They may also not understand the dynamics that are often involved with high-conflict families of divorce.

Finally, I worry about the children, for whom many decisions are being made with limited research data. I believe that their needs must always come before the competing demands of the parents and that the psychological development of the child is paramount.

I believe that, before someone can make decisions that affect the lives of children and families, he or she must have an understanding of the elements necessary for a child's healthy growth and development and must have knowledge about the impact that divorce, in particular high-conflict divorce, has on children and families. Evaluators must have a basic familiarity with the legal system in the community in which they work. If you are unfamiliar with your state's laws, I encourage you to talk with local judges and attorneys, contact government offices for the statutes, or look to the Internet for government pages that have those rules. Most states now have their statutes online. For example, at the time of publication, the California laws and regulations could be found at

http://www.ca.gov/s/govt/govcode.html

A Web page linking many states' codes can be found at

http://www.nasire.org/ss/STstates.html

I also encourage you to join local, state, and national interdisciplinary groups, such as the Association of Family and Conciliation Courts. Finally, I urge you to study the literature and obtain consultation when necessary.

It is my hope that this book crystallizes some of the critical issues that have been touched on in other places or ignored altogether in the past. With the information provided on these issues, custody evaluators can tackle increasingly complex tasks with more confidence and thoroughness. As with any work in this field, it is important to recognize that the research is still limited and our understanding grows each year. As we come to understand these complex issues in a more thorough way, the task for the courts and evaluators can grow easier over time.

What I said in the introduction of my previous book still holds true today.

> I have learned much since 1985, especially from the families with whom I work. I have learned that there are certain principles and standards which must be maintained when doing custody evaluations. I have learned that children cannot be viewed as property, and divorcing parents need to be taught to share their children, . . . and share in the parenting. More than anything, I have learned that we must understand the family divorce through the eyes of the children. We must understand how the children feel, what they fear and wish, and what makes conflict resolution difficult to achieve. We need to stay focused on the needs of the children, who are vulnerable to the actions of their parents, and who have the most to gain with a healthy resolution of the divorce conflict. (p. x)

I still have much to learn, and I expect to continue conferencing, training, reading, and networking with others in this burgeoning field. It is my hope that child custody evaluators, mediators, attorneys, and judges can learn more about the many complex issues in child custody work so that we can help parents make appropriate decisions for their children of divorce.

PART I

CHAPTER 1

Alienation and Alignment of Children

Prior to 1970, it was rare that parents disputed custody of their children. Beginning in the early 1970s, parents began litigating over child custody as a result of changes in societal factors and custody laws. In a divorce study group meeting of the American Orthopsychiatric Association in 1984, participants noted a rise in sexual abuse allegations within the context of divorce. Following that meeting, a number of researchers began to look at the question of sexual abuse allegations in divorce, with the first articles on sexual abuse allegations in divorce being written in the mid-1980s. (For more on that subject, see Chapter 3.)

In 1987, Dr. Richard Gardner, a psychiatrist in New Jersey who had previously written extensively on divorce issues and child custody, first outlined the concept of parental alienation syndrome. Since then, various researchers and attorneys have written about parental alienation, offering a variety of causes of and solutions to this growing problem. There is a significant dispute among the experts about whether parental alienation is a "syndrome," as well as about the causes and remedies of parental alienation. This chapter will describe the alignment and alienation of children, review the literature in the field, and provide a direction for the evaluator in approaching this issue, both during the evaluation process and with regard to recommendations.

For purposes of this chapter, I am accepting the premise that alienation exists and that the child is caught in the battle between the *alienating* parent and the *alienated* parent. Alienation can occur in both directions so that, at various times, the alienating parent is being alienated against and vice versa. Unfortunately, there is little research on the effects of alienation on children, including the long-term impact on a child being alienated from a parent, the long-term impact of a change of custody to remedy alienation, or even which qualities of the child help to mitigate against the alienating behaviors of both parents. Despite this lack of research, evaluators are being asked to address this complicated issue. It is my view that the primary tasks for the evaluator are to

❖ understand the emotional dynamics of all family members, including the alienating parent, the alienated parent, *and* the child;

❖ understand the impact of the alienation dynamics on the family system;

❖ explore the child's alignments with both parents, recognizing that these alignments may be caused by the behaviors of one or both parents or by psychological dynamics in the child;

❖ assess the existence and intensity of parental alienation; and

❖ help the family and courts develop recommendations that are consistent with the best interests of the child.

WHAT IS PARENTAL ALIENATION?

According to Gardner (1992),

> The concept of Parental Alienation Syndrome includes much more than brainwashing. It includes not only conscious but subconscious and unconscious factors within the preferred parent that contribute to the parent's influencing the child's alienation. Furthermore [and this is extremely important], it includes factors that arise within the child—independent of the parental contributions—that foster the development of this syndrome. (pp. 59-60)

Gardner notes that the child becomes obsessed with hatred of the alienated parent. He also suggests that the hatred takes on a life of its own in which the child may justify the alienation as a result of "minor altercations experienced in the relationship with the hated parent" (p. 68). Gardner differentiates between three categories of alienation: mild, moderate, and severe. He acknowledges that there is a continuum along which these cases actually fall, and he believes that fitting them into a single category is not easy. In general, it is the intensity of the reported alienation and the quality of the relationships between the child and each parent that differentiate families between mild, moderate, and severe alienation.

Mild Cases of Parental Alienation

In mild cases, there are subtle attempts at turning the child against the other parent and drawing the child in to the alienated parent's view of the other parent. This may be both conscious and unconscious, and usually the alienating parent is not aware of how this makes the child feel. However, the alienating parent is usually supportive of the child having a relationship with the other parent. Usually in these instances of mild alienation, the primary motive is to look better than the other parent in the eyes of the child. For most children, the consequences of such mild alienation are minimal, and the alienation manifests itself as a slight increase in loyalty conflicts or anxiety but no fundamental change in the child's own view of the alienated parent.

Moderate Cases of Parental Alienation

The motivation on the part of the moderately alienating parent is much more aggressive. These parents are quite angry and often vengeful in their behavior toward the alienated parent. Feeling hurt, the alienating parent often expects the child to take sides and be loyal to him or her. Such parents may actively interfere with visitation arrangements, be derogatory of the other parent to the child, and actively participate in a process designed to limit or interfere with the child's relationship with the alienated parent. In these moderate cases, the alienating parent will still support the *concept* of a relationship between the child and the alienated parent but will at the same time consciously and unconsciously attempt to engage the child in a process that limits and reduces that time to a minimum. In these moderate cases, the alienating parent will often ignore court orders if he or she can get away with it. During litigation, these parents are unwavering about their view that the other parent is unsafe or cannot be trusted, yet they are more subtle with the child, friends, and therapists.

Most of the children in these moderate cases are filled with conflict. They show many of the symptoms of children in high-conflict families described by Johnston and Campbell (1988) and Johnston and Roseby (1997), including anxiety, splitting, insecurity, distortion, and so forth. They often express their *own* frustrated views about the alienated parent, some of which mirror the allegations made by the alienating parent and some of which are borne from their own relationship with the alienating parent. They tend to view the alienating parent as the "good parent" and the alienated parent as the "bad parent." However, they are able to integrate and discuss some good traits about the hated parent and some negative traits about the preferred parent. As long as the alienation is limited, these children can sometimes enjoy their relationship with the alienated parent.

Severe Cases of Parental Alienation

In severely alienated families, there is a clear, consistent derogation of the alienated parent by the alienating parent and by the child. In these more severe cases, there is a combination of programming, brainwashing, and hostility that begins with the alienating parent and is taken on by the child against the alienated parent. In most of these instances, the child and alienated parent had previously had a positive and relatively healthy relationship, although the alienating parent can neither admit nor perceive this. Often, the alienating parent feels a tremendous bitterness and anger toward the other parent, usually related to feelings of abandonment and betrayal. These families are quite intractable and may be difficult to evaluate when there are simultaneous abuse allegations. The alienated parent is often confused and outraged at the change in the child and rarely understands how this has occurred, except to blame the other parent. Children in these families often get caught up in the brainwashing and programming and take on the hostility of the alienating parent, exaggerating and denigrating the other parent in quite hostile ways.

With these families, the evaluator quite often observes that the words and phrases used by both the alienating parent and the child are nearly identical. These more severely alienated families have drawn the greatest attention and controversy in the popular press and the professional literature. Although these families are intense, they are rather few in number compared with the mild to moderate alienated families in which alienation is not too severe. The task for the evaluator is to understand the family dynamics, determine where the family exists along the continuum of alienation, and differentiate between alienating behaviors and those behaviors that may appear (on the surface) to be alienation but actually have different dynamics. This may include a myriad of parental issues, dynamics of the psychological splitting, child development issues, and so on. These evaluations, and particularly finding workable solutions, are among the more difficult and complex faced by the child custody evaluator.

REVIEW OF THE LITERATURE

Gardner (1987) was the first to coin the phrase *parental alienation syndrome,* but Wallerstein and Kelly (1980) were the first to write about a process that they termed "alignment with one parent." In their breakthrough book, *Surviving the Breakup,* they wrote,

A very important aspect of the response of the youngsters in this age group (ages nine to twelve) was the dramatic change in the relationship between parents and children. These young people were vulnerable to being swept up into the anger of one parent against the other. They were faithful and valuable battle allies in efforts to hurt the other parent. Not infrequently, they turned on the parent they had (previously) loved and been very close to prior to the marital separation. (p. 77)

Since that time, there has been very little research on child alignment or parental alienation. Instead, most authors have written about these issues from a rather subjective view. Gardner's first use of the term *parental alienation syndrome* in 1987 was elaborated in his later books (1992, 1995). Clawar and Rivlin (1991) wrote about programmed and brainwashed children in a book published by the American Bar Association Family Law Section. Johnston (1993; Johnston & Campbell, 1988) wrote about children who refused visitation, and others (Cartwright, 1993; Dunne & Hedrick, 1994; Garrity & Baris, 1994; Lund, 1995; Turkat, 1994; Ward & Harvey, 1993) have written about the psychological issues of parental alienation.

Each of these writers focuses on a continuum of alienation as originally identified by Gardner and suggests that these families are quite troublesome for the courts. There is a theme in these articles that mothers are more typically the *alienating* parent and fathers more typically the *alienated* parent. The alienating parent is portrayed as feeling rage and vindictiveness toward the alienated parent, and the child gets, as Wallerstein and Kelly (1980) said, "swept up" in this rage. In the most severe cases, these parents are seen as having a fundamental psychopathology. The effect of this alienation is dramatic on children.

From the writings, it appears that the children who are most susceptible to alienation are passive and dependent and generally feel a strong need to psychologically care for the alienating parent. In both the child and alienating parent, there is a sense of moral outrage at the alienated parent, and there is typically a fusion of feelings between the alienating parent and child such that they talk about the alienated parent as having hurt "us."

The long-term impact of alienation on children and families has not been well researched. The general view is that children in such families are likely to develop a variety of pathological symptoms. These include, but are not limited to,

❖ splittings in their relationships,

❖ difficulties in forming intimate relationships,

❖ a lack of ability to tolerate anger or hostility with other relationships,

❖ psychosomatic symptoms and sleep or eating disorders,

❖ psychological vulnerability and dependency,

❖ conflicts with authority figures, and

❖ an unhealthy sense of entitlement for one's rage that leads to social alienation in general.

Others (Waldron & Joanis, 1996; Ward & Harvey, 1993) refer to parental alienation as a "family system defense mechanism." They believe that the function of the defense may be to serve several purposes, including any or all of the following:

❖ protecting the alienating parent's self-esteem,

❖ maintaining the alienating parent's symbiotic dependence on the child,

❖ managing the anger and revenge felt by the child or alienated parent, or

❖ avenging the alienated parent's abandonment of the family.

The relationships between each parent and the child are typically fragile, even if they were both positive prior to the separation. When children are brought into the tug-of-war between the parents, they have a diminished ability to maintain healthy boundaries and relationships. Ultimately, this dynamic causes the alienating parent to reject anyone who perceives things in a way that the alienating parent does not like. In most instances, the family is so heavily invested in the alienating efforts that the root causes may be difficult to understand.

In addition to identifying the extent of the alienation on the continuum and the possible causes and effects of the alienation, perhaps the most controversial aspect of the literature has been about the remedies. For families whose alienation appears to be mild to moderate and whose safety concerns have been eliminated, there is general agreement that recommendations should include most of the following:

❖ forced consistent time between the child and the alienated parent;

❖ parent education to help both the alienated and alienating parent understand the tragic impact of conflictual divorce on children;

❖ therapy for the child that includes conjoint work with the alienated parent;

❖ depending on the nature of the problems with the alienating parent and the alienated parent, therapy for that parent as well; and

❖ a structured court order that provides clear direction to the family.

However, within those families labeled moderate to severe, there is wide disagreement about possible solutions. Gardner (1987) touched off this debate by suggesting that the best solution is a change of custody from the alienating parent to the alienated parent, with an initial cutoff of all contact between the alienating parent and child. In a variety of court cases in which there were allegations of sexual abuse, he has testified that the sexual abuse allegation was a form of parental alienation and that a change of custody was clearly in order. Turkat (1994) supported Gardner's position and recommended this change of custody in cases of severe parental alienation.

Gardner's remedy has led to a number of articles written by attorneys (Isman, 1996; Mauzerall, Young, & Alsaker-Burke, 1997; Wood, 1994) who dispute Gardner's view. They perceive his recommendation as extreme and dangerous. They question the existence of parental alienation syndrome, suggesting that it does not meet any objective standard in the mental health community. They believe that changing custody on the basis of a "syndrome" that does not exist is potentially damaging to children.

Others (Garrity & Baris, 1994; Johnston, 1993; Johnston & Roseby, 1997; Kelly, 1997; Waldron & Joanis, 1996; Ward & Harvey, 1993) prefer a more cautious approach to these severely alienated families. They feel that caution is necessary to balance the risk of harm to the child from being cut off from one parent (i.e., the alienated parent) with the risk from cutting the child off from the other parent (i.e., the alienating parent). One solution does not fit all families because children and their parents are quite different. Cautious recommendations are likely to include many of the following:

- ❖ a court order that recognizes the value of ongoing contact between the child and the alienated parent and establishes structure around that contact;

- ❖ a mental health professional working with the child, the family, or both to therapeutically support the contact; or

- ❖ the use of a case manager, special master, guardian ad litem, or parenting coordinator who would monitor the cooperation with the order and have the authority to enforce compliance or report to the court quickly when one parent is out of compliance.

There are several other things that can be helpful. It is important to avoid changing custody as a corrective tool. Although there may be times when a change of custody is indicated, it is most useful if there are significant problems other than alienation. If the alienating parent is in therapy, it is important to be supportive to the parent but simultaneously provide a clear and consistent message that the alienation is harmful to the child. If the alienating parent is currently in therapy with someone who supports the position of the alienating parent (i.e., contact between the child and the alienated parent should be non-existent), it may be necessary for the court to order a change of therapists to someone who understands the dynamics and can become part of the treatment team.

Finally, in the most extreme examples, in which nothing seems to be working and the child appears to be at significant risk, it may be necessary to help the alienated parent therapeutically disengage from the child until such time that the child can more adequately reestablish the relationship. From the perspective of the child, this may actually be a less damaging recommendation than a change of custody.

If it is understood that alienation is caused by splitting within the family, it is critical that those who try to work with the family (the attorneys, the judges, and the mental health professionals) are in agreement in their approach. If evaluators recognize that alienated family systems are emotionally powerful, it is easy to see how the professionals involved can become split among themselves. In more extreme alienated families, the case manager will watch that the professionals do not succumb to the family's splitting, inadvertently escalating the split.

As indicated, there has been little formal research on parental alienation, though the concept has been observed and discussed for 17 years. This is an area in which research is clearly needed in the future.

THE EVALUATION PROCESS

When a referral is made alleging parental alienation, or if the evaluator suspects that such a process exists within the family, it is important for the evaluator to focus on several key elements. Not surprisingly, there are special dynamics to evaluate in the alienating parent, alienated parent, and, most particular, the child who is the object of the alienation. Observation of the child with each parent will be a critical element of the evaluation process.

The Alienating Parent

Though severely alienating behavior is fairly rare, I have found that it is quite easy to observe. Such signs of alienation include direct interference with visits, giving the alienated parent false information about school and the child's activities, and making inflammatory or critical statements against the alienated parent. Such parents may tell the evaluator,

> "I tell the kids that they don't have to go with their father if they don't want to, they always have a terrible time over there."

> "Everything she says is crazy, the kids simply can't trust her."

"The kids know that we can't do anything because he never pays his child support."

"We hate it when she has her boyfriend over."

In each of these examples, the evaluator will notice that the alienating parent makes absolute statements ("always" or "never") or merges his or her feelings with those of the children ("we hate"). These are two of the features that are most pronounced in alienating parents, the extremes of splitting (as observed in the absolute statements) and the problems with boundaries (as observed in the merged feelings statements).

When the evaluator hears such statements, it is important to ask for examples. If absolute statements are made, the evaluator needs to determine whether the alienating parent can be more positive or differentiate between the child's feelings and his or her own. These examples will either provide legitimate reasons for the feelings (e.g., the father is truly not paying child support, or there are specific visitation problems for the children when the mother's boyfriend is present) or will reflect the polarized feelings of the alienating parent. It is best if the evaluator's questions are subtle and less obvious, but if the parent is unrelenting, more direct questions will need to be asked.

The evaluator is looking to see whether or not the parent can recall more positive aspects of the relationship between the child and the other parent. In situations in which alienation is alleged but not occurring, it may very well be that the alienated parent has never really had a good relationship with the child, and the alienating parent can provide a detailed description of the problems in the relationship. On the other hand, if alienation is occurring, the evaluator can usually pinpoint a time frame or period in which a change occurred in the relationship between the child and the alienated parent. This change is usually associated with an intense emotional reaction on the part of the alienating parent (e.g., the discovery of a new girlfriend), among many other precipitating factors, including emotional need states within the alienating parent.

More difficult to assess, however, are the subtle behaviors and statements often made by alienating parents. It is unlikely that the evaluator will be able to determine whether alienation exists without exploring the concerns of the alleged alienated parent. For example, a father might report that mother always refers to him as "Smith" (his last name) to the children. The evaluator will look for clues that this is occurring and will likely ask questions that include the phrase "their dad" to see how mother responds. The evaluator might even ask the parent, "How do you think it affects the children when you refer to their father as 'Mr. Smith'?" Usually, an alienating parent will have no clue how it affects the children and is likely to respond with a statement reflecting the merged feelings, such as "Well, we know he's never been a very good dad, so they don't mind."

However, since the subtle signs can be numerous, it is important to follow up on all concerns raised by the alleged alienated parent. Most alienating behavior will fall into categories that include one or more of the following:

- ❖ unbalanced accounts of behaviors—talking in extremes and absolutes;

- ❖ merging of feelings between the alienating parent and children, such as "We don't like the Tuesday night dinner visit";

- ❖ denial of the relationship between the child and the alienated parent, as if he or she has no right to it anymore;

- ❖ behaviors that directly and/or indirectly thwart the relationship between the child and the other parent;

- ❖ intrusive behaviors such as frequent phone calls (e.g., two to three times per day or more) to the other parent's home during visits;

- ❖ encouraging the children to act as spies during visits;

- ❖ informing children about adult issues, such as child support, reasons for the divorce, and so forth;

- ❖ forcing the children to be messengers of communications;

- ❖ derogatory and blaming statements about the other parent; and

- ❖ tribal warfare in which other family members or family friends get brought into the battle between the parents.

Because alienating behaviors fall along a continuum, the evaluator must look for and explore as many indicators of the alienation that may exist. The evaluator will notice that the alienating parent is often very angry, vindictive, vengeful, extremely labile, or extreme in views, and struggles with emotional boundaries. In evaluating the alienating parent, it is critical to understand the rationale for those behaviors and what causes them. It could be that the alienating behaviors are the direct result of either *actual* or *perceived* shortcomings in the alienated parent. If real problems in the alienated parent are found, the evaluator will make recommendations to correct them. However, if the alienating parent is acting on the basis of perceived problems, it will be important to recommend interventions that encourage the alienating parent to alter his or her perceptions and recognize the many ways that the alienation is negatively affecting the children.

The Alienated Parent

For the alienated parent, there is a potentially different set of dynamics to explore. Alienated parents tend to fall into two groups. The first is a group of parents who had a healthy relationship with the child prior to the separation but are now being shut out of the child's life. These parents are truly being alienated from the child by the behavior of the alienating parent. The second group of alienated parents is those who claim that alienation is the significant source of the problems with their children, but who tend to be fairly defensive, avoid relationships, externalize blame, and have a very difficult time seeing their own role in problems with the children. Such parents are often very controlling and powerful and are used to having things their own way in their relationships. After separation, they expect their relationship with the children to be *as they want it to be.* These parents are often less child-centered and have less empathy than others. When the relationship does not work out the way they want, they are quick to blame the other parent for alienating the children and for creating problems with their children. I will discuss these two groups separately.

Alienated Parents Who Previously Had a Healthy Relationship With Their Child

Parents in this category seem to be truly alienated against. They may be insightful, able to reflect on a wide variety of possibilities for their children's behavior, and willing to look to themselves as a source of some problems. These parents have typically had a history in which they were close to their children and actively participated in their children's lives and activities. These parents can have a nurturing quality, though there may be a tendency toward some passivity and difficulty dealing with overwhelming emotions. These dynamics provide a fertile atmosphere for the alienation to flourish.

In these families, the alienating parent is typically extreme and emotionally overreactive, and the alienated parent is usually more passive, nurturing, and sensitive. The alienated parent is often overwhelmed and does not know what to do when faced with the alienating parent's behaviors. Rather than confront the alienating parent or reality to the child, these alienated parents have a tendency to detach. This detachment reinforces the alienating parent's vengeful behaviors. These parents may exhibit sensitivity to the children, nurturing behavior, passivity, insight, and a tendency to be overwhelmed with intense emotions.

Alienated Parents Who Previously Had a Poor Relationship With Their Child

On the other hand, many of these parents have had very little to do with their children prior to the separation and divorce. They may have been workaholics who came home late at night. They may have been fairly self-centered individuals who were more involved in their own activities than in the activities of their children. Many of these parents may be quickly involved in a new relationship and are insensitive to their children's feelings about this new relationship. Rather than recognize that their children may have their *own* feelings about their new partner, they are quick to blame the other parent for the children's feelings. Blame is common for these parents.

In exploring the history of the relationship between *these* parents and their children, evaluators often find that there is a general absence of a quality relationship in the formative years of development. There is a superficiality to the relationship caused by years of neglect or a history in which the other parent was truly the "primary parent" in the marital relationship. These parents may show up for the "Kodak moments," but they do so in a more self-centered way, often for their own enjoyment and interest rather than to participate with their children. These parents may report active involvement in activities such as coaching the children's sports, yet, on further exploration, the children often felt pushed into these activities and distant from their parent-coach. Often, these parents are not even that interested in the child after the divorce. They claim alienation primarily as a way of continuing the control and blame that they exhibited during the marriage. For these parents who are claiming alienation but are more likely to be the cause of the rift with their children, evaluators should look for indicators such as defensiveness, control, externalization of blame, self-centeredness, and superficiality.

As evaluators understand all of the alienated parent's dynamics, they can more objectively understand the nature of the alienation and related allegations.

The Children

Perhaps the most critical part of an evaluation in which allegations of alienation occur is the understanding of the children. Kelly (1997) observed that most children who become a party to the alienation process are in the age range of 7 to 15 years. It appears that many child variables contribute to whether or not they become entangled in the alienation behaviors of their parents. These variables may include the child's temperament, ego functioning, prior relationships with each parent, immediate reaction to the separation of his or her parents, and general level of anxiety and distress. When evaluating these children, the evaluator is going to be looking at all of these factors. In evaluating the nature of the child's current relationship with each parent, he or she needs to understand whether

- ❖ the child's alignment with one parent is the result of shared interests,

- ❖ there is a history of problems in the child's relationship with either parent,

- ❖ the child loves both parents and has little or no preference between the parents,

❖ the child is being alienated from one parent largely because of the actions of the alienating parent, or

❖ the child is alienated from one parent because of that parent's own actions and lack of ability to understand or improve the relationship with the child.

As with the adults, these children fall along a continuum. Questions directed toward the children are designed to help the evaluator understand the nature and severity of the child's negative feelings toward the alienated parent. One clue to suggest that the child is being alienated is if the child uses words that are identical to those of the alienating parent. Another indicator of alienation is when the child expresses moral indignation and outrage that seems more appropriate for a parent. Similarly, if the child uses absolute statements, such as "always" or "never," when criticizing the other parent, this is a clue that alienation is occurring. Statements such as the following would suggest that alienation is occurring:

"Things have been terrible since he left us."

"He's always mean to us."

"I can't believe she left us for that jerk."

"He used to be nice, but now he's always with *her* (the new girlfriend)."

On the other hand, some children tell very moving stories of how they have not liked or have been fearful of the alienated parent for a long time. They can give specific details of abuse, angry behavior, and so on, prior to separation. These children often feel relieved when their parents divorce because they are now free of those problems. The differential understanding will come from the child's clear account of inappropriate behavior, the detachment in the relationship, and a convincing sense of real problems (as opposed to the moral indignation of the alienated child).

When an evaluator listens to the children in those cases in which the child is detached from the alienated parent, there is little evidence that these children are put in the middle by the alienating parent. Rather, there is a sadness to these children, who wish (or may have wished in the past) for a different quality to the relationship with the alienated parent. Many of these children have observed significant spousal abuse during the marriage or have observed one parent being controlling and hostile to the other parent. It is the sadness and ambivalence about the lack of a relationship that are one of the key differential indicators that these children, though certainly aligned with one parent, are not being alienated.

For both of these types of children—those who are clearly alienated because of actual behaviors of the alienating parent and those who are primarily aligned because of significant problems in the past relationship with the alienated parent—there is usually a desire to have little or no contact with the alienated parent. The alienated children usually have no initial or ongoing legitimate reason for this, and their stated reasons appear on the surface to be flimsy, although they believe adamantly in their justifications. Those children who have a legitimate reason for being aligned against a parent are usually able to articulate this.

Another differential within these children will often emerge during the joint interviews and observations with each parent. The alienated child is usually enmeshed in the relationship with the alienating parent, often experiencing a hostile-dependent relationship with that parent. These children may feel a need to emotionally care for the alienating parent, and the refusal of visits is reflective of that need. The enmeshed and/or hostile-dependent nature of the relationship, or the "parentification" of the child, is usually apparent during the observations with the alienating parent. In the interviews with the alienated parent, these children will often be cold and indifferent to that parent, showing little ambivalence or remorse for their absolute lack of a relationship. Sometimes, if the joint interview is long enough, the evaluator might see a shift, or softening, of the child's alienated stance with a parent with whom he or she previously had a positive relationship. It is almost as if they finally allow themselves to have fun, when they think no one is noticing.

In contrast, a child who is aligned but not alienated usually has a fun and playful relationship with the alleged alienating parent, the boundaries are clear, and the relationship does not appear enmeshed. When the child is seen with the alienated parent, the sadness and ambivalence are more obvious. These children want the alienated parent to take responsibility for the problems in the relationship. They might want to rekindle the relationship, but only if the alienated parent would show some insight and understanding of his or her feelings.

Other Reasons for Alignment With One Parent:
What to Look for in the Children

There are two other dynamics that are important to look for in these children. First, many children seem to be aligned with one parent primarily because of shared interests or a "goodness of fit" in the personality dynamics with one parent. There is a natural affinity between an active, sports-oriented child and his or her active, sports-oriented parent. Other children may have a stronger affinity with the parent who has effectively been the primary parent, and they have a concomitant need to be with that parent. These dynamics have nothing to do with alienation but are related to the quality of the child's relationships with each parent. Unlike the alienated children, however, these children want to spend time with the other parent, though on a more limited basis. The evaluator will note that the child's reasoning is related to these interests or the quality of the relationship rather than imagined problems in the relationship with the "alienated" parent.

Second, conflict takes an emotional toll on children. As the level of conflict between parents increases and as children are caught in the middle of these conflicts, the child's level of anxiety and vulnerability increases. For many of these children, an alignment with a parent helps take them out of the middle and reduces their anxiety and vulnerability. When pressed, these children will prefer a relationship with both parents and show no real history of any significant problems with either parent. By making a choice to be primarily with one parent, these children are making a statement that they need to be free of the conflict. For some, it may not even matter which parent they live with as long as they are removed from the conflict.

In fact, when the child's anxiety is driving the split, the intensity and severity of the child's feelings may be greater than the intensity of the alienating parent's behaviors. Unlike children who are alienated primarily because of the alienating parent or children who are aligned because of a rift in the relationship with the alienated parent, these anxious and vulnerable children are experiencing alignment as a direct result of the conflict and behaviors of both parents.

SUMMARY AND RECOMMENDATIONS

As the evaluator nears the completion of the evaluation, he or she needs to understand each participant thoroughly. For the alleged alienating parent, the feelings and negative behaviors toward the other parent will be on a continuum from mild to severe. In evaluating the alleged alienated parent's behavior, the evaluator will be looking at the degree to which that parent has contributed to the rift in the relationship with the child, the need states of that parent, and whether that parent can see his or her own role in the problems. Finally, as the evaluator looks to the child, he or she is looking for clues along a continuum of alignment to alienation and for the degree of conflict to which the child has been exposed. The recommendations and the interventions will vary according to the dynamics observed. By carefully observing each participant's role in the alienation dynamics, the evaluator can help to pinpoint family recommendations that will hopefully work toward alleviating these problems for the child.

When Alienation Is Present

Given the wide range of situations in which alienation can manifest itself, the range of recommendations will also vary according to the dynamics of the family. However, there is one constant for all of these families that appears to be most beneficial. In cases in which some form of true alienation is functioning, it is important for all family members to participate in some form of parent education related to issues of divorce. Recent research on parent education (Arbuthnot & Gordon, 1996) suggests that, for all families, but especially those with milder forms of alienation, improvement can be made by helping the parents gain a better understanding of how their postdivorce behavior affects the children.

As alienation dynamics become more severe, it is equally clear that some form of direction from the court is critical in helping to ensure ongoing contact between the alienated parent and the children. When children are willing to go with the alienated parent, visits of longer blocks of time are often helpful, especially if there is little or no intrusion from the alienating parent. Long weekends several times per month and maybe 1- to 2-week blocks of time in the summer may help offset some of the alienating behaviors. When the court tells the parents and the child that there must be contact with the alienated parent, this also takes the child off the hook for having to decide. This may be quite helpful for those children who are feeling anxious but are less determined to avoid the alienated parent. Consideration of the child's temperament, age, and emotional functioning should be made whenever an evaluator recommends forced blocks of time for the child to be with the alienated parent. More information on child and developmental considerations will be addressed in Chapter 6.

When the alienation dynamics are at least moderately severe, the family might also need some form of court-appointed neutral decision maker or special master to help ensure that the family complies with the court orders. It is often helpful if this case manager has judicial-like authority to help implement the visitation plan and the opportunity to report to the court if one or both parents are not following through appropriately.

Often, therapy is indicated for some or all members of the family. Because the children are most vulnerable, having a therapist for the child who is sensitive to the dynamics of parental alienation is necessary. Primary goals of the child's therapy will be to help the child reduce the level of splitting, help with feelings of vulnerability and anxiety, help with his or her separation and age-appropriate autonomy, and help the child remain detached from the parental conflicts. It is very difficult to do this therapeutic work, because the therapist must balance the need to be supportive of the child's feelings while slowly confronting the splitting. This requires considerable experience because the confrontation could cause the child to reject the therapist.

When alienation is mild to moderate, it is often helpful for the child's therapist to work with the child and alienated parent at times to promote and help solidify the quality of that relationship. That therapist can also work with the child and alienating parent to help the alienating parent understand the child's emotional growth and the need for the child to have a healthier relationship with the alienated parent.

For the families whose alienation dynamics are more severe, it is usually wise to have the child's therapist be separate from either or both parents' therapists to prevent contamination and splitting within the therapy. In those circumstances, it may be wise to have a family therapist assigned to help deal with the dynamics associated with the child and each of his or her parents. In that way, when the case manager forces visits and the family therapist is raising issues with the child and either parent, the child's therapist is free to be a supportive and nurturing force who can simultaneously support the child's feelings and help the child understand why he or she has to go along with the court orders.

As for the parents, in addition to parent-education classes, it is often helpful for the alienating parent to have some therapeutic encouragement in letting go of his or her vengeful and angry feelings and in separating his or her feelings from those of the children. Unfortunately, because many of the more severely alienating parents exhibit symptoms of other personality disorders, such efforts are often met with extreme resistance. With those parents, it is likely that the combination of a case manager, parent education, and a therapist for the child will be the most successful in countering the alienating process.

Although these recommendations are ideal, insurance companies, health maintenance organizations (HMOs), and managed care organizations usually do not support elaborate therapeutic interventions. In some jurisdictions, necessary services can be developed within a university setting. One new paradigm for treating alienation can be found in group treatment. For example, a therapist can treat three alienating parents and three alienated parents (from different families) in one group, while the other set of three alienating parents and three alienated parents meets the next night. This may be far less costly than individual therapy. Communities need to become inventive until research provides answers to the multiple needs of these families.

When the Child Is Aligned and Alienation Is Not Present

In circumstances in which the child has provided a sound reason for his or her feelings of being aligned primarily toward one parent and wanting little or nothing to do with the other parent, the therapeutic efforts need to be focused on the parent who is claiming alienation where little exists. Even for these families, a case manager is often helpful to provide a measure of protection for the child and the alleged alienating parent against the controlling, inappropriate, and intrusive demands of a problem parent.

The primary focus will be therapy for the parent who claims alienation but who has little insight into his or her role in the problems. Primary goals of the therapy will be to help increase the parent's empathy toward the experiences of the child and to help that parent recognize that the child has his or her own feelings and is not simply a mouthpiece for the other parent. Therapeutic efforts designed to help this parent take responsibility for his or her behavior, apologize to the child, and encourage the child's forgiveness are also beneficial. Once this is accomplished, the child and parent can work together to improve their relationship and find activities and interests that they can share. Having the child tell that parent how he or she feels and why these feelings exist is part of the therapeutic healing that needs to take place.

Parentectomies: Do They Help?

As indicated earlier, perhaps the most controversial element of all the alienation literature has been Gardner's (1987) recommendation for a swift change of custody in those families identified as exhibiting severe parental alienation. In these cases, there may also be a severe limitation on the child's contact with the alienating parent, at least for the first few months after the change of custody. Although there are certainly times when an evaluator might recommend a change of custody from one parent to the other, doing so solely on the basis of a finding of severe parental alienation may not be in the child's best interest. When a child has a strong attachment to the alienating parent, even if the attachment is an unhealthy one, it can be emotionally damaging to the child if the relationship is abruptly terminated.

It is important to remember that children in these families are often in an enmeshed relationship with the alienating parent and often feel a strong need to protect that parent. They may be in a hostile-dependent relationship with the alienating parent. An abrupt change in custody may cause significant problems for the child. The evaluator must be careful that the proposed solution to alienation does not cause more problems for the child than did the alienation. I have never seen a change of custody by itself lead to a reduction in conflict and improvement in the situation for the child. Although it may temporarily help the relationship between the child and the alienated parent, it often comes at an exorbitant price for the child.

Even with case manager and therapeutic support, many of these children continue to long for a relationship with the alienating parent. Sometimes these dynamics will resurface several years later. Rather than a complete change of custody, I believe that a more balanced time-share in which the child has time to be with each parent for a relatively equal period of time in larger chunks (such as 2-week blocks or most of the summer) may be more beneficial to the child. Even when this is difficult to achieve, I would always consider the impact to the child of the change of custody and whether this solution will be worse than the alienation that is occurring.

For some families, it will be impossible to help the alienated parent ever have a viable relationship with the child, despite the best therapeutic and structural efforts. Some courts are taking to punishing children, placing them in juvenile halls and psychiatric hospitals because they do not see a parent. I do not agree with this approach. I believe that these children should be in therapy, with part of the therapeutic work centered on the alienated parent withdrawing from the child's life. It is important to do this carefully so that the child does not feel abandoned by the alienated parent. The alienated parent needs to be taught to say the following to the child (in his or her own words, but with the overall intent completely clear):

> I know how hard it is for you when you feel pain. I know that you and I don't see things the same way, and maybe we never will. I am sorry for whatever I have done to cause you to feel pain, and I know that our divorce has been terrible for you. I love you and don't want you to be in the middle of the war between your mom (or dad) and me. I know it's terrible for you, and rather than have you continue to experience that pain, I am going to withdraw for a while.
>
> I want you to remember three things. First, I do love you and want what is best for you. Second, I will always be there for you if you need anything. Third, if you ever change your mind and want to rebuild our relationship, nothing could make me happier. I'm only withdrawing for now to help you feel less pain and take you out of the middle of our war. I'll keep in contact with you every few months or so. I'll keep sending you birthday and Christmas cards. I hope you get them, and I hope you'll write back. I'll always make sure you know where I am and how to reach me if I move. More than anything, I want you to have peace in your life, and, someday, I hope I can be a part of it. I love you and I always will.

Although this is a painful thing for an alienated parent to do, sometimes it is the only viable solution for an intractable situation. I would certainly encourage such a child to remain in therapy, at least periodically, to explore how the situation is working out. I would also encourage the parent to continue sending the cards, inviting a reunification with the child. At the present time, there is no research on these children and families to know if this actually helps, but anecdotal evidence for some children suggests that it might.

CASE EXAMPLE: The D Family

This couple had been married for 12 years. They had two children, Johnny, who was 11 at the time of the evaluation, and Mary, who was 9. There was a great deal of splitting in this case, and the daughter was unwilling to visit with the father. As is often the case, both parents had a role to play in the children's alignment, though the mother's alienation efforts from a very early age were quite evident. Psychological testing also identified consistent personality dynamics.

The following summary and recommendations from my evaluation provides an outline of these dynamics and the recommendations that I made. As this case example shows, precise recommendations are difficult to make. The use of the special master was designed to help adjust the recommendations as the children's needs change. Therapy for the girl was also a significant factor in the recommendations.

Given the complexity of this case, it is important to outline the various components that are contributing factors to some of the problems for the children. It is this examiner's observation that these factors include the following:

♦ both parents' tendency to be rigid and defensive and to externalize blame onto the other;

♦ both parents' tendency to be angry and impulsive in their expression of anger;

♦ Mr. D's history of passivity in regard to the children and his limited involvement in Mary's life, in particular;

♦ Ms. D's tendency to view things in extremes and, in particular, her extremely strong and negative view of Mr. D, with the belief that the children would be fine if he had little or no role in their lives;

♦ Ms. D's tendency to be obsessive, overinvolved, and overprotective of the children in *their* lives;

♦ Mr. D's tendency to avoid conflict at all costs because of his perception of Ms. D's irrationality; and

♦ Mary's own feelings of frustration with her father and both children's view that they don't know their father very well, if at all.

Through the course of this evaluation, there were numerous allegations made by both Mr. and Ms. D about the other. It is my observation that both of them have a tendency to be impulsively angry. Ms. D is more emotional and therefore seemingly more irrational compared with Mr. D, who seems extremely logical and relatively disconnected from his emotions. Except for the issues noted above, I see no evidence of significant psychopathology in either Mr. or Ms. D, no evidence of difficulties with reality testing, and no evidence of irrational thinking on the part of either parent.

It is this examiner's observation that Ms. D's view of Mr. D is affected by her tendency to view things in extremes and to overreact emotionally. Mr. D's view of Ms. D is affected by his tendency to be very logical and overly rational in his approach. Both of them have gotten more rigid toward each other over the years.

Mr. D believes that Ms. D is alienating the children against him. Parental alienation is a syndrome in which an alienating parent actively or subtly discourages a relationship between the child and the alienated parent. His or her behavior is viewed by the child in such a way that the child has an increase in anxiety, and that anxiety gets transferred to the alienated parent. At the same time, there may be a rift of some kind between the child and the alienated parent, often caused by the alienated parent's behavior. In addition, a frequent component in parental alienation is the child's increased anxiety and insecurity in the relationship between the child and the alienating parent. Often, this insecurity is caused by problems in the dependency attachment, usually as a result of a hostile-dependent relationship between the child and the alienating parent. As the child's insecurity increases, the split between the parents occurs, and the child cannot emotionally tolerate relationships with both parents. Over time, even when the alienating parent encourages the child to have a relationship with the other parent, the insecurity about that initial relationship is overwhelming. In fact, the dynamics seen in parental alienation are not unlike those typically seen in children with school phobia twenty or more years ago.

Given the issues noted above in this evaluation, it is this examiner's opinion that there *are* elements of parental alienation taking place. Ms. D is extremely angry at and has expressed her hatefulness of Mr. D toward and in front of the children for many years. At the same time, Mr. D has had a very strained relationship for years with Mary, and, as such, there has been a longtime rift in the relationship between them. He doesn't understand Mary, Mary feels neglected by him, and she is very angry at him. Finally, it is this examiner's observation that Mary has a moderately fragile relationship with her mother, in large part because of the overprotective and at times hostile-dependent relationship between them. With this pattern, it is likely that Mary feels an emotional need to take care of her mother, for fear of incurring her mother's anger and rejection. All of these factors are contributors to the parental alienation pattern in this case.

Given these dynamics, it is this examiner's observation that solutions for Johnny and Mary are difficult, especially for Mary, who appears to be the more fragile of the two children in terms of their relationship with Mr. D. In cases in which parental alienation and high conflict exists, it is usually necessary to have a blend of therapeutic and structural recommendations that will assist the children in improving their relationships with *both* parents and assist the parents in doing a better job of parenting. In addition, it is important to view both short-term and long-term goals for the children and the family. Given the above, I offer the following recommendations:

1. Mr. and Ms. D to share joint legal custody of the children, with Ms. D having primary physical custody.

2. Adjusting the children's schedules as follows:

Johnny: I would recommend that Johnny spend every Monday overnight and the second and fourth weekends with his father. I would define the weekend as being Friday after school (or when Mr. D can arrange to pick him up) until return to school Monday morning. As such, on the weekends that Johnny is with him, they would have four nights in a row together. In addition, I would recommend that Johnny be with Mr. D every Thursday for a 3-hour block of time for dinner and homework. I would recommend that Johnny be with his mother for the remainder of the time, including the first, third, and fifth weekend of every month (except for adjustments because of holidays and vacations).

Mary: At the present, I would recommend that Mary be with her father every Thursday for the same 3-hour block of time as Johnny and on the second and fourth weekends of every month. For the present, I would recommend that Mary spend the rest of her time at her mother's, reserving the addition of Monday overnights (as with Johnny) pending therapeutic progress (see below).

3. I would recommend a three-pronged therapeutic approach for this family. First, Ms. D could benefit from short-term therapy designed to help her deal with her feelings of rage toward Mr. D and learn to accept him being more actively involved in the children's lives. She has a lot of hurt inside, sometimes with good reason, and she needs to begin disassociating her own feelings about Mr. D from the children and their needs. Most important, she needs to lower the intensity of her rage toward Mr. D.

Second, I would recommend that Mr. D be in therapy himself to help him deal with his feelings of depression and his own feelings of hostility and anger. In addition, he needs help in understanding ways to improve his relationship with the children, separate from Ms. D's behavior toward him in regard to the children. A therapist specializing in parent-child relationships would be beneficial.

Third, and most critically, Mary needs a therapeutic opportunity to help her with the multitude of issues affecting her. She needs assistance in helping her separate in a healthier way from her mother and in dealing with her anger at her father for the many years of his passivity and lack of involvement in her life. She needs to work with Mr. D in expressing herself to him and helping him become more the kind of father she wants him to be.

It is this examiner's observation that, if this multitiered therapeutic approach is in place, the relationships should improve.

4. Another critical component in the improvement for this family is a special master. It is this examiner's observation that a special master can assist in the communication between Mr. and Ms. D. First, I would recommend that they be required to meet conjointly with the special master at least once per month to discuss the children and their needs. Second, I would recommend that the special master have sufficient authority to resolve day-to-day disputes between Mr. and Ms. D and adjust any scheduling discrepancies that might arise. This will assist Mr. and Ms. D to lower the level of conflict between them and resolve their disputes in a way that will be more healthy for the children. Third, and equally as important, the special master can monitor the therapeutic progress of each of the participants and recommend changes in the time-share as needed. Finally, if the special master determines that either Mr. or Ms. D is significantly inhibiting Mary's progress, the special master can report back to the court with an alternative set of recommendations regarding her time with each parent.

5. In approximately 9 months, if the special master feels that it will be helpful, a brief reevaluation would be indicated to assist in understanding everyone's progress and whether or not a significant change in parenting time is indicated.

Several months later, I had a conversation with the special master and the therapist to discuss this case. It appears that the mother had not changed her position. However, Mary was beginning to understand her own psychological splitting and was much more willing to be with her dad, at least some of the time. Mr. D was beginning to get more involved with Mary, he stopped blaming his ex-wife, and he was concerning himself only with his relationship with Mary. Johnny was beginning to express concern about his mother but was beginning to spend less time with his father. This shows how transient the symptoms of alignment can be when one of the parents has some significant emotional pull with the children.

CHAPTER 2

Domestic Violence

In the past few decades, there has been an increased focus on understanding domestic violence and its various components and how it affects the family, particularly children. As the debate about what conditions precipitate domestic violence has grown, so has the social awareness.

The issue of domestic violence received major focus following the murder of Nicole Brown Simpson, one of the most watched and publicized trials in the United States. Since that time, there has been an increased awareness of the need to understand the effects of domestic violence on children and the issue of domestic violence within the context of divorce.

Newmark, Harrell, and Salem (1994) studied the issue of domestic violence as it related to custody cases. They focused on the issue of empowerment and whether domestic violence issues affect the power differential in mediation. The American Psychological Association sponsored a Task Force on Violence and the Family in 1996. Perhaps the two most respected researchers in this area are Susan Hanks, Ph.D., and Janet Johnston, Ph.D., both of whom have written about domestic violence in the context of marriage and divorce. Independently of one another, each developed a typology of domestic violence families. All of this research has helped bring about a more thorough understanding, not only of the domestic violence within the family but also of the impact on children.

As various state legislatures have explored the issue of domestic violence, more have included domestic violence as one of the factors to be considered in definitions of "the best interests of the child." At the time that this book was written, 13 states have a rebuttable presumption that a parent who has been found to have committed an act of domestic violence should not have either sole or joint legal or physical custody, unless the courts still find that it is in the child's best interest. The intent of such laws is to protect children, but I have a concern when any *single* issue has such significant weight that it forces judges into any particular custody or visitation arrangement.

I prefer the legislation in California, in which judges continue to have leeway in their orders. Under the new California law, when there is an allegation of domestic violence in a contested custody matter, the judge must state, for the record, that he or she addressed the issue of domestic violence. If the judge grants joint or sole custody to a parent who was violent, he or she must also state the reasons that such an order was made. If there is a conflict between them, the health, safety, and welfare of the child (as they relate to issues of abuse) take precedence over frequent and continuing contact with a parent.

As the debate continues over presumptions and other laws, legislatures and courts are understanding that domestic violence hurts children, regardless of whether the child is a witness or directly abused. Because it is often difficult for courts to understand the subtleties of domestic violence issues and the truthfulness of the allegations, these families are increasingly being referred for evaluation.

Custody evaluators have not kept pace with this trend in state legislatures. A recent survey of custody evaluator practices by Ackerman and Ackerman (1996) revealed that domestic violence was the second least likely reason for not giving someone custody. Nearly 75% of respondents recommended against custody for a parent when there were findings of parental alienation syndrome. Since 1998, custody evaluators in California have been required to take training in domestic violence issues in order to be appointed by the court. The purpose of the law and the training is to inform evaluators about the dynamics of domestic violence, the effects of domestic violence on children, the California laws on domestic violence, and treatment resources for families. This chapter will help custody evaluators understand issues of domestic violence within the context of the divorcing family, understand special techniques for evaluating the allegations of violence, and recognize when the allegations might be false or exaggerated, and it will suggest a range of recommendations that might be made when findings of domestic violence exist.

APPROACHING THE FAMILY'S DOMESTIC VIOLENCE ISSUES

Violence within the family can take on many forms. Physical abuse can include behaviors such as hitting, kicking, biting, slapping, spitting, pushing, shoving, pulling hair, throwing or breaking things, and other forms of physical abuse.

More harmful violence can include stabbing, shooting, actions that lead to internal injuries, the use of weapons, and strangling. For the most part, when we think about domestic violence, we are often drawn to thinking about these actions. In many of these families, the primary goal for the abuse is power and control in the relationship.

A second form of abuse is emotional. This can include name-calling, badgering, controlling, making someone think he or she is crazy, humiliating, threatening to harm or commit suicide, verbal assaults on one's self-esteem, constant criticisms, and other behaviors that are violent to the psyche. This can be just as devastating as physical violence. Children who experience such violence develop maladaptive coping mechanisms, perhaps becoming depressed, afraid, or withdrawn or becoming abusive themselves. Such coping mechanisms are pathological if they are reactive to the violence in the family.

A third form of family violence is economic. When one parent controls the money, the other tends to feel more isolated and insecure. Restricting access to community funds, giving an insufficient "allowance" to manage the household, having to ask permission to have or use money, and financially depriving the children in retaliation for a partner's behavior are all examples of economic abuse. Many women stay in abusive relationships because they fear becoming homeless or being unable to feed their children if they were to leave.

A fourth form of violence can be sexual. Controlling, pressuring, and intimidating sexual behavior by one spouse toward the other is considered a form of violence. Marital rape, being forced to engage in sexual behaviors that are abhorrent, being forced to have sex when one does not want to, or having unwanted violence as a part of the sex act are all forms of sexual violence. Sexual abuse can be more devastating to a woman's self-image than other forms of physical abuse.

Violence is most devastating when several of these patterns are combined. The victim and children in such families live in a state of intimidation and fear that can be debilitating. Even when the physical violence has diminished, continued threats of such violence, with occasional acting out, are perhaps the most traumatic for children and families. When there is a blend of psychological, physical, economic, and other violence that is perpetrated in an intermittent fashion over time, often with little or no apparent cause or warning, the abuse is perhaps the most devastating and overwhelming.

In a few families, the violence may appear to be mutual. True mutual violence is fairly rare, and an exploration of who is the primary initiator and who lives in more fear will usually help the evaluator determine whether the violence is mutual or whether one person is reacting in self-defense to the violence of the other.

Categories of Domestic Violence

Research on violence within the context of divorce suggests that the violence can take on many forms. Johnston (1993; Johnston & Roseby, 1997) has written about five typologies of domestic violence that she uses to understand the most commonly seen categories in her research with families of divorce. These typologies will provide a foundation for my discussion of the issues in the rest of this chapter.

Ongoing Episodic Male Battering

This is a category that most closely resembles the battering spouse–battered wife syndrome that is typically described in both the literature and popular press. In these cases, the batterer is always the husband (or boyfriend) and the victim is always the wife (or girlfriend). Typically, the violence seems to originate from a combination of the man's intolerable tension and chauvinistic attitudes. These men are frequently jealous, quick to blame, have very limited tolerance to frustration, and have poor impulse control. In Johnston's (1993; Johnston & Roseby, 1997) research, alcohol or drugs exacerbated this type of violence in approximately half the families.

The victim women in these families generally do little, if anything, to initiate or provoke the abuse and are frequently quite surprised when the next attack occurs. Some women do attempt to defend themselves, though the defense is typically intermittent. The attacks in these families are the most frightening and severe, sometimes rising to dangerous, life-threatening levels. The batterer shows little restraint, as he might threaten or use weapons, throw or break household objects, punch or beat the woman as well as verbally and emotionally demean and abuse her. When confronted with their abuse, these batterers blatantly deny it, again blaming the victim.

Hanks (1992) found that many of the men in this category are narcissistic and that the violence is a response to an emotionally overwhelming narcissistic injury (real or imagined). One such rejection can be reduced attention as a result of pregnancy or childbirth, when many of these men become abusive for the first time. They feel vulnerable and can be emotionally dependent on the women they abuse. Separation can be a particularly dangerous time and may stimulate a violent attack, stalking, and renewed threats of violence, including threats of violence to the children. They may threaten suicide as a way to control the partner. This threat is a reflection of the immense pain these men feel at the time of separation. In general, these men have no recognition of the effect of their behavior on others and no empathy for the emotional experiences of their children, and they feel little or no guilt. If they express any upset, it is usually related to the impact on themselves from demands made by the legal system.

In Johnston's (1993; Johnston & Roseby, 1997) research, some of the older girls who experience such violence took a stand against the violent father, aligning with the mother. Although many of these men claim that the mother is "alienating" the child against them (see Chapter 1), it should become clear to the evaluator that these fathers have alienated themselves by their abusive behavior. Older boys in these families tend to be oppositional and difficult and are often simulating similar controlling behaviors toward their mothers. These older boys tend to be identifying with the aggressive behaviors of their fathers. Younger children, both boys and girls, tend to feel anxious, insecure, and confused, and they may worry about their mother's safety. A particular subgroup of the men in Johnston's research exhibited poor boundaries with their daughters, alternating between being seductive and aggressive in their behaviors.

Children who have experienced such violence generally experience strong feelings of vulnerability and insecurity, mostly because of the unpredictability of the father's behavior. Unfortunately, there is little long-term research on the effects of this abuse on children, except that it is likely to result in maladaptive defenses of one kind or another. These fathers are prone to child abuse, given their poor impulse control, low tolerance for stress, and externalization of blame, which is such a fundamental part of their personalities.

Female-Initiated Violence

Although numbers were much smaller than in the other categories, in this category the physical attacks are always initiated by the women. As with the men in the previous category, the attacks are usually caused by an intolerable internal state of tension and stress. This violence is also the result of rejection, often because their partner does not fulfill their emotional needs and expectations. Many of the male victims in this group are very passive, sometimes passive-aggressive, and this passivity seems to provoke the explosive temper outbursts. At the time of separation, this could be exacerbated during conflicts over custody and financial settlements.

The relationships between the mother and her children are often erratic and unpredictable. The children are fairly insecure, demanding, and anxious. Boys may mimic their passive-aggressive fathers and may also be depressed, suppressing their rage at their mother. These women tend to be psychologically disturbed.

Male-Controlling Interactive Violence

This category of domestic violence is seen as arising primarily out of a conflict of interests or disagreement between spouses, which escalates out of control. Although either the man or the woman might initiate physical aggression, men seem to do so in greater numbers. Once aggression is initiated, the overriding response by the man is to assert control. The man views his assertion of control as his legitimate right, and, during the relationship, the physical aggression is seen by both parties as an accepted way of resolving the interpersonal dispute. These men generally do not beat up their wives, using only as much force as needed to maintain control. They may use as much restraint as force in their physical interactions. Alcohol use was found in more than half the families researched, and when alcohol was involved, the violence tended to be more severe.

Many of the women in these situations seem to become "hysterical" (as perceived by the man), and the men use physical force to control the woman's "overreaction" (again, as perceived by the man). Johnston (1993; Johnston & Roseby, 1997) found that the violence in these families tends to cease after separation, especially when there is little opportunity for new provocation.

Johnston also found that the children in these families often feel over-whelmed because of the ongoing lack of ego control and anger management in the parents. Because these parents model fighting and arguing rather than reasoning as a means of settling disputes, the children often engage in power struggles as well. Boys in particular are difficult to discipline and seem to have little respect for authority. Girls tend to alternate between being assertive and demanding or retreating into a more passive response. In general, both parents in these families have little ability to set reasonable limits or control their tempers when their children begin acting out. Both parents are inconsistent in their limit setting, and, frequently, both mothers and fathers attempt to control their children, much like the way the men in these families control their wives.

Separation-Engendered and Postdivorce Trauma

This subgroup includes families in which there are relatively infrequent difficulties with violence or control until the point of separation. For the aggressors in this group (both men and women), the separation is particularly traumatic and psychologically overwhelming. Feeling desperate and vulnerable, these adults act out, usually to try and hold onto the rejecting partner. The other partner is often shocked by such behavior, and such actions serve to reaffirm that leaving this "crazy person" made sense. Unfortunately, such behaviors cause the victim parent to crystallize a negative view of the other parent, as if this individual violent act now becomes a central point of the other person's personality.

Forgotten in such families are the years of relatively reasonable problem solving and judgment that may have existed prior to separation. In this group, violence is neither ongoing nor repetitive. Though the individual incidents can be quite serious, they are generally limited to no more than a few incidents around the time of separation. One of the most important distinctions in this group, as opposed to the earlier groups, is the openness to which perpetrators will admit the violence and feel shame or embarrassment in so doing. They feel genuine guilt and remorse, recognizing that they have hurt another human being, and they seem to understand the impact of this behavior on their children.

Johnston (1993; Johnston & Roseby, 1997) found that the children in these families are noticeably inhibited and constricted. They typically experience symptoms of posttraumatic stress. Because violence is so atypical in these families, the symptoms are typically briefer. She also found that there is a good prognosis for both the emotional response of the children and the parenting ability of the parents.

Psychotic and Paranoid Reactions

For a very small proportion of families, the family violence is generated by some type of disordered thinking, delusions, or drug-induced psychosis. In nearly all such cases found by Johnston (1993; Johnston & Roseby, 1997), the separation itself triggered the acute phase of the violence. In this category, both the men and women who are violent believe that the former spouse intends to harm them or their children. Because of a perception that the ex-spouse plans to hurt them, these adults have an urgent need to counter the perceived hostility that they expect. They often feel justified in seeking revenge, often feeling forced to protect themselves from the former partner's expected attacks. The level of violence in these episodes ranges from moderate to severe, and the violence is frightening because it is unpredictable. People in this group tend to generalize the violence and acting out, and they may feel that those who help victims of their abuse are involved in a conspiracy. The helpers may become targets of violence or threats, as well.

For a more in-depth understanding of these dynamics, I refer the reader to Johnston and Roseby's (1997) book *In the Name of the Child.*

ISSUES IN DIFFERENTIAL DIAGNOSIS

History of the Family's Domestic Violence

The first step in differentiating between these types of families is taking a good history. It is important to get a separate history about all aspects of the marital relationship from each parent. Because so many parents (both victims and perpetrators) are good at hiding family violence, it needs to be explored in all evaluations, not only when it has been alleged by one of the parents. It is important to ask questions that will elicit information about the nature and extent of any violence, be it physical, emotional, economic, sexual, and so on.

Even when there are no corroborating documents (i.e., police reports, medical reports, etc.), allegations of abuse should be taken seriously and thoroughly investigated. In custody evaluations, it is common to hear disparate stories from each parent, and it may be difficult to sort out the truth until a rather complete picture is generated. Hanks (1998) reports that women tend to overreport their violent behavior and men tend to underreport their violence. At times, there will be police and medical reports or statements from therapists and others, pictures of injuries, taped threats, or other clear evidence that may help the evaluator in determining "the truth of the family." At other times, however, there may be none of the above, and sorting out these truths may be more difficult. Lack of collateral evidence does not mean that violence has not occurred, but collateral documents should always be reviewed before forming an opinion on the veracity of the allegations. Psychological testing may also be useful. Although such testing cannot confirm or refute an allegation of abuse, it can shed some light on the personality dynamics of the parents, which may also be used in forming an opinion on truth.

In the individual interviews with each parent, the evaluator will need to ask questions that help gather information about the pattern of abuse, any trigger events, and the first, most recent, and worst of such incidents. When emotional abuse is alleged, ask questions to elicit information about violence, physical aggressions, or assaults on a person or object. In some families, intimidation is ongoing and severe, and there does not need to be physical violence to exacerbate the intimidation within the family. It is important to remember that victims of violence may exhibit posttraumatic stress disorder, giving incoherent and emotional histories. Some violent acts may not be perceived by either party as violent. Other symptoms may include incapacitating depression, being angry at the children, and being traumatized by the children when they act violently.

Evaluators are looking for patterns and history that help differentiate between families who have a risk of ongoing assault and those who do not. The most robust predictor of violence is past behavior, which is much more useful than personality traits. The evaluator wants to know the age of the perpetrator at the first offense and whether or not the person is currently on, or has a history of, probation or parole. A history of probation failures is a positive indicator of future risk, as is the involvement of other agencies (e.g., Child Protective Services). Check criminal histories, if allowed in your jurisdiction, looking for charges of abuse, assaults, and so on. Get copies of any restraining orders because they are likely to provide specific data regarding the abuse. There is greater risk of future violence when violence has been long term; there has been no treatment; the perpetrator externalizes blame, denies problems, or both; and the perpetrator focuses on the victim.

There is a lower risk of renewed violence when there is acknowledgment of the violence; guilt and remorse that focuses on the impact on the victim, the children, or both; responsibility for violent behavior; empathy for the effect of the violence on the children; awareness of the children's needs; an understanding that the abuse has served to maintain control in the relationship; and a motivation to change.

If there has been violence, it is important to differentiate between which type, as outlined above.

Finally, it is important to differentiate between different levels of lethality. The Conflict Tactics Scale can be used to understand the intensity and frequency of violence between partners. Lethality also needs to be assessed. According to the Pennsylvania Coalition Against Domestic Violence (1990), assessment of lethality is tricky and never foolproof. However, the likelihood of a homicide is greater depending on the existence and intensity of the following factors:

- ❖ threats of homicide or suicide;
- ❖ fantasies of homicide or suicide;
- ❖ the presence of weapons;
- ❖ the presence and use of drugs, alcohol, or both;
- ❖ "ownership" of a battered partner;
- ❖ significant dependence on the partner;
- ❖ separation violence;
- ❖ depression;
- ❖ access to the battered woman, family members, or both;
- ❖ repeated involvement of law enforcement;
- ❖ escalation of batterer risk; and
- ❖ hostage-taking behavior.

If the evaluator sees a risk for domestic violence and assesses lethality, the evaluator can provide the family and the court with direction to reduce the violence and meet the needs of the children.

Specific Questions to Ask Parents

There are a number of questions that evaluators might ask to elicit a better understanding of the violence issues. Some of them are obvious and directly connected to the issue of family violence. Others are designed to get an understanding of the parents' empathy and attitudes about themselves. Some are related to specific incidents. Possible questions include the following:

- ❖ How did your parents deal with conflict? What did you see?
- ❖ How do you think your child feels when you and your spouse are angry (or violent) with each other?
- ❖ What do you like most about your child?
- ❖ What was the most tender moment with your child?
- ❖ When was the last tender moment with your child?
- ❖ When was the last time your child got angry at you? How was it handled?
- ❖ When was the last time you got angry at your child? How was it handled?
- ❖ Give five adjectives to describe your childhood. Why did you pick them?
- ❖ Define *discipline* and what it means to you.
- ❖ Has your child ever tried to intervene in your fights? Has your child ever tried to call the police? What happened?
- ❖ Has your child ever been directly threatened or injured? How?
- ❖ Have you or your spouse ever blamed the fight on your child?
- ❖ Has your child ever been threatened with loss of toys or pets or told to keep secrets?
- ❖ Has your child ever been forced to watch abuse?
- ❖ Has your child ever been abducted to gain compliance by the other parent?
- ❖ Is your child having problems in school, especially being frequently tired in school?

For specific incidents, ask the following:

- ❖ What did the child see, hear, and do?
- ❖ How close was the child to the violence?
- ❖ Did he or she hide, flee, or try to intervene?

The Children in These Families

A critical issue with domestic violence is how much the children have witnessed, both directly and indirectly. Even when children are not direct witnesses of violence, they may experience symptoms of posttraumatic stress, regression, vulnerability, and other forms of psychological injury. If abused themselves, they are likely to exhibit many of the psychological signs commonly seen in abused children. However, many children who witness domestic violence between their parents but who are not themselves victims of abuse exhibit psychological symptoms as well. Many of these children are in love-hate relationships with both parents.

In families with more than one child, it is common for each child to have a different reaction to and role in the violence. Siblings may become abusive with one another or may soothe one another. Violence is overwhelming for children, and parents may or may not have the capacity to soothe the child. The severity of the violence is not directly connected to the experience of trauma with the child. If the child does not see the violence and does not intervene, the trauma is connected more to the child's vulnerability and perceptions than to the actual event itself.

These children need a differential assessment that helps in understanding their vulnerabilities and future needs. They typically exhibit a range of emotions, including hopelessness and guilt, rage, depression, vulnerability, hypervigilance, fear, and so forth. Because the family violence may be a secret, it is important to speak to collateral sources who can help in providing information on the child's relationships with peers, parents, authority figures, and others. Talk to the teachers and find out if the child sleeps in school. Many of these children are hypervigilant at night and sleep during the day.

Parents will often provide a very different view of their children, and the evaluator will need to form his or her own opinion of the level of pathology in these children. Because this population of children is at a high level of risk, a thorough, independent assessment of the child is critical. The assessment of the children in these families may also help in the understanding of the family's pattern of violence. Interviews with the children may provide the evaluator with necessary data to understand the family pattern of conflict.

Finally, evaluators need to look at the extent to which the children are at risk themselves. This might be a risk of child abuse, but it might also be a risk of abduction or a threat by an angry and vindictive parent. The levels of both the direct threat that the child is exposed to and the perceived threat to the child himself or herself need to be understood. In families with a history of domestic violence, it is not uncommon for children to express fear of being around a violent parent, and the assessment of difference between the real risk and the child's perceived risk (if there is a difference) is important before formulating a custody and/or treatment plan for the family. The evaluator must assess and understand ways in which the child can feel more secure and less vulnerable, a task that will be important in protecting these children. By understanding the direct and indirect impact of the family violence on the children, the level of the child's psychological vulnerabilities, and the risk that these children are exposed to (either real or perceived), evaluators can help formulate a careful plan for access and custody and treatment for the family.

AN OBJECTIVE RANGE OF ACCESS AND TREATMENT RECOMMENDATIONS

As indicated in the beginning of the chapter, many states are now taking a rebuttable position that perpetrators of domestic violence should not be eligible for legal or physical custody of their children, either joint or sole. These presumptions require the judge to specify why he or she grants custody to an offender and for what reasons this custody decision is in the child's best interest. Because some research has shown that as many as one half to two thirds of all divorcing families experience some level of abuse around the time of separation, such laws could preclude perpetrators of abuse in those families from having any custody of their children. In other states, such as California, where the court must address why custody is given to those perpetrators when there are allegations of domestic violence, the stakes are clearly high as they relate to the children.

The first task for the custody evaluator is to try and determine the veracity of the allegations. The next step is to look at the broad range of issues, including the facts of the alleged violence, and provide a recommendation for custody and access regarding the children. Although some psychologists and judges prefer that evaluators do not make recommendations regarding the ultimate issue (i.e., custody), I believe that a thorough custody evaluation provides an opportunity for the evaluator to make recommendations that are in the best interests of the children. In the context of family violence, the evaluator needs to address the issue of how the violence has affected the children and provide insight to the court on the dynamics that contribute to the violence. Once the violence is understood, appropriate recommendations can be made.

For families in which domestic violence is an issue, the key is to understand the extent of the domestic violence, the form it takes, the overall parenting ability of both parents, and the impact of the domestic violence on the children before making a recommendation. Other important factors to consider include the quality of the relationships, developmental needs of the children, and parenting capacities. Evaluators need to pay attention to the laws of their state and integrate the data into the recommendations that they make. Recommendations will usually be very specific so that the courts, the police, or both can enforce the order, ensure safety at transitions of the children, and limit the contact between the parents. Police departments are not good options for the exchange because they are often busy with other business, and it sends a message to children that something is wrong and that their parents are incapable of providing safety without police intervention.

Access Issues

When there is real danger to the children, in the form of violence, emotional abuse, or threat of abduction, supervised or limited visitation might be indicated. Supervised visitation might be necessary regardless of the form in which the violence occurs. It is recommended for male batterers whose violence extends directly to the children and for delusional parents who have made threats of violence or abduction and whose pathology is currently out of control. When there has been a finding of child abuse, supervised visitation will be needed until the factors that contributed to the child abuse have been ameliorated. Very limited or no visitation would be appropriate when the perpetrator does not acknowledge his or her violence and when the child is fearful of even supervised visitation. Supervised visitation is generally seen as a short-term situation until an identified problem has been corrected. When supervised visitation is set up as a result of a child's perceived risk, therapy will probably be needed to reduce the child's fears and normalize the relationship and contact.

At times, this supervision can be provided by a family member (such as a grandparent or other relative of the child) or a family friend with whom the child feels safe. However, it may be difficult for relatives and friends to adhere strictly to the court order. The violent parent may pressure these nonprofessional supervisors into ignoring parts of the order, putting children at risk. To reduce this risk, professional supervision is an alternative. Many communities now have a network of trained visitation supervisors who can follow court orders and provide safe and appropriate supervision of the visits until supervision is no longer needed. The professional supervisor can also be a help to the court or evaluator when there is a need to know how cooperative the parents have been with the supervision arrangements. Though there is a financial cost to professional supervision, it is often a significant help.

Another intervention that is sometimes necessary is a supervised transfer of the children. This is most likely to occur when there is no need to protect the children from direct violence but a threat of a violent episode exists between the parents. Typically, the same professionals who provide supervised visitation are able to provide supervised exchanges of children. In these circumstances, one parent drops off the children at a prescribed time and the other parent picks up the children 15 minutes later. The exchange is supervised at the other end as well. This reduces the likelihood that both parents will be in the same place at the same time and thus reduces the risk of violence.

Sometimes, the risk of violence is even less, so the exchanges may be scheduled at a neutral site or with a trusted family member or friend present. This might be the neighborhood McDonald's or some other public place. This at least allows both parties to be more comfortable that the risk is reduced because there are observers available at the time of exchange. In addition to providing safety for some young children in particular, having a neutral site may reduce a parent's anxiety and, hence, make for a smoother transition.

When the risk of violence is low but the risk of turmoil is high, it is often best to schedule exchanges away from the parents altogether. When one parent drops off the child at school at the beginning of the day and the other parent picks up the child at the end of the day, the parents are not together at the time of exchange. In such instances, it will certainly be necessary for the child to have access to his or her things at both parents' houses, and arrangements may need to be made for the transfer of some of the children's items, such as schoolwork, special clothing, athletic equipment, and so on. For some families in which there is a risk of conflict, specific recommendations should be made that allow for the transfer of the child's things yet still reduce the likelihood of exposing the children to turmoil.

As with any family, a determination must be made regarding the frequency of visitation or length of contact with each parent. Johnston's (1993; Johnston & Roseby, 1997) research suggests that if the child's relationships with each parent are relatively equal and there is little risk to the child in spending time with each parent, it is often better to arrange for longer but less frequent blocks of time with each parent. This would be especially true for children who are at least 6 years of age.

Thus, the evaluator has available a range of time-share options that might include supervision of the visitation, supervision of the exchange, monitoring of the exchanges, less frequent exchanges, and longer blocks of time with the noncustodial parent. In each situation, the evaluator will be making recommendations according to the dynamics of the family, the risk of real or perceived threat, and the typology of violence noted. As far as access is concerned, "safety first" is important, followed by reducing the risk of turmoil and violence between the parents.

It is important to point out that these structures are not a solution to the problems of the domestic violence. Although they may reduce the manifest conflict, the child may still be caught up in a web of violence that is damaging to his or her development. Bringing an end to the violence and encouraging therapy is needed before the child can heal.

Therapeutic and Structural Interventions

For most of these families, the evaluator will likely be making some form of therapeutic recommendation. With abusive parents, a 52-week batterer's program is currently seen as an ideal stratagem. This helps perpetrators become aware of precursors to their battering behaviors, recognize that violence is a choice they do not have to make, learn new ways of dealing with their impulses, and increase their empathy for their victims and the children in these families.

In the absence of violent behavior but when anger problems remain, a shorter anger-management program may be the treatment of choice. Such a program will focus mostly on stress-reduction techniques and teaching skills to help impulsive parents learn more appropriate outlets for their anger.

When impulse-control problems and violence are secondary to a psychiatric problem or substance abuse, medication, treatment, or a combination of medication and treatment for the substance abuse or psychiatric problem would be indicated. Because many perpetrators experience strong feelings of inadequacy, dependency, and vulnerability, psychotherapy may also be a useful adjunct. However, it is important to point out that therapy alone is usually not sufficient with men who are in the category of episodic male battering. These men are likely to require a lengthy batterer's treatment program that is significantly focused on the issues of domestic violence.

For the adult victims of domestic violence, treatment is often needed to build ego functioning, help raise awareness around issues of domestic violence, and improve one's self-esteem. Many of these victims do not know how to recognize that they are in danger, and therapy that focuses on the risks of violence is important to preclude or prevent involvement in future violent relationships. For the small number of families in which there is mutual battering and for families in which the violence appears to be separation-engendered and related to the postdivorce trauma, it is often helpful for both parents to participate in some form of anger-management work. The goals of this work are to reduce the likelihood of provocation, increase the likelihood of empathy for one's children, and reduce the extent to which each parent contributes to the cycle of domestic violence. Just as the perpetrators of domestic violence might benefit from individual psychotherapy, victims may need insight into how their own personal issues contribute to their victimization. Parenting classes may be necessary for many parents with a pattern of violence in the family.

It is quite likely that the children in these families will benefit from individual or group psychotherapy. There is certainly evidence to support that they can benefit from group interaction to help normalize issues of divorce and help them focus on and understand issues of violence within the family. An example of such a program is Kid's Turn, a nonprofit program in the San Francisco Bay Area described by Bolen (1993). In this group program, children participate with one another in age-appropriate groups to understand their feelings associated with the dynamics of divorce; violence, when they have experienced it; and how these issues affect friendships, relationships, and so on. At the same time, parents must meet in separate groups to learn about the impact of the conflicts on their children. Because many of these children are anxious and experience feelings of vulnerability and inadequacy, individual psychotherapy may be indicated.

For many of these children, reunification with the violent parent may be healthiest and safest if it occurs in therapeutic sessions in which the child can express his or her fears and feel reassured by the violent parent. Once the child recognizes that he or she is safe and the parent has taken responsibility to control his or her assaultive behavior, it will then be possible to begin unsupervised and increasingly frequent contact. In the most severe cases, therapeutic work is a necessity before any meaningful visitation can take place.

Finally, as indicated above, there is a strong need for a structural intervention in the form of a clear and direct court order. Just as with the families experiencing alienation described in the previous chapter, many of these families benefit from some form of special master or case manager.

CASE EXAMPLE: The V Family

Mr. and Ms. V were married for 13 years. He was a computer engineer, and she was a housewife. They had two boys and a girl. Their relationship was in constant turmoil, with a great deal of arguing and periodic violence. Typically, Mr. V would become upset and hit Ms. V "to put her in her place." He would occasionally hit the boys when they were disrespectful of their mother or teachers. He was very controlling, and Ms. V and the children were terrified of him.

Finally, Ms. V decided to leave him. She took the children and went to a shelter. She was still ambivalent and went back to him about 2 weeks later. As their arguing escalated over the next month, she threatened to leave again. One night, he came home and Ms. V and the children were getting ready to leave. He lost control, went into the kitchen, and grabbed a knife, allegedly threatening Ms. V. The older son, 11 at the time, called 911, and the other son (age 9) screamed at his dad to leave their mother alone. Their daughter (age 7) hid in the closet, terrified. When the police arrived, they arrested him. He arranged a plea bargain in which he served very little jail time but agreed to a 52-week batterer's treatment program.

The couple separated, Ms. V got custody of the children, and Mr. V was granted supervised visitation. He moved to a community about 500 miles away, where he started a new job. He enrolled in a local 52-week program and began his supervised visits, once per month. However, he was quickly frustrated with the supervision requirement and also became upset with things he was hearing from the children about their mother. He was worried that she was dating a man who was violent. He wanted custody of the children, believing that he would provide a better environment for them.

At the evaluation, he denied ever threatening his former wife. He reported that she exaggerated the incident and stated that he was suicidal at the time, never intending to harm her. He acknowledged being distraught that she considered leaving him at that time. He reported that his boys were more afraid of their mother's screaming and that, if she was not so upset, the police would not have come to the house. He was remorseful about the incident, yet he showed no evidence of remorse for the history of violence in the family. He was clear that he would never harm his children, and he loved them very much. He wanted custody of the children, but he would settle for unsupervised visitation twice per month. He felt that the boys missed him and needed a positive male role model, and he worried that his daughter was anxious and doing poorly in school. He blamed all of this on his wife.

Ms. V was quite upset about having to go through this evaluation. She denied his claim that she was currently in an abusive relationship, and, when her current boyfriend and the children were interviewed, there was no evidence of this. She reported that she was in a lovely relationship with a man who supported her. They were in counseling together, as she was working to overcome the terror of her marital relationship.

The children were doing poorly. The middle boy (now age 10) was depressed and angry. He had little impulse control and was constantly in fights at school. The older boy (now age 12) was doing well academically but had few friends. He wanted to stay home most of the time. The girl (now age 8) was anxious, refusing to go to school. She had multiple symptoms of stomach problems, sleep disturbances, and fear. She was afraid of her 10-year-old brother, who would frequently pick fights with her. All of the children were angry at their father, though they were afraid to tell him, even during the supervised visits. In fact, they would sometimes tell him that they wanted to live with him despite the fact that they were afraid of him.

The evaluation revealed several things. First, it appeared that Mr. V was a classic example of an episodic violent person. The incident that led to his arrest was directly related to the narcissistic injury he felt when Ms. V threatened to leave him. Projection and externalization of blame are common in men who exhibit this pattern. What was very interesting was the way he remembered the incident as a suicide threat rather than a threat against his wife, while the children (and the police report) clearly suggested it was a homicide threat. He blamed Ms. V for brainwashing the children about that. The police at the time thought the terror of the children was quite genuine. The other critical element with Mr. V was his absolute inability to have empathy for what the children were experiencing. He had no awareness of the terror they had felt or the reasons for their current symptoms.

Ms. V was clearly showing signs of posttraumatic stress disorder. She had little awareness that she was dating a man who, although not being physically abusive like her husband, was still controlling her a great deal. She exhibited many symptoms, including denial and a tendency toward overreaction in relationships. Some of her symptoms were related to issues in her childhood. Her mother had been physically abused by her father, but she was in denial of the impact on her and her younger sister, just like she had been in denial of the impact of her husband's abuse on her children. She decided to leave him only when she began to see that the children were terrified because he was becoming abusive to them. She had little ability to be independent, was clingy in her relationship with her new boyfriend, and depended on the children emotionally.

As could be expected, the children were experiencing problems related to both of their parents. The oldest boy was the family caretaker. He was afraid to make mistakes and was afraid to leave his mother alone after school. He isolated himself in his room and was quite detached from his feelings. He had little awareness that he was angry, internalizing it into his symptom of perfectionism. He did not allow himself the opportunity for friendships because he needed to be perfect as a student and a substitute father. He did not like his mother's new boyfriend but could not articulate any reasons for this. When he visited with his father, he tried to please him, focusing on his academic success and his goals for college. He wanted to be an engineer, something that pleased his father very much.

The middle boy was quite expressive of his anger. He identified with his aggressor father and acted out his rage everywhere. He was abusive to his sister, struggled with authority figures at school, and was very disrespectful of his mother. He cooperated with her boyfriend, more out of fear than anything. At the same time, he expressed tremendous anger toward his father, verbally bullying him during the supervised visits. Mr. V did not know how to manage his son's rage. All he could do was blame his mother. He was referred to therapy but refused to attend, saying he was not crazy like his father. He was clearly afraid.

The daughter felt all of her emotions and was overwhelmed. She never knew what happened the night her father was arrested, as she had hidden in the closet until the police arrived. She had not talked with anyone, mostly because she was afraid, and her mother hoped she would not remember (just as she had not wanted to remember her own parents' fighting). Because of the terror that was never talked about, she experienced nightmares and somatic symptoms, including stomachaches, and school phobia. She was very clingy to her mother, who was too involved with the new boyfriend to give her enough attention. She tried to be "good," but it was hard for her.

This was a family who required multiple interventions. The middle boy was hospitalized for several weeks until he could learn to manage his rage. He learned that he was identifying with an unhealthy part of his father's personality and that there were healthier ways to deal with his anger. He actually made the most short-term progress. The oldest boy remained quite isolated and perfectionistic, though he began to get involved in the music program in his junior high school. This took him away from home a bit, and he enjoyed his new autonomy. He still maintained a strong need to be perfect. The daughter began therapy and was slowly working to understand her feelings and build a healthier ego base for herself. Unfortunately, it was still very scary for her mother to talk about the family violence, which made it difficult for more progress to be made. She did break off with the boyfriend, but not until an incident in which he threatened to beat the middle son. Once she broke off that relationship, however, she discontinued her own therapy. As a consequence, she never really came to understand how she was perpetuating the experiences of her childhood. When the evaluator pointed this out to her, she acknowledged it briefly but continued her pattern of denial soon thereafter.

As for Mr. V, he continued his 52-week program, convinced that he was not a threat to anyone. He reported being less depressed. He could not understand why his children were angry at him. He never understood their terror or learned empathy for their feelings. He never learned that his efforts to take custody were a function of his need to control his ex-wife and continue his dominance over her. Because he had never internalized any remorse or understanding for what he had put the children through and because they continued to be angry and terrified of unsupervised visitation, the supervision was continued.

CHAPTER 3

Allegations of Sexual Abuse

Theresa M. Schuman, Ph.D.

Over the years, the pendulum has swung from the theory that children's accounts of sexual abuse are products of fantasy to the notion that whatever children said about abuse is true and should be believed. As professionals, we have been taught to examine our personal feelings about the sexual abuse of children. It was thought that unconscious forces, in part, prevented health professionals from detecting abuse. We did not want to admit that parents could do such horrible things to their children. Through the attention given to sexual abuse and the protection of children, in the media, in child abuse prevention programs, and in our graduate studies, the world has become acutely aware of abuse and accepting of the unfortunate fact that harmful things sometimes occur to children at the hands of their own family members. Although it is a breakthrough for U.S. society that our communities are acutely aware of the dangers to children, there also appears to be an anxiety, if not hypervigilance, generated by the increased awareness.

Over the past 15 years, allegations of sexual abuse in the context of high-conflict divorce have forced us to examine elements that might prompt a child to say that a trusted, loved parent hurt him or her, when, in fact, the event may not have occurred. Have we become so prepared to deal with whatever may come down the pike that we are seeing abuse when it really is not there? Are we looking closely enough at alternative explanations as to why children might say that a parent touched their "pee-pee"? Are we able to make the important distinctions so that we can diagnose sexual abuse when it is present and accurately label false allegations? Have we progressed enough in our knowledge of the field that we can lower the margin of unsubstantiated claims?

This chapter addresses these questions and explores a systematic way of examining sexual abuse allegations that occur in the context of families plagued by high conflict during and subsequent to the divorce process. In addition, this chapter discusses the controversy surrounding interview techniques and the use of anatomically detailed dolls. Child and parent factors will be considered, as will ways of collecting and interpreting the data, arriving at conclusions, and making appropriate recommendations. Other considerations such as supervised visitation and reunification therapy will also be discussed.

Although alleged perpetrators can be of either gender and can be parents as well as adolescent siblings or members of the extended family, the most frequently occurring scenario in my experience is that of the mother as the accuser and father as the accused. The research, as will be seen, suggests that over half of the sexual abuse allegations in the context of divorce appear to be true. I believe that the child custody evaluator needs to approach each evaluation with the equal possibility that the allegations will be deemed true or false or will still be unclear when the evaluation is completed. It is from this perspective that this chapter will unfold.

BACKGROUND AND REVIEW
OF THE LITERATURE

Knowledge about sexual abuse in the context of divorce evolved from what is known about both intrafamilial and extrafamilial child sexual abuse. We originally drew on knowledge from incest families and attempted to use that criteria as they related to families in high-conflict divorce presenting an allegation of sexual abuse. We know that sexual abuse more frequently occurs at the hands of someone the child knows and trusts (Peters, 1976; Tsai & Waagner, 1981), often a caretaker or parent substitute (Meiselman, 1981). We know that offenders attempt to get the child's confidence in a variety of ways and attempt to keep the abuse a secret (Segroi, 1982). Children are less likely to disclose when close relatives or friends are perpetrators (Landis, 1956). More often than not, sexual abuse is revealed by the child after the abuse has stopped because the child is no longer living with the perpetrator and feels safe to disclose (MacFarlane & Waterman, 1986). We know that disclosures are more often than not delayed and that the child's account is likely to be inconsistent in certain ways. We also know that some children who were abused recant because of the distress following disclosure (Summit, 1983).

For every allegation, there is often a defense by the perpetrator, who denies that the abuse occurred. We expect offenders to initially deny (Gebhard, Gagnon, Pomeroy, & Christanson, 1965; Guttmacher, 1951; Peters, 1976; Rader, 1977; Swanson, 1968). We know that offenders are not men in trench coats hiding behind a tree with a bag of candy in hand waiting to lure unsuspecting children. We know that offenders cannot be profiled (Schuman, 1987) and that they come from all walks of life and all socioeconomic categories. Sometimes, they may be the more effective of the two parents, having a closer attachment with the child and better parenting skills than the other parent. However, much of what we have learned may not be generalized to allegations of sexual abuse made in the context of highly conflictual divorces.

Regarding sexual abuse allegations in such a context, one of the largest and most frequently cited studies is the Association of Family and Conciliation Courts Research Unit's (1988) tracking of 9,000 families with custody and/or visitation disputes, 1.5% of which involved allegations of sexual abuse. Of these 169 cases, nearly half were allegations brought by mothers against fathers. Alleged victims were mostly girls, and, in most cases, the allegation was of recent and multiple episodes. Abuse was probable in half (85 families) of the cases, not probable in one third of the cases (56 families), and not known in the remainder of the cases (28 families). Of those deemed not probable, 14% (8 families) were thought to have been deliberately false reports.

In a sample of 215 cases of allegations of sexual abuse in the context of divorce, Faller and DeVoe (1995) found that the discovery of sexual abuse was followed by divorce in 14% of the cases; sexual abuse was ongoing during the marriage but discovered after the separation in 25% of the cases; and sexual abuse started during or after the separation in 27% of the cases. Of the 21% of cases that appeared false or possibly false, nearly 16% were classified as misinterpretations, and 5% knowingly made false allegations. In 13% of the cases, the allegations were unrelated to the divorce dynamics.

Faller (1990), in a sample of 136 cases of allegations of sexual abuse in the context of divorce, found that the discovery of abuse prompted a divorce in 8%, sexual abuse was ongoing but discovered subsequent to separation in 19%, the divorce process preceded sexual abuse in 38%, and 14% were false allegations. Only three of these false allegation cases were deemed purposeful.

Jones and McGraw (1987) examined 576 protective services referrals and found 6% of the allegations made by adults and 2% of allegations made by children were false. A large proportion of these were made during divorce custody disputes.

A number of explanations are given to account for sexual acting out or precocious sexual knowledge in children that could lead to allegations of sexual abuse. In their initial study on divorce, Wallerstein and Kelly (1980) offered possible explanations that include cases in which

- ❖ a parent was sexual with the child,

- ❖ a child witnessed promiscuity or allegations of promiscuity by one or both parents,

- ❖ there was increased visibility of a parent's sexual behavior,

- ❖ anger led to a rise in sexual acting out,

- ❖ sexual activity was an extension of the parent's unconscious or conscious needs or impulses,

- ❖ there was increased anxiety about sex on the part of the children, and

- ❖ it was found that incest fantasies were projected by one parent onto the other and then shared with the child.

Wallerstein and Kelly also found that parental instructions, inquiries, and fantasies frequently prompted questions that contributed to an increased eroticization of the relationship between the parent and child and reinforced the child's anxiety about sexual things. Parents who were previously discreet in their sexual activities before separation were less so after. Their children became preoccupied with sexual thoughts and fantasies.

It has been thought that the very structure of marriage helps to maintain and preserve boundaries. When a marriage dissolves, many impulses are no longer contained, and a parent's sexuality might be expressed in new ways (Wallerstein & Blakeslee, 1989). Though the thinner incest barrier that exists between children and stepparents may not necessarily lead to sexual abuse, it may raise sexual tension in the household.

COMMON SCENARIOS IN THE PRESENTATION OF FALSE ALLEGATIONS

Recently divorced or separated parents may be raising their children as single parents for the first time. Divorce is difficult for most people, but some divorces carry more than the usual amount of animosity and bitterness. Typically, one or both parents lose their perspective, distortions run high, and people jump to conclusions. They each recall injustices done to the other in the relationship and worry that the child is being treated in the same manner. Feelings of rejection or abandonment predominate and may be sealed over by rage and bitterness. In this highly volatile situation, the child arrives home from a visit complaining of a red or sore bottom, has a bladder or yeast infection, and/or makes a general statement about daddy being bad or a more specific claim that daddy touched his or her private parts. These incidents often occur in the phase of separation and divorce in which trust is at the lowest point. The overload from responsibilities of the newly single family is more than the mother can bear. She telephones her ex-spouse, relatives, or Child Protective Services and becomes very worried that her child has been hurt and that the father might be the perpetrator. Once convinced, she may seek the help of several attorneys, social workers, and therapists in an effort to find someone who will believe her.

The father, on the other hand, may be hurt, depressed, and forlorn about losing his marriage. He becomes incensed by the thought that his ex-wife would make such an allegation against him. He becomes increasingly certain that his ex-partner is making up these awful allegations as a way to keep the children from him, turn the children against him, or show her hate for him. He concludes that she is crazy. He might recall that she promised to get even, that this is a ploy to prevent visitation or a scheduled vacation. Occasionally, the father accuses the ex-partner's new mate or adolescent son.

As more people become involved, the child is put in the middle of an extremely stressful and confusing situation and may side with one parent as a way of maintaining some semblance of security. Added to the allegations of sexual abuse are a variety of complaints that the parent does not bathe or feed the child well, does not require the child to wear a seat belt, and so on. Some of these complaints often have validity. Very often, both parents appear credible when they are interviewed separately and have a chance to tell their own side of the story. Concerns about the child are inadvertently left by the wayside, despite the fact that each parent professes that his or her actions are in the best interest of the child.

This chain of events leads to the child being interviewed by a variety of strangers. Not only may the child be confused about the parental separation, but he or she then has to talk to police, social workers, attorneys, and therapists. By the time the matter is in the hands of a child custody evaluator, it feels much like the game of telephone—that is, the concluding message may be totally different from the beginning one. However, unlike the game, allegations of sexual abuse have devastating and widespread impact on children and families and set a course that can affect the child and the accused parent for many years to come. Allegations of sexual abuse are always serious and can be traumatic, even when they are false. The lasting effects that such accusations have on families and children can be devastating. There is increased risk that a child will be alienated from the other parent.

The uproar and chaos that occur in high-conflict families confound the evaluator's ability to sort through why a child is making a particular statement. The difficulty is compounded by the fact that, frequently, there are also allegations of domestic violence, physical or emotional abuse, neglect, substance abuse, or all of the preceding. Child Protective Services and the police might be called many times. Often, there is either insufficient evidence with which to sustain a petition at the juvenile court level or the allegations are deemed false, and the case is closed. If the agency feels that the child is adequately protected or receiving therapy, or both, the case will be closed and referred to the family court for adjudication. After a period of time, an evaluation may be ordered.

PARENT FACTORS ASSOCIATED
WITH FALSE ALLEGATIONS

While sexual abuse is suspected of being transmitted intergenerationally (Brown, 1979; Gelinas, 1983; Meiselman, 1981; Summit & Kryso, 1978), it also appears that parents with unresolved issues of trauma or sexual abuse may be more hypervigilant and vulnerable. The anxiety generated by the suspicion that their child is being molested may prompt some parents to conclude that their child is being victimized on the basis of incomplete or biased information. A mother who was not protected as a child vows to protect her own child and break the cycle of abuse. This *is* important for a mother to do if her child is being hurt. However, if the child is not being hurt and such protection is not necessary, the atmosphere of danger is likely to be a distortion of the reality. In cases in which parents are unable to differentiate their own feelings and needs from their child's, the child's actual needs do not get addressed.

When the allegations are false, it appears that a parent's unresolved childhood victimization might play a role in this. For example, a mother who feels discomfort with normal, adult sexual relationships might choose a partner who does not make sexual demands on her because his primary sexual attraction is to children (Faller, 1990). Similarly, a father's unresolved victimization might result in blurred boundaries and, along with other factors, might increase his vulnerability to cross the boundaries and be sexual with his own child (de Young, 1981; Groth & Hobson, 1983; Groth, Hobson, & Gary, 1982). Sometimes, parents might be sexually addicted, sexually preoccupied, or unconsciously seductive. This could stem from actual or perceived sexual victimization or from other factors such as parents who had extramarital affairs or parents who were philanderers. Although these parents may not molest their children, the sexual focus can be communicated to children. Transmission occurs in ways that we cannot put our finger on scientifically.

It is common in my experience as well as the experience of my colleagues and others (MacFarlane & Waterman, 1986) that a parent, grandparent, or other person may overreact to something the child says or does for a variety of reasons. Such overreaction may lead to

- ❖ a parent's reluctance to allow the child to separate for visitation,
- ❖ hypervigilance and increased anxiety prompted by the divorce, or
- ❖ alarming reactions to the child's touching of his or her genitals or a comment from a child.

For example, a child returns home from a visit with her father and has a mark on her neck. The grandmother inquires, and the child responds, "Daddy kissed it." After a few more leading exchanges with the child, that innocent comment is translated into "Amanda's father gave her a hickey." This is followed by normal behavior such as the child touching herself. Combined with the overreaction, it can result in an allegation of child sexual abuse against the father. Once evaluated, it appeared that the child had fallen and the father "kissed it to make it better," a very common parenting practice.

Desperate parents attempting to determine whether their child was abused sometimes resort to behavior that is intrusive and has as great an impact on the child as molestation. Such intrusive behavior may be considered abusive in some circumstances or, at the very least, inappropriate. This behavior may include the following:

- ❖ photographing children on their return from visits,
- ❖ repeatedly inspecting the child's genitals after visits with the other parent,
- ❖ recording their statements on audiotape or videotape,
- ❖ bringing them to the pediatrician for repeated sexual abuse examinations, and
- ❖ barraging the child with questions after visits.

If the child was abused, such behavior can reinforce victimization. If the child was not abused, such behavior contributes to the child's sexualization because children learn things about sex when parents put them through these intrusive actions. They may learn things that they might not have previously known. The fact that the parent goes to such extremes is a sign of poor judgment. At the very least, such behavior creates an atmosphere of anxiety, danger, lack of safety, and alienation.

As watchful as parents think they are, recently single mothers or fathers going through the stress of divorce are likely to be preoccupied by financial, social, and child care concerns. As a result, they may be lax about supervision or appropriate child care. The sense of panic that a single parent feels when the child care person cancels just before he or she must leave for work may contribute to the parent's making poor choices about child care. All of this creates opportunities for children to be exposed to gestures or language from watching other adults, observing adolescent baby-sitters or siblings with poor impulse control, watching inappropriate material on TV, or walking in on a parent while they are watching adult movies or while they are having sex.

Although there may be no intent to abuse the child, some parents have a style that unwittingly engages in inappropriate behavior. Examples of such behaviors are encouraging nudity, taking baths or showers with school-age children, sleeping in the same bed with the child, or having sex in the room while the child is asleep. These behaviors can be sexually stimulating to children and may stir sexual fantasies that can become projected in a variety of ways. Single parents who are dating again may inadvertently create a more sexual environment at home.

Some coaching or sexualization may be inadvertent or unconscious. A mother with unresolved trauma in her background looks through a pair of toy binoculars in the playroom. Staring at a blue rug, she states, "That's scary!" to which her 3-year-old looks through the binoculars and repeats, "That's scary!" with the same affect. This may occur even though there was no indication of anything in the room being frightening. A woman who is pouring her heart out to a friend on the phone about her ex-spouse's infidelities or drinking might be oblivious to the fact that her 5-year-old got out of bed and is listening to this adult conversation. Bits and pieces of adult conversations may turn up in a child's statements and convince an outraged father that his ex-partner is viciously turning his child against him. Children may become privy to inappropriate information that is likely to be confusing or disturbing to them. Young children may repeat words such as *sex, drugs,* or *drunk* without understanding what they mean. For example, a very young child reported to me, "My daddy is a drunk." Further inquiry revealed that the child did not know what the word *drunk* meant but knew that it was something bad. She had overheard her mom talking on the phone.

Many times, parents embroiled in highly contested divorce proceedings become intractably rigid. Highly anxious, and perhaps overwhelmed, their attitude and values appear so well fixed that they may adhere to an untenable position despite significant evidence to the contrary. This is usually evident in the clinical interviews and may also be corroborated by the psychological testing. These parents are difficult to convince that their children are not being molested. They are also less amenable to therapy because therapeutic interventions may not be easily integrated.

Whether one agrees with Hoppe and Kenney (1994), who maintain that people in high-conflict divorces suffer from a transient relational disorder, or

Masterson and Klein (1989), who maintain that an arrest in early development results in long-standing personality disorders, it is common to observe that rigid parents who engage in high-conflict divorce exhibit primitive defenses of splitting and projective identification. As a result of an intolerance to containing good and bad feelings within the self, they project their own worst parts onto the other spouse, who becomes the container for all of their problems and all of their bad feelings.

OTHER PARENT FACTORS IN THE ALLEGATIONS OF SEX ABUSE

Periodically, parents will present a past history of having sexually abused an older child in the family or a child in another family, and the question becomes whether they are at risk of molesting their own child. In this case, an offender risk assessment needs to be conducted. This includes not only standardized psychological testing but other assessment instruments recommended by Salter (1988), including a review of relevant police and probation records and possibly a polygraph, phlethysmograph, or the Abel Assessment for Sexual Interest.

Though the majority of child custody and visitation cases with allegations of sexual abuse occur during the divorce, there does not have to have been a marriage for similar issues to be raised. With marriage, there is the assumption that there was a time when the couple shared a deep commitment. In many cases of unmarried partners, a brief or dating relationship resulted in a pregnancy in which the parents did not know each other very well or share parenting experiences. Grandparents petitioning the court for custody or visitation may also be the accused or the accuser.

It is thought that some parents resist urges to be sexual with their children by using external inhibiting factors (Finkelhor, 1984). However, when a father lives in a small apartment with an adoring child, he may be unable to resist these urges. He may then rationalize his behavior as a way of justifying his actions to himself and the child (MacFarlane & Waterman, 1986).

Sometimes, when parents suspect sexual abuse, they might draw closer to the child, give them more attention, or increase nurturing behaviors. This encourages a child to repeat what he or she did or said prior to receiving the attention. Younger children may be especially vulnerable to these response reinforcement patterns. This may also contribute to the children sounding more rote in their disclosures (MacFarlane & Waterman, 1986).

CHILD FACTORS IN THE ALLEGATIONS

When a 5-year-old reports that she dreamed that her father peed in her mouth and further inquiry reveals that the pee was yellow and, moreover, the dreams are recurrent, especially during periods of increased anxiety, a myriad of thoughts go through an evaluator's mind. These may include the following:

- ❖ Did she really have a dream?

- ❖ Could she be dissociating or fantasizing?

- ❖ Did she observe something that she could not comprehend, such as "golden showers," and then integrate it into her thinking?

If it is also discovered that the child's mother directed the grandparents to lock her in a garage as punishment, she witnessed her parents in violent arguments and observed her father chase her mother down the street with a knife, and she has two drug-abusing parents, how is an evaluator to sort out the layers and uncover whether this child was sexually abused? In such a scenario, the child is being subjected to multiple types of abuse. In such a highly disorganized, chaotic, and violent environment, sexual abuse allegations may not be the most important of the issues.

Child factors encompass a number of variables such as normal and abnormal sexual behavior, memory, suggestibility, lying, motivation, attachment, and bonding, as well as developmental level. When applied to allegations of child sexual abuse, these child variables take on even greater importance. One has only to read the developmental research, including Piaget, Mahler, or Stern, to realize how our views about the way children learn have progressed over the years. Our knowledge about children's responses to trauma (Terr, 1990) has increased, not to mention the ever-expanding body of literature about children's memories (Bruck, Ceci, & Hembrooke, 1998; Ceci & Bruck, 1995; Ney, 1995).

Behavioral indicators of sexual abuse have long been delineated in the literature and include sudden changes in personality, depression, withdrawal, acting out behavior, and the like. In my opinion, it is dangerous to diagnose or report sexual abuse on the basis of behavioral indicators alone without clear statements that a child was touched inappropriately. Likewise, it is dangerous to diagnose sexual abuse on the basis of drawings alone or on the basis of one psychological test. Behaviors that trigger suspicion and require careful investigation are sexualized behaviors, precocious sexual knowledge, sexual acting out, and direct statements by the child that he or she was molested. In this vein, it is important to consider what is known about normal sexual behavior.

Young children may locate and rub their genitals as part of their normal exploration of their bodies. Sometimes, children are born with genital abnormalities or have illnesses that bring focus to certain parts of the body. Toilet training brings about increased attention to genital areas. If there is great stress at the time that a child is exploring his or her body or toilet training, the child may turn to the pleasurable genital sensations for soothing. Such behavior can become quite compulsive in nature if the child does not have other outlets for expressing the mounting tension.

Sexual exploration between children is thought to be normal if the children are roughly the same age and size and the exploration is what the children arrive at by virtue of their own imaginations and experience, such as playing "doctor" or "house." The key is that the behavior originates from the child's limited knowledge of sexuality. As the acts become more invasive, the situation becomes more suspicious. Sexualized behavior such as humping furniture, licking and kissing genitals, and kissing with tongues goes beyond the norm for young children. The presence of these behaviors does not necessarily mean that a child was sexually abused. However, it raises serious suspicion and warrants an investigation to uncover where a 4-year-old might gain such knowledge. Gil and Johnson (1993) devoted an entire book on the topic, entitled *Sexualized Children*. Although one parent might be eager to assume that the other parent is a molester, the task for the evaluator is to find out how or through what means the child gained the knowledge.

There is no research-based information to help determine when a child's specific sexual behavior is indicative of sexual abuse and when it is not. In addition, no sexual behavior is observed only in sexually abused children (Ney, 1995). Ney cites 15 sexual behaviors that are cause for concern. These include the following:

- ❖ sexual behaviors between children of different ages or developmental levels;

- ❖ sexual behaviors that are out of balance with other aspects of the child's life;

- ❖ children with too much knowledge about sex or those who behave in sexual ways that are more consistent with adult expression;

- ❖ behaviors that are different from those of age-mates;

- ❖ sexual behaviors that continue after a parent says to stop;

- ❖ sexual behaviors that occur in public or in places where children have been previously admonished;

- ❖ behaviors that are eliciting complaints from other children or adults and that are adversely affecting their relationships;

- ❖ sexual behaviors that progress in frequency, intensity, or intrusiveness over time;

- ❖ behaviors associated with fear, shame, and guilt;

- ❖ those that cause physical pain;

- ❖ sexual behaviors that are preceded, followed, or accompanied by anger or physical aggression; and

- ❖ sexual behaviors involving coercion, bribery, manipulation, or threats.

Once the behavior has been identified, an evaluator must find the best way of eliciting the most complete account possible about what occurred. Much has been written about children's suggestibility and the type of interview techniques that will yield the most reliable information. Most would not refute the idea that preschool children are more vulnerable to suggestion than are older children and adults (Ceci & Bruck, 1995). There is some controversy over whether some interviewing conditions or certain events the child is recounting increase the reliability of their reports. It appears that children may not be as suggestible about personally experienced actions that involve their own body.

Across studies, it appears that children provide more information in response to specific rather than open-ended questions (Bruck et al., 1998), but accuracy rates are higher for responses to open-ended questions. Young children need to be cued to direct their attention and help them focus (MacFarlane & Waterman, 1986). Questions that limit the response to "yes" or "no" do not offer the child the opportunity to elaborate on his or her experience. This may result in a loss of valuable information. Older children are found to be more accurate in response to both specific and leading questions. Delays between the actual event and the interviews may result in children leaving out information. They may also result in the inclusion of information that was not part of the original account. Inconsistency in a child's reports should not be taken as a hallmark of unreliability. Ceci and Bruck (1996) summarized data that suggested children may not provide all of the elements in one interview. Additional details may be provided in subsequent interviews. However, prolonged, repeated, and leading questioning may taint the interviews and result in inaccurate information. This is based, in part, on a child's wanting to please the adult interviewer.

Children appear most accurate when they are interviewed by a neutral evaluator who asks few leading questions and when there is no motivation to produce distorted reports. An 8-year-old girl was eating a large chocolate chip cookie in my presence while she was describing, in detail, the way that she and her mom baked the cookies. It was clear from the packaging that they came from a local bakery. After confirming with the mother that the cookies were purchased, I inquired as to why she might tell me differently. The child replied that her father had said so many bad things about her mother that she wanted me to think that she had a good mother. Her lying was motivated by wanting me to think of her and her mother in the most positive terms. She was also motivated to alleviate the guilt she felt for expressions of rage toward her two inadequate parents.

The research on suggestibility provides a great amount of information about children's memories and the elements that affect reliability. However, concern has been raised about how generalizable the research may be. To be ethical, experiments must limit any long-term impact on a child. As such, the scenarios in the research may be different from situations in which sexual abuse has occurred. I believe that the research is valuable as it provides a greater understanding of these issues.

Another issue that is important with children is interviewer bias, the concept that the beliefs of an interviewer can elicit desired information from children. This is applicable to anyone who questions a child, even parents. Interviewers who are biased and who believe in advance that the allegation is either true or false may attempt to obtain affirming information that supports their hypothesis but leave out evidence that might prove the hypothesis wrong (Bruck et al., 1998). In Bruck et al.'s research, children exposed to repeated misinformation over the course of a year not only incorporated the misinformation into their reports but made other inaccurate claims that were not suggested. The authors concluded that young children may use suggestions in highly productive ways to reconstruct and, at times, distort reality about unpleasant bodily events.

Bruck et al. (1998) cite a series of studies by Poole and Lindsay (1996) that show that mildly suggestive techniques that are repeated by parents in the context of reading a book to their children can result in substantial memory distortion in the 3- to 8-year-old range. In my opinion, this research is consistent with clinical situations in which the parent may not be directly coaching the child but influences the child with subtle communications in small, steady doses that span a long period of time. Such experiences may eventually lead to alienation of the child from the other parent.

Bruck et al. state that the use of repeated interviews with suggestive components prompted children to correctly assent to previously denied events, but it also prompted children to assent to events that never occurred. There appears to be support for the hypothesis that patterns of disclosure that begin with secrecy and denial and that eventuate in disclosure may reflect the use of suggestive interview techniques regardless of whether the reported event did or did not occur.

It is thought to be quite difficult to detect errors when children have come to believe what they are telling adults. Bruck et al. (1998) reviewed a number of studies and concluded that, under certain circumstances, children are capable of providing accurate, detailed, and useful information. The absence of suggestive techniques allows even preschoolers to provide highly accurate reports although sparse in the number of details. Factors that increase the likelihood of accurate reporting include a neutral tone by the interviewer, limited use of misleading questions, and the absence of any induction, motive, or bias for the child to make a false report. It has been determined that when preschoolers are interviewed by unbiased, neutral interviewers, when the number of interviews and the number of leading questions are kept to a minimum, and when there is an absence of threats, bribes, and peer pressure, the reports are at "considerably less risk for taint" (p. 146).

When there is clear medical evidence, there may be fewer variables to question. Much of the time, there is no medical evidence because the alleged acts involve fondling, oral copulation, or exhibitionism that does not leave evidence. In many cases, the findings are inconclusive because the scarring, anal fissures, or abnormalities could be caused by other means besides sexual molestation by penetration. It is always important to have a thorough examination by a reputable clinic or physician trained in the examination and interpretation of medical evidence pointing to sexual abuse.

Another important factor is the age of the child. The younger the child, the more difficult it is to sort out what occurred because of the limits in cognitive ability and language. A 3-year-old who said "Jim hurt my butt with ice" prompted me to bring ice to the session in an effort to clarify. Likewise, a preschooler who says "Daddy hurt my pee-pee with a red stick" but cannot differentiate colors leaves much to be determined. Such very young children may not know their colors either because they are too young or because they suffer from developmental delays. These delays in development can be caused by sexual abuse, if the allegations are true. They may also occur in children who experience a particularly high-conflict divorce of their parents characterized by violence or the threat of violence and accompanied by repeated police involvement to settle domestic disputes or civil standbys to enforce visitation. Parents who become alarmed and take their children to several different agencies to tell their accounts eventually wind up with rote children who have little affect in presentation and appear as if they are trying to remember something that was told to them.

Children who are alienated from one of their parents may develop the defense of splitting, in which all of their negative feelings are projected onto the alienated parent. That parent becomes the container for all of their negative feelings, including those they may have toward both parents or other relatives.

APPROACH TO THE INVESTIGATION: EVALUATION

A basic distinction needs to be made between a child sexual abuse assessment and a custody evaluation that contains a sexual abuse assessment. The former usually refers to the first stage of psychotherapy in which the therapist is a consultant for parents who are concerned that their child was molested in a context other than custody and are seeking treatment. The latter refers to a full custody evaluation that involves a sexual abuse assessment.

Confused parents in the midst of a divorce and convinced that something is terribly wrong with their child may want to bring the child in for therapy in the hope of the therapist finding an abnormality that can stop visitation. Of course, there are times when therapy is indicated as a separate process from and not as a substitute for an evaluation. When evaluations are conducted in cases of suspected sexual abuse, a neutral court-ordered appointment is the best course of action prior to beginning the evaluation. The court may order a sexual abuse assessment without a full custody evaluation. In either case, an order of the court ensures that the evaluator is neutral and is not working for one parent against the other. One-sided custody evaluations, which unfortunately occur in some jurisdictions, may result in the child having to be evaluated more times than is advisable.

In addition, I have found it to be a sound policy for each attorney, in coordination with their clients, to submit a list of questions to be addressed in the evaluation. This is especially important when the court order does not delineate a specific focus. Such questions usually relate to the psychological functioning of the parents; whether the child was sexually abused and, if so, who the perpetrator might be; and, if the child was not sexually abused, what might account for the symptoms presented by the child. The questions might also relate to specific treatment recommendations, visitation schedules, or changes in custody.

Child Protective Services and police investigations are generally conducted soon after allegations of sexual abuse are reported and are usually conducted in one session. By the time the matter is referred for a custody evaluation, a substantial period of time might have elapsed, the child may have been interviewed by many people, and the situation is likely to be complicated by the escalating feud between parents. The child may have increased difficulty at transitions and may refuse to go on scheduled visitation. Visitations may have been temporarily halted by the court pending the outcome of the evaluation. Because of all of these factors, it is necessary that the investigation proceed in a step-by-step fashion and that sufficient time be allowed for the facts to unfold and for a determination to be made.

As a result, a typical child custody evaluation in which there are allegations of sexual abuse may take 3 months. The primary concern is that of the child and not of the parents. If the child is already in therapy, it is often recommended that the therapy be temporarily suspended pending the evaluation in order to not overwhelm the child with therapeutic contact and not dilute the process. It is also crucial to the outcome of the evaluation that there are no changes in custody or visitation during the evaluation process, except as necessary to ensure the child's safety. The process of evaluation is much like a research project, and consistency ensures the most accurate outcome. Changes such as increased visitation or unsupervised visits in the middle of the evaluation might confound the findings, making it impossible to differentiate whether the findings are the result of the change or the sexual abuse. Changes that need to be made should wait until the findings and recommendations are reported to the parties and the court. If the situation between the parents is highly volatile, an attorney for the child or guardian ad litem may be warranted to ensure that the child's best interests are served.

The evaluation begins with a thorough history of the parents' relationship as well as a detailed account as to how the allegations have come to light. More complete information about the allegations is likely to be obtained if the parents are interviewed separately. Unlike general child custody evaluations, when there are allegations of physical abuse, sexual abuse, or domestic violence, many parents refuse to be in the same room with each other. There may be a restraining order prohibiting this, as well. Safety must take precedence over observing parental interaction. Psychological testing is recommended because the dynamics are likely to be complicated and because factors such as reality testing, impulse control, coping skills, anger and aggression, depression, empathy, and the like can be more completely assessed.

The history of the child includes events surrounding the pregnancy and delivery as well as developmental factors. The purpose of such detailed information is to create a context in which the child can be interviewed and understood. Valuable information is received by testing the parents' recollection of their son's or daughter's early childhood. It also may reveal how involved each parent was at the time of the child's birth. The etiology of nonspecific symptoms such as withdrawal, depression, and anxiety should be carefully explored. The evaluator should be well informed about what the child has stated, be familiar with the child's routines, and know the names he or she uses to label private parts. Unless there is a restraining order, it is important that the child be brought to sessions alternately by the mother and father because it allows the evaluator to see the interaction between the child and each parent in the waiting room and at the point of separation. Another purpose for alternating who brings the child is to evaluate whether the information the child discloses is dependent on who brings the child to the sessions. It is helpful to observe the parent and child together when a problem arises during the course of the session and the child wants the parent's assistance. If one parent has supervised visitation, the supervisor can accompany the parent and the child to the session. If one of the presenting complaints is that the child experiences extreme reactions a day or two following visitation, one or two sessions might be timed following the visitation.

It is recommended that there be five to eight individual sessions with the child and one child-parent observation session with each parent. The sessions are spaced to ensure that sufficient time is allowed to

- ❖ assess developmental issues;

- ❖ introduce the anatomical drawings or dolls;

- ❖ ask the child to name body parts;

- ❖ discuss good, bad, and confusing touch;

❖ conduct specific techniques such as time lines, projective drawings, and using the dollhouse to walk through the child's day at each home; and

❖ talk about secrets.

It is also necessary to evaluate and clarify the child's responses to the questions and to note the child's patterns in play. On or about the sixth visit, a parent observation session should be included, followed by a session alone between the evaluator and the child, followed by the observation session with the other parent. There should be one or two sessions to clarify, recap, and terminate. Fewer sessions may be needed for older children because they have a better ability to communicate and respond to the interviewer's queries.

Within the given time period, the evaluator must accomplish certain tasks. First, there must be an assessment of the developmental level of the child (i.e., Does the child know his or her colors? Can he or she count? Can the child articulate who is in his or her family? What is the child's verbal ability and ability to understand communication?). Important in the assessment of sexual abuse is whether the child knows important prepositions such as *underneath, on top of, inside, outside,* and *next to.* One also should not assume that a child understands certain key words, such as *touch,* for example. Colors can be determined by using color flash cards or pointing to colorful objects in the room. Knowledge of prepositions can be tested using blocks and a paper bag.

It must be determined whether the child knows the difference between the truth and a lie or between fantasy and reality. Although a differentiation between the truth and a lie may be necessary for the court to allow hearsay testimony about a child's statements, I favor approaching the question about fantasy and reality, especially with younger children. The implication of the former is that the truth is "good" and a lie is "bad" or something for which the child will get in trouble. Once that is established, the child is unable to change his or her mind without having the feeling that he or she has done something bad (lying) and, as a result, might get into trouble. It locks the child in place and makes previous statements irrevocable. On the other hand, distinguishing between what is "for real" and what is "pretend" is a more neutral way to question a child about the events. Examples should be given, such as, "If I said my hair is green, is that real or is that pretend?" It is important to be careful in the use of examples. For example, with a question such as "Is Mickey Mouse real or pretend?" a child who has visited Disneyland and seen someone in a Mickey Mouse costume may not be able to distinguish between real and pretend in that situation. For that child, Mickey Mouse is real.

Interviewing children about sexual abuse is a controversial issue with many differing viewpoints among clinicians who do this work. Faller (1990) points out that a custody evaluation with allegations of sexual abuse focuses on minimizing possible pressure on the child to make a false statement. The interviewer must determine whether anyone has suggested to the child what to say. A main focus is on the alleged victim's ability to provide detail. Questioning children about adult figures in their life other than the accused helps determine whether other perpetrators may have been involved. It also temporarily shifts the focus from the accused and creates a more neutral frame.

MacFarlane and Waterman (1986) recommend finding out at the outset what the child wants to have happen, does not want, is afraid of, and who it was that gave him or her the ideas. It is also important for children to be able to change their answers during the course of the interviews.

I follow a pattern of creating the most general atmosphere thought possible to elicit a disclosure. A structure is created so that if the child was sexually molested, it can unfold during the process. If the discussions about time lines, dollhouse play, puppet play, or activities at home do not elicit a disclosure, then questions become more narrowly focused and more direct. Some researchers have thought that young children cannot disclose sexual abuse with open-ended questions because their cognitive development is such that they need to be cued (MacFarlane & Waterman, 1986). This view is criticized by others (Ceci & Bruck, 1995). Steinmetz (1997) recommends using questions that begin with the words *what, who, how* or *how come, where, when,* and *what* as a way to avoid potentially leading questions. She suggests avoiding the question of *why* because it implies blame and may lead a child to make a leap in understanding something that he or she does not really understand.

It is important to directly tell the child that "I don't know" is an acceptable answer so that children do not feel the need to make up an answer or to respond with "no" when they really mean "I don't know." If an evaluator asks a child the same question repeatedly, the child is likely to think either that the evaluator did not like the answer or that he or she gave the wrong one. Therefore, it is important to make a clarification statement, "Let me see if I understand," or "I am a little confused, can you tell me . . ." An evaluator's attitude can help the child feel less apprehensive. It is important for the evaluator to use a straightforward, nonjudgmental, matter-of-fact tone that communicates to the child that the evaluator expects to hear what has happened to find out what is going on.

Language is another important aspect of the evaluation of children. Young children need questions and comments to be short and words to have few syllables. A general rule of thumb is to use the number of words in a sentence equal to the child's age plus one or two. For example, when speaking to a 3-year-old, use sentences that are four words long. This concept seems simple, yet it can present a challenge for the evaluator.

Neutrality is perhaps one of the most important earmarks of a sound investigation. Many evaluators were trained to reassure children that they did the right thing in telling and, as a result, inadvertently reinforce that "it is good to tell." It is only good to tell if something happened. The evaluator must communicate in whatever fashion possible that it is OK if the child tells and that it is OK if the child does not. Often, there is substantial pressure on the evaluator to find out "the truth." There is also pressure on the child to please adults.

It is especially important for the evaluator to find out what the child knows and not give the child any more information about divorce, anatomy, or sexuality than the child already possesses. The point is to not traumatize the child during the evaluation and to have it be as painless as possible.

The use of anatomically correct dolls is a controversial issue. The American Professional Society on the Abuse of Children's (1995) *Practice Guidelines* conclude that anatomical dolls are both a useful and an accepted tool in investigating cases of sexual abuse if

- ❖ the evaluators are knowledgeable and experienced in conducting such interviews,

- ❖ they are prepared to describe the role the dolls played in the interview, and

- ❖ the use of the dolls is not overemphasized, relied on exclusively, or used as a diagnostic *test* of sexual abuse.

There is little support for the position that the dolls are too suggestive or overly stimulating to be useful, and there is little empirical evidence that exposure to the dolls induces nonabused, sexually naive children to have sexual fantasies or act out sexually in a way that one might conclude they were abused.

Similarly, the Anatomical Doll Working Group of the American Psychological Association (Koocher et al., 1995) supports the use of anatomically detailed dolls as a communication or memory aid for children 5 years of age and over. It points out that there is a potential risk of errors if misleading questions are used. Greater caution is needed with preschool children because of greater suggestibility and difficulties with symbolic representation. Their use is not ruled out with these children, even though preschoolers are more prone than older children to false reporting.

As summarized by Sattler (1998), critics of the use of anatomically detailed dolls maintain that a child's behavior with the dolls may be difficult to interpret, may not provide valid or useful information, or may induce false memories. Sattler reports that the dolls are useful as an interview aid but not useful as the basis for diagnostic decisions regarding sexual abuse.

However, Ceci and Bruck (1995) conclude that "an assessment tool should only be used if it provides reliable additional information" (p. 184). They believe that there is no evidence to support the clinical or forensic diagnosis of abuse made primarily on the basis of a very young child's interaction with anatomical dolls. Not only do they object to the use of these dolls, but they express the view that the dolls impede children's reporting and can lead to false judgments about the status of abused and nonabused children. They urge that the dolls not be used diagnostically with very young children.

I agree with those who conclude that the best use of anatomically correct dolls in an evaluation is as a tool for children to demonstrate what happened *after* making a verbal disclosure (Ney, 1995).

No investigation can be conclusive without the valuable information received from collateral contacts, especially because parents involved in custody disputes are potentially biased. Parents are asked to provide a list of people in the child's life. Such a list may include grandparents and extended family members, teachers, the pediatrician, the day care provider, family friends, a visitation supervisor, the parents' therapist, and the child's therapist. An investigation of child sexual abuse must be thorough. In one case, in which there had been allegations that the perpetrator sexually abused the child *and* the family pet, the evaluator checked not only the child's medical records but the pet's to ascertain the validity of the allegations and the reliability of the accuser. Though this case represents an extreme example, it points to the need for thorough investigation that may go beyond what many of us have been trained to do in graduate school.

To the extent possible, information should be kept confidential to encourage people to be as open and honest as possible. Local court rules may prohibit this practice, however, because it can result in testimony that cannot be corroborated or cross-examined. My experience is that most sources are forthright and usually honest. Oftentimes, they are able to provide a perspective about the child that cannot be provided by either parent. Older siblings in a family can provide an important perspective of family life. A review of medical records and a discussion with the physician who conducted the physical examination of the child are especially important even in cases in which there are no physical findings. Such consultation might provide information about the child's demeanor during the examination, the physician's contact with the parents, and the parent-child interactions. It is especially important to talk to individuals other than the custodial parent to whom the child may have disclosed abuse. Information from collateral sources helps create the context in which the sexual abuse allegations can be evaluated.

PARENT-CHILD OBSERVATION SESSIONS

Ground rules for joint sessions include telling the parents in advance that the session is an opportunity for the evaluator to observe parent-child interactions and not to discuss the divorce or sexual abuse allegations. If a parent has supervised visitation, the supervisor and the parent should bring the child. If there has been no contact between the accused parent and the child for some time, care should be taken so that the child does not accidentally meet the accused parent in the evaluator's office. This is important for three reasons. First, it is not healthy for the child to be surprised at seeing the accused parent unexpectedly. Second, observing the child's initial reactions to seeing the parent often provides useful information. Third, these reactions could be affected by the surprise. I use a smaller waiting room in an out-of-the-way upstairs location where the accused parent can arrive a half hour ahead to avoid having both parents arrive at once. The parent who is accused should be instructed not to initiate any contact but to wait for the child to initiate the contact. This parent should not bring toys, Christmas presents, or birthday presents to the session.

During the session, I watch the interactions, being careful not to intrude. I direct activities and discussions when necessary. It is important to observe whether the parent can take the child's lead in directing the play, how the parent responds to the child's anxiety, and whether the parent can contain his or her own anxiety. The parent's style is important to evaluate. The level of attunement between parent and child is a useful indicator of how well the parent can read the child. Assessing whether the child can say "no" to the parent or resist parent directives is important in understanding whether the child can resist inappropriate parental influences. Observing how the parent reacts when the child mentions the other parent allows the evaluator to assess which parent might be more likely to allow the child access to the other parent. It is important to observe whether there is room for the child to have the idea of mommy and daddy in the presence of the other parent. It is also important to notice how dependent or independent the child is in the presence of each parent and whether either parent encourages age-appropriate independence.

There may be occasions when the accused parent has not seen the child for a long time, has great difficulty managing his or her emotions, and seems awkward about playing with the child. When I observe this, I follow the observation with an interview with that parent and brief him or her on appropriate behavior. I then schedule a second session to see how much the parent was able to integrate. In addition, some parents are unable to maintain appropriate behavior in the presence of the child and the evaluator. A parent who cannot follow directions when the evaluator is in the room is likely to have difficulty adhering to appropriate behavior during unsupervised visitation.

Finally, there may be times when a child has not seen the accused parent for several weeks, months, or years and the custodial parent informs the evaluator that the child does not wish to see the other parent. It is my policy not to traumatize children during the evaluation and to keep the child's best interest first. I try to explore whether it is the parent, the child, or both who are anxious about the observation session. I talk to the children about their concerns and reassure them that they can stop the session any time they want. The majority of the time, this reassurance is sufficient. If the anxiety of the custodial parent is too high to warrant a comfortable session between the child and the accused parent, a trusted third party might transport the child to the session. In these instances, a structured session that gives the child as much control as possible is the most helpful. Children might be more comfortable meeting with the parent after taking a peek at that parent through the window or meeting him or her at a favorite fast-food restaurant with the evaluator present. If the child continues to be uncomfortable, I will try, over several sessions, to assess whether this might change. However, if the child continues to refuse to see the accused parent despite all my efforts to calm and reassure the child, I will discontinue the effort to make such contact happen.

INTERPRETING AND REPORTING THE RESULTS

High-conflict custody disputes are likely to produce a range of symptoms in children that closely parallel many symptoms of child sexual abuse. These symptoms can include regression, lapses in toilet training, increased genital stimulation, fearfulness, clinging, withdrawal, depression, and anxiety. Exceptionally provocative or aggressive sexual behavior or overtly sexual behavior is not common to divorce. However, it is common to sexual abuse (Koocher et al., 1995). The evaluator should explore the etiology of both the nonspecific symptoms and sexually specific behaviors.

The problem with indicators is that they do not apply in every case. Because there is no sexual behavior observed only in sexually abused children and no research-based information to help determine when a child's specific sexual behavior is indicative of sexual abuse, it is important to understand the pattern of distress in the child and to use multiple sources of information before reaching a conclusion.

There are several possible reasons why children might lie about or misrepresent sexual abuse. These may include the following:

❖ the adolescent child who acts out of revenge,

❖ the child who wants to please an adult,

❖ repeated interviews,

❖ pressures from parents,

❖ heightened sexual stimulation that can lead to behaviors that point to abuse, and

❖ young children misreporting who is responsible for abuse because they fear retaliation.

Evaluators with many years of experience may reach a conclusion based on an unscientific method. They use their gut feeling or a single psychological test. This is a Russian roulette approach that does not take into account a range of factors or possibilities. The literature has failed to arrive at indexes that discriminate between those who molest and those who do not. It is as risky to base conclusions of perpetration on a set of personality characteristics as it is to diagnose sexual abuse based on general emotional symptoms of a child.

Before reaching a conclusion, the evaluator must understand the context in which the alleged abuse occurred. Sexual molestation usually occurs in a context. Stranger molestation is often opportunistic in that the perpetrator is primarily seeking sexual gratification and chooses random children. This is the least common form that sexual molestation takes. Scenarios in which a family member or acquaintance molests a child have a different context that usually includes grooming by the perpetrator, a special relationship, and a pattern of dysfunction described by many.

Therefore, context becomes an extremely important element. The evaluator must ask parents to explain the context in which the allegations were made. Disclosures may be made by children to angry mothers or fathers who easily concede, "I wouldn't put anything past him or her." In this context, there is usually significant distortion by the parent in which the child's original communication is lost. Frequently, a child makes statements to one parent that, when taken out of context, casts them in a different light. Unless an evaluator has interviewed both parents and has observed the child alone and with both parents, differentiation based on context cannot be adequately examined.

It is tempting, at times, to assess a 3-year-old in a high-conflict divorce and automatically conclude that nothing sexual has occurred. However, the evaluator must then explain the symptoms and statements of the child. The fact that the allegation was made is always serious. Whether it can be substantiated is a separate matter. As described earlier, the 3-year-old who insists that daddy did something with red sticks but cannot distinguish colors needs a closer look.

As such, it is not adequate merely to identify whether the evaluator concludes that abuse has occurred or not but to offer a rationale that explains the range of possibilities and the reasons why one explanation makes more sense than another. Often, the allegations do not stop after the evaluation is completed and the parents have met with the judge. Allegations frequently resurface until the underlying problem is directly addressed. Statements by children that they were sexually abused need to be corroborated by the child's affect and behavior, and there must be a meaningful context in which they were made. Prior to reaching a conclusion, it is crucial to examine every hypothesis, including the equal possibility that abuse has, or has not, occurred. The evaluator must write a report that offers a rationale as to why one solution is more plausible than any other. This allows the reader to understand the thinking process behind the conclusions offered in a report.

Although clinicians generally agree that there is no psychological profile of an individual who molests children, there is a practice, still used by some, of stating that people with certain characteristics such as poor impulse control, difficulty monitoring emotional reactions, excessive self-centeredness, strong dependency needs, and poor judgment are similar to individuals known to molest children (Bresee, Steams, Bess, & Packer, 1986). The custody evaluator might conclude that these characteristics were consistent with those of child molesters. Though it may be true that many sexual offenders have such characteristics, these traits might fit any number of problems such as domestic violence, child physical abuse, character disordered parents, and substance abuse problems.

When a child is coached, he or she may not have more than a few words to describe things, because the child has no real knowledge beyond that which has been coached. The child's details usually validate the experience or give away that the child does not know the meaning of what he or she is talking about. There is a developmental inability for preschool children to fabricate much factual content about sexual acts with adults. Likewise, it is difficult to get young children to remember what they are supposed to say. Coached children use adult words or phrases whose meaning the child may not understand; they repeat their statements repeatedly; and they cannot elaborate on the actual experience or tell about their feelings. Children also should be asked to describe the taste, smell, or feeling of their alleged experience to rule out pornography as an explanation for precocious sexual knowledge.

It is important for the evaluator to use the conclusion section of the evaluation to discuss the findings regarding the major evaluation questions, including the specific allegation of the sexual abuse. It is important to list the possibilities that were considered and offer a rationale for the conclusions reached. The recommendations should easily flow from the data and conclusions. If the evaluator does not find the presence of abuse, it is crucial to explain why not. It is also important to offer explanations for how the allegations came to be. The rationale should be backed by data arrived at from research, the history, the clinical presentation, and the psychological test data.

There may be times when the allegations of sexual abuse have resulted in either a mild disruption in the child's relationship with the accused parent or a more pronounced alienation (as described in Chapter 1). Recommendations should address a plan for restoring the relationship. Frequently, an exonerated father will expect that the relationship will resume where it left off prior to the allegations. However, the child may not yet feel comfortable relinquishing a supervisor, if there is one. In cases such as these, a gradual reduction in the amount of supervised time is recommended, perhaps having an unsupervised visit every other time or increasing the length of unsupervised visits over the course of several weeks. Frequently, a child may need a family therapist who is willing to alternate joint sessions between the child and his or her mother and father to help facilitate the child's attachment to the alienated parent while being able to discuss concerns with the alienating parent.

Finally, there are times when even the most experienced evaluator cannot sort out whether the allegations of sexual abuse are valid. In these instances, protection of the child should be foremost. For the young child, it may be helpful to recommend that he or she attend preschool. This can reduce family isolation, encourage independence, and offer the child a structured setting to get away from the conflict of the parents. The preschool setting can serve as a safeguard. A recommendation for the child to be in therapy can also be helpful. Sometimes, a disclosure of molestation will be made in the therapeutic setting, even though it was not uncovered during the evaluation.

VISITATION RECOMMENDATIONS

Supervised visitation is a common recommendation when the protection of the child is in the forefront. It can be a safeguard for protecting children in a number of situations that might be dangerous and in which their best interests may not be protected. In cases in which there are allegations that a parent molested a child, the best use of supervised visits is during the time period when an evaluation is being conducted and the court must be sure that the child is adequately protected. Such supervision usually has a specific time frame. However, should there be a finding that sexual abuse has occurred, such visitation is usually stopped until the offender, victim, and nonoffending parent have had adequate treatment and the victim is ready for reunification with the offending parent. I believe that continuing supervised visitation subsequent to a finding of sexual abuse repeatedly exposes the victim to the person who molested him or her. This exposure in other than a therapeutic setting may interfere with the child being able to deal with the abuse adequately. It implies to the child that he or she should pretend to act normal with the abusing parent and go on activities without the molestation ever being addressed. I believe this perpetuates the abuse dynamics.

Others disagree with that approach. Faller (1990) states that it is important to preserve the child's relationship with the offending parent because there are likely to be aspects that are worthy of preserving. She adds that it affords the child an opportunity to work through feelings about the sexual abuse and the divorce, and it encourages a realistic view of the offending parent. Though these are important long-term goals, I believe that therapeutic intervention for all of the parties should be the first priority.

Supervision is an attempt to control the situation. If the situation requires monitoring, then it can be appropriate. If the situation does not require monitoring, then it can be damaging. Children need emotional access to both parents for identity formation. Their future lives and relationships depend on having an internalized mother and father with all of the loving and angry, positive and negative features integrated. Supervised visitation, when not absolutely necessary for child protection, is an unfair intrusion into the parent-child relationship and promotes the idea that the parent is "bad" in some way.

REUNIFICATION THERAPY

There are times when children are convinced that they were inappropriately touched, but the evaluator does not think that child sexual abuse is the most salient explanation for the situation. In cases in which children appear convinced that they were molested, the most straightforward approach is not to talk them out of their position but to have the parent meet them at their level and reassure them that they will not harm them. When a parent holds clearing his or her name or proving the other party wrong as more important than reassuring the child, the child's needs are not met. When one parent is ready to move ahead with reunification, the other parent may be putting on the brakes, creating a difficult situation for all concerned, including the therapist. Such cases generally require a clear court order, the use of a neutral decision maker to enforce the reunification, and the parents to be in therapy so that they can work toward addressing their child's needs more directly.

CONCLUSIONS

Ultimately, whether the allegations of sexual abuse are true or false, they are seen as an indicator of emotional risk for a child (Bresee et al., 1986). A child's emotional health is equally threatened when a parent abuses him or her or when a parent is overreacting or lying. The responsibility of an evaluator does not end with proving or disproving the allegations. With that in mind, the evaluator must protect children from parents who would sexually abuse them but also from parents who would lie.

I have a strong opinion that, in general, parents know their children best, and, therefore, they are the best people to make decisions for their children. However, when parents, for whatever reason, are unable to exercise this role, the job falls to others, and the parent loses something valuable. The children's best interests demand that evaluators act in a manner that helps the parents move toward reclaiming their rightful place. It also behooves us, as professionals, to stay abreast of the research and continue receiving feedback from one another to ensure high-quality work.

CHAPTER 4

Move-Away Evaluations

An increasingly mobile society often forces parents to choose between a career and family. When one parent needs (or wants) to move and the other parent needs (or wants) to stay, children become victims in a battle over parenting time, custody, and visitation. In increasing numbers, judges are seeking the assistance of child custody evaluators to determine "the best interests of the child" in these relocation cases. For the child custody evaluator, move-away cases are among the most difficult and emotionally sensitive, often because there is no middle ground that can reduce the conflict or potential risks to the child.

REVIEW OF THE LITERATURE

As with many areas of family law and child custody evaluation, there is a scarcity of research or writing on move-away evaluations. In California, as in many other states, the courts have been grappling with the issue of relocation following divorce and with its impact on custody and visitation.

Wallerstein and Tanke (1996) wrote an amicus brief for the California Supreme Court regarding a move-away case. Wallerstein drew on her research on the effects of divorce on children and applied it to her analysis of moves. Their brief was the primary source of information used by the California Supreme Court in its decision in *Marriage of Burgess* (1996). Miller (1995), an appellate judge in New York, addressed many of the issues facing the court in move-away cases. With no adequate research of the effect of relocation on children, both Wallerstein and Tanke and Miller wrote theoretical articles outlining the dilemmas facing the courts and families in such cases. Berkow

(1996), a family court commissioner in Contra Costa County, California, outlined what issues the court and ultimately the child custody evaluator need to look at when understanding how relocation issues will affect the best interests of a given child. I will describe their writing in detail and follow it with an analysis of some of the societal issues that influence the courts and an analysis of the California Supreme Court decision.

According to Wallerstein and Tanke (1996), children of divorce often experience feelings of anxiety and self-blame for the marital failure, and, though the legal system "pays lip service to their needs with the best interest standard" (p. 306), all too often those needs are obscured by the advocacy of warring parents. The court needs to assess the impact of possible disruptions on the child. The court needs to extend its understanding of best interests to include the potential impact on the child if a move does take place as well as if the move does *not* take place. The best interest of the child cannot be identified without a consideration of the child's feelings, as understood by sensitive and caring adults who are independent of the battling parents.

Wallerstein and Tanke claim that the psychological adjustment of the custodial parent has consistently been found to be related to the child's adjustment, but the psychological adjustment of the noncustodial parent has not. Although they state that they do not wish to diminish the important role of the father in the child's growing up years, they believe that there is no significant connection between frequency of visits and time spent in the father's home and the development of the nurturing father-child relationship on the positive outcome in the child or adolescent. When a court prohibits a move by the custodial parent, it may force that parent to choose between custody of the child and possible opportunities (e.g., a new marriage, an important job opportunity, or a return to the help provided by extended family) that may benefit the entire family unit, including the child. They add that children are not Ping-Pong balls and that travel plans need to be tailored to the age, temperament, and wishes of the child. Wallerstein and Tanke state that the best interests of the child are best served within the nurturing and protection provided by high-quality parent-child relationships and that the needs of children should have greater protection than the rights of the adversarial parents or the process. They concluded that, "especially at the time of the contemplated move, the court should be responsive to the child's voice, amplifying it above the din of competing parents" (p. 323).

Justice Miller (1995) notes that, as early as 1981, the New York Court of Appeals apparently recognized the legitimacy of considering a parent's right to a "fresh start," among other factors bearing on the child's best interest. The most significant message contained in various New York cases is the court's unequivocal concern for the child's welfare above all else. New York courts have typically held a two-part test to determine whether relocation would deprive the noncustodial parent of "regular and meaningful access to the child" (p. 347). If there is deprivation, exceptional circumstances must be shown to allow the move. If there is no deprivation, the custodial parent need not show exceptional circumstances. However, if the court finds that the relocation will deprive the noncustodial parent of meaningful visitation, a presumption arises that relocation is not in the best interest of the child. Miller feels that, once it has been determined that the custodial parent has demonstrated the requisite exceptional circumstances to justify the relocation, the focus then becomes whether the relocation is in the child's best interests. Whether a given relocation is in the best interests of a child is based on the given facts in each case. Central to this inquiry is an analysis of the quality and quantity of visitation enjoyed by the noncustodial parent and child prior to the proposed move and whether the relationship can adequately be preserved at a greater distance with less frequent, but more intensive, prolonged visitation.

Miller (1995) suggests that the court must look at the following five factors in determining what is in the best interests of the child:

1. whether the move is likely to enhance the quality of life for both the custodial parent and the child;

2. the motives of the custodial parent who wishes to move, to determine whether the motive behind the move is to defeat or "frustrate" visitation;

3. the noncustodial parent's motives for opposing removal;

4. the noncustodial parent's visitation rights, because it is in the best interests of the child to have a healthy and close relationship with both parents as well as with other family members; and

5. whether a realistic and reasonable visitation schedule can be reached if the move is allowed.

Justice Miller believes that there should be no presumptions for or against a proposed move. The custodial parent desiring to relocate shall bear the initial burden of coming forward with evidence that the motivation underlying the move is one of good faith and is not sparked by a desire to interfere maliciously with the relationship or visitation schedule of the child and noncustodial parent; that a rational basis exists for believing that the relocation will provide a better life for the family unit, the parent, or the child; that the child will enjoy a healthy, decent lifestyle in the new community (i.e., adequate schooling, housing, financial support); and that the proposed visitation program will provide the noncustodial parent with sufficient visitation to permit and encourage the development of a meaningful relationship between the noncustodial parent and child. Miller's most important point is that the flexibility implicit in the recommended approach to relocation cases permits the courts to weigh the relative importance to the child of such close relationships with the noncustodial parent against all other factors in determining whether to permit the move, alter visitation, or even change custody. The basic change proposed is not a matter of preference between fathers and mothers, but rather one of focus on the child considering all factors impacting upon that child's best interest unimpeded by rigid preconditions. (p. 387)

Commissioner Berkow (1996) notes that judges perceive relocation cases to be "nightmare" cases. She outlined social policy issues raised by these cases, as they represent

the latest battlefield between feminists advocating the right of the primary custodial parent (often but not always the mother) to move whenever or wherever they like and the father's rights groups advocating the right of the non-custodial parent to always keep the child in the current location. (p. 18)

She adds that "both miss the point," because the issue is not "what either parent may desire but which custodial plan is in the best interest of the child in a given case" (p. 18).

Berkow (1996) discussed several appellate decisions in California related to move-away cases. Essentials with which the courts in all recent move-away decisions concurred include that both parents should have certain procedural safeguards requiring custodial parents to provide at least 45 days' prior notice of an intention to change the child's residence; if mediation is unsuccessful, there should be a right to a custody evaluation; and the moving parent should show that the move was necessary and in the child's best interests. In cases in which there is a strong emotional bond with the other parent, the working shared custody arrangement, and established ties in the child's school, neighborhood, and community, denial of permission to move away has been upheld.

Just as Wallerstein and Tanke (1996) point out the benefit of a custody evaluation to hear "the child's voice," Berkow (1996) believes that a custody evaluation "is very helpful to the court in determining several factual issues critical to the best interest analysis" (p. 19). While pointing out that it is not the job of the custody evaluator to make a legal assessment of whether the proposed move is or is not in the best interests of the child, Commissioner Berkow believes that an evaluation focused on certain issues is critical to the court's making an intelligent decision in a move-away case. These issues include whether there is a working shared custody arrangement; what the reasons for the move are, both stated and unstated; the history of the moving parent either facilitating or interfering with the noncustodial parent's access to the child; the child's developmental and individual needs at this point in time and how they can be expected to change in the future; the child's significant relationships with siblings, stepsiblings, teachers, playmates, and others, and what impact the proposed relocation may have on these relationships; the child's special needs, if any, and how they might be affected in the new location; what a child wishes in the context of the age and ability to formulate an intelligent preference; whether there are any less-disruptive alternatives to the proposed relocation; and if there are alternative parenting plans under the proposed relocation considering the financial and logistic circumstances. Berkow believes that child custody evaluations that focus on such relevant issues are a major contribution to the judicial decision for these families.

SOCIETAL ISSUES

What are the societal issues that the custody evaluator needs to understand in addressing these cases? Most parents who want to move cite employment, remarriage, and economic hardship as their reasons. The nonmoving parent often claims that the move is designed to interfere with the relationship between him or her and the child.

Employers and the military are not necessarily family friendly. Most people change jobs several times during their adult life; corporations downsize; companies move various operations; and military bases close. When this occurs, parents are faced with choosing between the other parent's access to the child and their own career options and enhancement. The courts have long recognized the necessity and rights of parents to move for employment reasons, and, as previously noted, they are likely to grant a move for such reasons to a primary custodial parent.

Parents may wish to move for a remarriage. Many parents get involved in a relationship that requires a move. The stepparent, or soon-to-be stepparent, may already reside out of state or may be transferred to another location. Some stepparents may be unemployed and need to find a job in another state. For these families, it is the blend of remarriage and employment economics that forces the move. Given the relative lack of value placed on stepparents in the courts, these cases may require a somewhat different analysis. The courts and the evaluator are usually concerned about the direct impact on the relationship between the biological parent and the child.

Economic hardship may cause a move. In high-cost-of-living locales, a single parent may need to move in with relatives (often a parent) or to a location with a lower cost of living, even if there are no relatives nearby. In such cases, the court will often assess the reality of the hardship before allowing the move.

In contrast, there is usually only one primary reason that parents oppose moves: Moving may make it difficult for the noncustodial parent to maintain frequent and continuing contact with his or her child. Twenty or 30 years ago, when it was more common for mothers to raise children and for fathers to work, it was not unusual for the noncustodial father to move away from his children sometime after the divorce. Although many of those fathers continued their relationship with their children, they were less concerned with the frequency of such contact, as long as they could maintain some relationship with their child. As modern-day fathers have become more directly involved in child rearing and are participating more fully in their child's day-to-day lives, it is not surprising that they find themselves in opposition to proposed moves.

Some parents allege that the other parent wants to move to control or interfere with the child's relationship with him or her. They maintain that there is no legitimate reason for the move; instead, they believe it is borne out of revenge or spite. They oppose the move because they can see no positive impact that a move could have on their child.

Often ignored in this debate is the parent who *chooses* to move away from his or her child, regardless of the reason. Noncustodial parents are often upset with the desire of the custodial parent to move, but no one seems to object when the noncustodial parent moves. Yet such moves may be very difficult on the child. The child can experience feelings of abandonment, anger, disappointment, and resentment and may wish for the return of the relocating parent. This may worsen the child's adjustment to the divorce. Though it is rare, for the potential custody evaluator, there could be an increasing number of evaluations to address appropriate visitation issues for these families.

ISSUES FOR THE COURTS

As can be seen by the above analyses by Justice Miller and Commissioner Berkow, the issue for the court is still the best interest of the child. Using California appellate decisions, I will provide a review of several judicial cases and discuss the reasoning that was used in making these decisions. Although the legal implications of these decisions are primarily limited to California, the rationale is important for custody evaluators to understand regardless of where they practice.

Typically, the primary focus of a traditional best-interest determination is in the child's emotional rather than economic needs. In the absence of compelling reasons, courts are reluctant to disrupt established patterns of care and emotional bonds. For a number of years, the California courts considered whether a move was necessary and in the child's best interests or whether it was "essential and expedient" and for an "imperative" reason. The courts have ruled that parties have an equal right to travel or not to travel. Typically, they have found that a move for the custodial parent's or that parent's spouse's new job was "necessary." The appellate courts have encouraged trial courts to evaluate the necessity of such a move, and, as Commissioner Berkow (1996) indicated, "necessity" may simply be the absence of a willful intent to interfere with the other parent.

In April 1996, the California Supreme Court made a decision on the issue of relocation (*Marriage of Burgess*). In the *Burgess* case, the children had previously had almost daily contact with both parents, although the children had been in the sole physical custody of the mother when the trial court issued its custody decision. The trial court originally supported the mother's right to move, but the court of appeal overturned the ruling on the grounds that her relocation was deemed not to be "necessary." The Supreme Court determined that "in an initial judicial custody determination based on the best interest of minor children, a parent seeking to relocate does not bear a burden of establishing that the move is necessary as a condition of custody" (p. 5). It went on to state that

> after the judicial custody order is in place, a custodial parent seeking to relocate bears no burden of establishing that it is necessary to do so. Instead, he or she has the right to change the residence of the child, subject to the power of the court to restrain a removal that would prejudice the rights or welfare of the child. (p. 8)

Using Wallerstein and Tanke's (1996) amicus brief as its guide, the Supreme Court found that a parent who has been the primary caretaker for minor children is no less capable of maintaining his or her responsibilities and obligations of parenting "simply by virtue of a reasonable decision to change his or her geographical location" (p. 7). The decision continued,

> Once it has been established that a particular custodial arrangement is in the best interest of the child, the court need not re-examine that question. Instead it should preserve the established mode of custody unless some significant changes in circumstances indicates a different arrangement would be in the child's best interest. . . . In a move-away case, a change of custody is not justified simply because the custodial parent has chosen, *for any sound good faith reason* [italics added], to reside in a different location, but only if, as a result of relocation with that parent, the child will suffer detriment rendering it essential or expedient for the welfare of the child that there be a change. (p. 9)

Ultimately, the California Supreme Court concluded,

> Each case must be evaluated on its own unique facts. . . . The trial court . . . may take into consideration the nature of the child's existing contact with both parents—including de facto as well as de jure custody arrangements—and the child's age, community ties, and health and educational needs. Where appro-

priate, it must also take into account the preferences of the child. . . . A different analysis may be required when parents share joint physical custody of the minor children under an existing order and in fact, and one parent seeks to relocate with the minor children. (p. 10)

I have had numerous conversations with judges and attorneys who believe that the court's ruling in the *Burgess* case was designed to set a standard in which appellate courts would overturn trial courts only for procedural errors and to discourage the appellate court from making judicial policy regarding such cases. The end result of the Supreme Court decision in the *Burgess* matter is that the trial court must continue to establish best interest in relocation cases. When there is a primary custodial parent, this ruling is likely to support a reasonable request by that parent to move. A trial court may still find that there is no basis for moving and that it is not in the child's best interest to move. This would most likely occur if the court finds that the requested move is designed more to thwart the child's relationship with the other parent than to meet a specific need for the custodial parent. This ruling does little to address the needs of families in which there is joint physical custody and one parent seeks to relocate. California law provides that there is neither a preference nor presumption for or against joint legal custody, joint physical custody, or sole custody. The law allows the court and the family the widest discretion to choose a parenting plan that is in the best interest of the child.

Since that decision by the state supreme court, there have been two more appellate decisions in California involving relocation issues. In the first case, *Brody v. Kroll* (1996), the parties enjoyed a joint physical custody arrangement, and the trial court originally allowed the mother to move with the child from California to Connecticut. The case was sent back to the trial court because "the court should have determined whether it would be in the child's best interest to give the mother virtual sole physical custody" (p. 1732) rather than continue the joint custody. The appellate court ruled that the trial court never addressed the issue of the child's best interest. It ordered mediation and, if mediation was unsuccessful, a new hearing to determine whether a change of custody was warranted.

In the second case, *Cassady v. Signorelli* (1996), the mother was the primary custodial parent, but the trial court ruled that it would not be in the child's best interest to move from California to Florida, in large part because of significant psychological problems of the mother. In this case, the appellate court upheld the trial court decision because a determination of best interests had been made.

Other states have made legislative decisions about relocation. For example, the Florida legislature adopted a rule (Fla. 97-242; text available at http://www.flcourts.org) in 1997, which states,

No presumption shall arise in favor of or against a request to relocate when a primary residential parent seeks to move the child and the move will materially affect the current schedule of contact and access with the secondary residential parent. In making a determination as to whether the primary residential parent may relocate with a child, the court must consider the following factors:

1. Whether the move would be likely to improve the general quality of life for both the residential parent and the child.

2. The extent to which visitation rights have been allowed and exercised.

3. Whether the primary residential parent, once out of the jurisdiction, will be likely to comply with any substitute visitation arrangements.

4. Whether the substitute visitation will be adequate to foster a continuing meaningful relationship between the child and the secondary residential parent.

5. Whether the cost of transportation is financially affordable by one or both parties.

6. Whether the move is in the best interests of the child.

For child custody evaluators, one significant implication of these rulings is the likelihood that courts will seek the assistance of evaluators in most of these matters. Trial courts will need to address the question of best interests, and, given the multiple issues in these cases, the courts will look to the evaluator for guidance. Attorneys may now be reluctant to encourage clients to agree to a parenting plan in which the other parent has primary physical custody. Even before a move is contemplated, more families could experience contested custody hearings to prevent one parent from moving with the children as they get older.

The rest of this chapter will focus on the specific issues that evaluators need to address in these evaluations.

FACTORS FOR THE EVALUATOR TO CONSIDER

Given the issues noted above by Wallerstein and Tanke, Miller, Berkow, the legislatures, and the courts, it seems that there are a variety of issues that child custody evaluators must look at when evaluating families for relocation. These can be separated into two types of issues: child and family issues and move issues. In this section, I will outline and provide a brief description of these issues. The purpose of the evaluation will be to assist the court in making a ruling in the best interests of the child.

Child and Family Issues

 Nature of child's relationship with each parent: pre- and post-separation

One of the most important issues for the evaluator to understand is the *actual* relationship between the child and each parent during the marriage, the early stages of the divorce, and presently. This helps to establish a baseline from which to assess the potential risk to the child's relationship with the other parent if the child were to move. The evaluator will be trying to understand the qualitative and quantitative aspects of the relationships and how much the child relies on each parent for day-to-day needs. This will help the evaluator determine whether the parents have been practicing joint physical custody or whether one parent has been the primary custodial parent. In many jurisdictions, this analysis is critical for understanding the potential impact of a move on the child, and it will be a significant factor in the best-interest analysis.

 What is the *actual* custodial arrangement now? How well does it work? What are the problems? Why does someone have primary custody?

Once the evaluator understands the history, he or she can then assess the qualitative nature of the relationships. The evaluator will want to know who participates in day-to-day activities, such as helping with homework, reading at bedtime, driving to activities and doctor's appointments, and other daily tasks. The evaluator will want to know to whom the child goes when afraid, excited, angry, or hurting. The evaluator will assess the relative attachments and the extent to which the child feels closer to either the mother or father or whether the child feels equally close to both. By understanding these facts, the evaluator can better understand the current nature of the relationships between the child and each parent.

The evaluator also needs to assess the relationship between the parents. If they share joint legal and joint physical custody, how is their coparenting arrangement working? If one parent has primary physical custody, the evaluator will want to know how that parent encourages the relationship between the child and the other parent and whether the custody was established voluntarily or as a result of a previous court decision. Because the court is likely to allow a primary custodial parent with a reasonable motive to move or allow a move when joint custodial parents share an unworkable plan, this information is critical.

Developmental stages of the child and the child's capacities to maintain a relationship with distance (i.e., interplay of move and developmental tasks)

Once the evaluator has assessed the custodial relationship, it is important to understand the developmental issues of the child. As will be described in Chapter 6, children of different ages have varying developmental needs. For example, with young children, it will be important to understand how they can be expected to maintain and increase the attachment with the noncustodial parent if distance becomes an issue. Certainly, before age 5, a young child requires relatively frequent contact with each parent to establish and maintain a relationship. The evaluator must understand how each parent perceives relationships being affected by a move. The evaluator will want to understand the child's capacity to maintain a relationship when significant time might pass between visits.

For school-age children, the evaluator must assess the potential impact on the relationship between the child and the noncustodial parent if the child can visit only for blocks of time, such as vacations, holidays, and summers. The evaluator will want to understand the child's capacity to use the telephone, fax, e-mail, and other technologies that might be useful in maintaining an established relationship. The evaluator will also want to know how the noncustodial parent can foster and maintain the relationship with the child at a long distance.

Adolescence may bring a whole range of new issues, such as the adolescent's lack of desire to relocate away from his or her friends. Teenagers are able to hold and maintain relationships over long distances, but the impact of those relationships is reduced when much of their time is spent with friends. As evaluators encourage and guide adolescents toward adulthood, it is important to understand how each parent will be able to contribute to this task, especially at a long distance. Adolescents may state a preference to stay in their community because of strong attachments to friends. This can pose a problem for the evaluator when there are siblings and the evaluator attempts to meet the needs of all children. Another dilemma is found with teenagers who want to be with the parent who gives them the most freedom but does not necessarily provide the best structure to meet their needs.

Whatever the developmental issues, it is important for the evaluator to understand and integrate them for the particular family.

 Gender, temperament, and fit between each parent and child

Another issue to understand is the extent to which gender, temperament, or psychological fit is an issue for the family. Although there is no specific research that differentiates between the relative value of mothers or fathers for boys and girls, the move might stimulate a problem that is gender related. For example, it might be more detrimental for a teenage son to be moved from his noncustodial father than it would for a teenage daughter because the father's ability to be a male role model will be limited by the move. A similar scenario might be problematic for a latency-aged daughter, but the impact could be different, and the evaluator needs to understand the gender issue.

Similarly, although many children adjust to a variety of circumstances, some have a temperament that makes adjustment more difficult. The evaluator must understand the child's temperament and whether it might affect the child's adjustment to the proposed move. For some children, especially those who have had difficulty adjusting to significant changes in their life, a move from one's home and community could be detrimental. A child who had trouble adjusting to the divorce itself may have difficulty adjusting to a family change related to the move. The evaluator must bring an understanding of these issues to the court's attention.

The "goodness of fit" reflects the extent to which a parent and child blend or clash in their personalities. For example, a child who is very athletic and interested in sports might miss a parent who is a part-time coach differently from another child who is artistic like one of his or her parents would. Similarly, a child who is temperamentally fidgety may do better with a parent who is temperamentally calming. Because many families are being evaluated for the first time and a judicial custody determination has never been made, the evaluator can lend insight to the court on the quality of the relationships and on the psychological connections between each parent and the child. This is important for all custody evaluations, but it is especially crucial in move-away cases.

 Potential meaning of the loss to the child: What is the child going to experience if the proposed move does or does not take place?

With a proposed move, one of the significant issues is the expected loss to the child. The evaluator in these cases is being asked to assess the nature of the expected loss. This is related to the previous issues, such as the extent and quality of the attachments, the involvement of the noncustodial parent in the child's day-to-day life, goodness of fit, and child development. It is common for the parent who is left behind to express a fear that the child will lose a significant relationship and that such a loss will be detrimental to the child. In contrast, the parent who wants to move typically states that the loss will be minimal to the child. The task for the evaluator is to understand his or her own assessment of this loss and what the child is likely to actually experience rather than what either parent is alleging will occur.

At the same time, it is important for the evaluator to assess the impact on the child if the move is not allowed to take place or if there is a change of custody and the previously custodial parent moves. In their amicus brief, Wallerstein and Tanke (1996) cite the example of a mother, the primary custodial parent, who wanted to return to school and become a doctor. The move was denied by the court. Wallerstein and Tanke suggested that the child, a school-age girl, might feel guilty that she prevented her mother from going to medical school. If the girl's mother becomes depressed because her goal was thwarted, they suggest that this will also negatively affect the child. This example illustrates the importance of evaluating any potential negative impact on the child if the move does not take place and not merely the impact if the move does occur.

 Mental health of the moving parent and whether he or she will facilitate a positive relationship with the other parent over time. What is the history of the moving parent's facilitating or interfering with the other parent's access?

A significant factor to evaluate is the mental health of the moving parent, especially if there have been problems with that parent facilitating a relationship with the other parent. Relatively healthy parents who have encouraged and supported the child's relationship with the other parent are likely to continue that pattern after the move. On the other hand, parents who have a pattern of interfering with visitation may use the relocation to further the interference. The evaluator will want to consider if this is really the primary reason for the move. For some families, this may be the determining factor in whether the court allows the move.

With regard to mental health issues, the evaluator needs to understand the level of pathology in the parents, the level of conflict between the parents, the extent to which the move is primarily designed to get away from the other parent, any pathology in children due to the parents' high conflict or emotional disturbance, and whether the child will be more or less affected by the reduction in conflict as opposed to the change in relationships.

 The child's special needs and if there are siblings, activities, or friends that will represent other losses to the child. What is the impact a move will have on such relationships, needs, or activities?

Among the child factors to be evaluated are the other relationships that are likely to be affected by the move. Many children have close friends or may be involved in cherished activities (such as Little League, dance, music, etc.). I have had many children express an unwillingness to move because of their preferred activities. Other potential losses for the child would be stepsiblings, stepparents, and other close family members. The evaluator needs to understand

and report to the court about these potential losses and evaluate the extent to which the child will be hurt by these losses.

Occasionally, children have special education or medical needs that require specialized programs. An assessment of available services in the potential new location should be made. A comparison of the available services in both parents' communities should be considered when this is an issue.

 Given the child's age and ability of self-expression, what are his or her wishes?

As stated by Wallerstein and Tanke (1996), it is important to understand the child's feelings. As children get older, their ideas and wishes sometimes become the overriding determinant. Some children clearly express their wishes concerning the proposed move, even if it means a change of custody to the other parent. When evaluating the child's statements, it is important to evaluate the reasons that are articulated by the child. Some children have very clear and obvious reasons for their wishes, whereas others appear to be lobbying on behalf of one of their parents. Differentiating this is an important task of the evaluator. Other children are reluctant to state their feelings and may be more concerned about protecting one of their parents than stating their own feelings. Especially for children over the age of 10, it is important to understand the child's stated wishes and feelings and incorporate them into the recommendations being made.

Move-Related Issues

Just as there are significant factors related to the child and family that need to be addressed, there are significant factors related to the move itself that need to be understood by the evaluator. These include the following:

 What are the reasons for the move, both stated *and* hidden?

The court needs to understand the reasons for the move. Parents might state their reasons to the court in their formal declarations. The task for the evaluator is to understand whether there are hidden factors not being discussed by the parent. For example, a parent might state that he or she wants to move to be closer to out-of-state relatives. However, the evaluator might actually learn that there is more family close by, and it might appear that the primary reason for the move is to interfere with visitation. Often, there is no hidden agenda in wanting to move, but, if there is one, it usually relates to interfering with the other parent's relationship with the child. Some parents may hope to get an increase in child support if they move. By taking the time to explore these issues with the parents, the evaluator can be secure in stating whether or not there appears to be a hidden agenda.

 What are the realities of visitation if the move is to proceed: for example, money, geography, flexibility of parents?

Another variable to be evaluated is the logistic realities for the parents. Some moves will make it more complicated for the child to visit the other parent. Evaluators need to understand how frequently the child can easily visit, whether travel will need to be by plane and how easy it is to arrange flights, and whether the parents can afford to pay for frequent visits. For very young children who cannot travel by themselves, it will be important to understand how the moving parent envisions that visits can take place. Some parents are quite rigid when it comes to visitation plans, and others are quite flexible. Flexibility is an important trait when trying to facilitate long-distance visitation.

 Is the move representative of stability or a pattern of instability on the part of the moving parent?

Divorce is a time of instability for many children. Whether this move is representative of more instability is a critical variable to understand. Changes brought about by divorce are very stressful to children. Changes brought about by moves are stressful as well. If the requested move is part of an ongoing pattern of instability, the evaluator must note that to the court. For example, I have seen children who have moved four or more times in 3 years following the initial separation, which is reflective of instability. A move out of state might represent more instability or may be the necessary step to reaching relative stability. The evaluator should assess this. The move might be reflective of instability if the reason for the move is questionable. In such a situation, the evaluator might anticipate another move of continued great distance in the future. Because children require stability following their parents' divorce, the relative stability of each parent will need to be assessed by the evaluator before making a recommendation.

 Given the circumstances, are there any alternative parenting plans that might be suggested?

Finally, in many circumstances, alternatives to the proposed move may make sense. For example, a parent who wants to move a 3-year-old might be encouraged to wait until the child is at least 6 years old. This would help facilitate a growing bond between the child and the other parent, and then, if a move is still desired, the timing might be better. Some parents who are forced to make job transfers might have a variety of possible locations. The evaluator might explore with that parent which location would be the least problematic to the child. Communicate with the employer if possible, as there may be circumstances in which the employer would be willing to delay a relocation if the parent needs it. Although most relocation requests have few alternatives available, the evaluator should explore if a more appropriate alternative is possible. Also, consider whether the nonmoving parent would be willing to make a move to keep him or her close to the child.

In all the years that I have done evaluations, none is more difficult than the move-away case. This is because few alternatives are available, the impact on the child is potentially severe, and parents tend to be rather rigid in their positions. The parent who wants to move sees no other alternatives, and the nonmoving parent often experiences sadness and distress at the loss of his or her child. For many families, one parent feels he or she must move, while the other feels that he or she must stay. There is little room for negotiation, and one parent usually feels a victory while the other parent feels a loss. The sad reality in most relocation cases is that one parent does gain, one parent does lose, and the child almost always suffers, no matter the outcome. If the evaluator can maintain the perspective of the best interests of the child, address the multiple factors noted above, keep in mind the multiple needs of the child and focus them along a hierarchy (see Chapter 6), and provide the parents and the court with a consideration of the benefits and risks of moving, parents and judges can make informed decisions on behalf of the child.

For the remainder of the chapter, I will provide examples of three different evaluations. In the first, I made a recommendation in favor of the move. In the second, I made a recommendation against the move (and for a temporary change of custody). In the third, I felt that the issues were sociological and did not lend themselves to a recommendation. These examples reflect the varying nature of cases that evaluators often see in questions of relocation.

CASE EXAMPLE: The S Family

In a recent evaluation, I was faced with the task of addressing the possible relocation of Joey, a 6-year-old boy, from California to Chicago, Illinois. The boy lived primarily with his mother and her new husband (Mr. and Ms. N), who had been transferred there. Mr. S, Joey's father, wanted his son to stay and opposed the move. In addition to that, his mother joined in on the case, citing grandparent's visitation rights. The requested evaluation was focused on these issues. It is important for readers to keep in mind the California Supreme Court decision referred to earlier in this chapter when reading the case. The recommendation to support the move was made within that context. Under different laws, it is possible that a different recommendation would have been made.

The report findings were as follows:

In addressing move-away evaluations, it is this examiner's observation that it is critical to address numerous questions associated with the child and family as well as questions related to the move. In looking at these issues, it is then easier for the court and the evaluator to understand how best to settle issues related to the "best interests of the child." At the same time, it is also important to understand the reasons for the move and the resistance to the move, especially when some aspects of the move-related issues seem more clear-cut.

It is this examiner's observation that the precipitant for the move is Ms. N's desire to move as a result of her husband's new job. The resistance to the move is Mr. S's sense of loss, his fears for his relationship with Joey, and the way in which his own childhood experiences have affected him. It is this examiner's observation that, if Ms. N and her husband were to move to a closer locale, or if Mr. S had previously had a more secure father-child relationship in his own life, these issues would be less problematic. This is not to say that Mr. S is fine with Joey leaving; in fact, it is the opposite. He loves Joey very much, has enjoyed a growing relationship with him, and does not want anything to disrupt this relationship. It is for these reasons that this examiner believes he is attempting to block the move of Joey to Chicago.

Looking at other issues related to the proposed move, it is expected that Joey will handle the change associated with the move reasonably well. He is functioning quite well, is generally adaptable, and shows no evidence of any unusual anxiety or stress. He *will* feel a loss associated with his father, extended family, and peers. However, his adjustment should be fine if he is allowed to maintain these relationships (even if on a long-distance basis). Visitation is unlikely to be problematic, as both families can set aside the moneys that they are currently spending on private school to enable a series of trips throughout the year.

Among the child and family issues that are relevant in a move-away case, it appears that Ms. N is and has been Joey's primary custodial and primary psychological parent. Though his father has been active in Joey's life, he has not taken a direct parenting role as Ms. N has done. In fact, from Joey's standpoint, the current custodial arrangement has worked quite well, enabling Joey to have a secure and stable relationship with both of his parents. He has moved to a developmental level in which he can clearly maintain a relationship with his father, even with the distance, and looks forward to writing him, having him share in his new life, and seeing him for longer blocks of time during visits. There is no evidence in this evaluation to suggest that Ms. N will impede the relationship with Joey and his father. Except for rare glitches in the communication between the parents, it appears that Ms. N has supported Joey's relationship with his father. Although there is conflict at the present time, there is little evidence that this conflict will be exacerbated by the move, as long as both parties can adjust as need be.

Regarding the potential impact to Joey if the move does not take place, I believe that Joey is wanting to move because he sees it as important to his mother. He is close to his mother, and there appears to be a very good fit in how they relate. Their attachment is strong. If his mother is unable to move and either the new marriage dissolves or there is a change of custody, *and if Joey perceives it to be his fault,* there is the risk that Joey will feel guilty if the move does not take place. In addition, if for some reason Ms. N becomes depressed as a result of the fact that she cannot move with Joey, this could negatively affect Joey as well. It is this examiner's opinion that the potential negative impact on Joey if the move does not take place is greater than the potential negative impact on Joey if he does moves.

If the move takes place, it is critical for both parents to maintain a working relationship (as they generally have during their divorce) and for Mr. S to continue in an important parenting role with Joey. It would obviously be devastating to Joey if his father were to respond to the move just as his father's biological father responded to *him* when his mother remarried after his parents divorced. The growth and facilitation of the relationship between Mr. S and Joey is essential, and it is this examiner's observation that Mr. S and his wife will make this happen. In addition, maintaining relationships with extended family, in particular Mrs. S (paternal grandmother), is also indicated for Joey's mental health.

As expected from the above analysis, I recommended that Joey be allowed to move with his mother, and I also recommended very specific visitation plans including times for Joey to return to his father during school breaks and opportunities for the father to visit Joey in Chicago. I recommended that the parents get computers with fax and online capability so that Joey and his father could communicate regularly. Letter writing and frequent phone calls were encouraged. Ms. N was encouraged to communicate with Mr. S regarding school and medical information, and Mr. S was encouraged to participate in decision making for Joey. Finally, I recommended a brief updated evaluation 1 year later if either parent had concerns about Joey's adjustment or if problems developed in the coparenting relationship. I also suggested a reevaluation at perhaps age 10 if Joey expressed a desire to live in California with his father.

CASE EXAMPLE: The B Family

In this case, Ms. B wished to move with Erica, her 9-year-old daughter, from California to Connecticut so that Ms. B could attend college in a unique program in Eastern religions. She maintained that she was unable to work in California and needed to go to school *in that program* so that she could earn a living. Mr. B opposed the move because he felt her only real reason for moving was to thwart his relationship with his daughter. He had previously petitioned the court on several occasions because of his concern that she was interfering with his visitation. He was also concerned about the extent to which his daughter was taking care of Ms. B emotionally. Although this evaluation was done prior to the *Burgess* decision in

California, the issues and recommendations would most likely still apply. The report summary and recommendations were as follows:

> Overall, Mr. B and Ms. B have different views of this situation. Ms. B is responding to her need for professional growth and a change in her career. She sees moving to Connecticut as a way to solve these problems and help with her depression. She is angry at Mr. B for interfering with her life goals, and she perceives that he is controlling her and trying to keep her in limbo. In contrast, Mr. B is focusing largely on his daughter and his perception that moving will be detrimental to her. He has turned down opportunities to improve his own career because it would mean moving away from her, and he believes that Ms. B should do the same. Although this oversimplifies the situation somewhat, it is at the heart of the differences between them.
>
> In addition to this, there has been absolutely no communication between this couple for years. Neither trusts the motives of the other, and neither believes that the other has been a responsible parent. Ms. B feels that Mr. B is controlling and manipulative and that his new marriage is very unstable. In contrast, Mr. B believes that Ms. B has led an unstable life and feels that this instability has disrupted Erica's life. He also believes that she acts with little thought to Erica's well-being. He believes that Ms. B's recent sale of her condo with no place to move reflects this trait. Each believes that he or she is the best parent to have primary physical custody of Erica, though both acknowledge that Erica needs an ongoing relationship with each parent. Finally, though it appears that Mr. B was controlling in his relationship with Ms. B in the past, it appears that he is less so now. In some ways, it seems that Ms. B has remained stuck in her perception of Mr. B and remains depressed and dependent, while Mr. B appears to have moved forward, remarried, and settled his life in positive ways.
>
> This examiner is struck, however, by the conflicting statements of Ms. B. On the one hand, she reports that there is nothing wrong with taking Erica to Connecticut and that she is going to be there only for several months while finishing her degree. At other times, however, she knows it will be difficult for Erica to be away from her father. Though she says she intends to return to California, she acknowledges that, given the right opportunity, she would stay in Connecticut. It appears that she doesn't plan for what lies ahead. I share in Mr. B's concern that she sold her condo with no specific plans and continues to disrupt Erica's life.
>
> More than anything, however, I am concerned about the way in which she seems detached from Erica and her emotions. As indicated, it appears that Erica provides her mother with a great deal of emotional support, and this is detrimental to Erica. Ms. B has a hard time separating her own needs from those of Erica and doesn't respond too well to Erica's emotional needs for stability and security. Although I know that she loves Erica, and appears to do a "good enough" day-to-day job of taking care of her, it seems that her depression and dependency are taking their toll on Erica.

Though Mr. B appears to be defensive and detached from his own emotions, he appears more connected to Erica's feelings and better able to separate his issues from hers. I see no evidence of any trouble between Mr. B and his wife that might add to Erica's tension. He appears to have stabilized his life, and he appears stable for Erica.

All of this leads to a difficult dilemma. On the one hand, it may be best for Erica to maintain the status quo, not move to Connecticut, and continue the current time-sharing plan. In my view, a move to Connecticut would certainly be detrimental to Erica because of her attachment to her father, the instability of Ms. B's plans, and the strong possibility that Ms. B might wish to remain there. As such, I cannot support it. Certainly, Ms. B can go to Connecticut and pursue her education and career plans, though, if she does, it will be important that she does not reject Erica. However, I am concerned that Erica will miss her, and I do not recommend it.

The question remains as to how to handle the custody and time-share if Ms. B remains. They could continue the status quo, but Ms. B has already sold her condo, and she and Erica will be forced to move somewhere. In addition, I have concerns about the ways in which Ms. B is dependent on Erica and how this and her depression interfere with her ability to meet Erica's emotional needs. It seems that she uses poor judgment, causing Erica emotional pain.

However, moving Erica to her father also creates potential problems. It is disruptive, at least initially, and it would likely cause Ms. B to be even more depressed. She already perceives that she is victimized by Mr. B, and this would add to such feelings. Because Erica tends to be her emotional caretaker, it may also be hard for her because she might feel that she has let her mother down. If she does not move out of state, we don't know where Ms. B will settle locally and whether it will be close to Mr. B.

These issues create a situation in which there are no "perfect" solutions. Nonetheless, given all of the above, I offer the following recommendations.

As you might gather, I recommended that Erica not move and that she stay with her father during the school week and with her mother every other weekend, either until Monday or Tuesday depending on where her mother moved locally. I also recommended a dinner visit once per week with her mother, along with a specific holiday and vacation plan. Given the emotional issues observed, I recommended that Ms. B continue her therapy and work on her depression and dependency issues, learn to separate herself emotionally from Erica, and develop better impulse control and planning and better judgment with Erica. I recommended that Erica get in her own short-term therapy to learn to understand her own needs and feelings and learn that she is not responsible for soothing her mother's depression and dependency. It appeared that she shared her feelings only with her stepmother because she is afraid of upsetting either her mother or father. Finally, I recommended a brief update in the future if Ms. B stayed locally and made the therapeutic gains, to see if it made sense to increase Erica's time with her mother.

Ms. B did not move to Connecticut and about 9 months later petitioned for an updated evaluation. She and Erica had both improved, especially in regard to issues of Erica's separation, and because Ms. B had settled near Mr. B, I recommended a more equal parenting arrangement for Erica and her parents.

--------------------◆-------------------

CASE EXAMPLE: The L Family

In this case, Jill, a 5-year-old girl, lived in northern California under a relatively equal joint custody time-share with both of her parents, who had divorced when she was an infant. They had frequently adjusted the schedule according to Jill's needs, and they generally worked well together on behalf of Jill. They clearly had a well-functioning joint custody arrangement.

When Jill was 2 years old, each parent remarried. Her father and his wife (Mr. and Ms. L) had a new daughter who was almost 2 years old. Her mother and her husband (Mr. and Ms. Z) were expecting a new baby. Jill was very close to all four of her parents, loved her little sister at her dad's house, and appeared excited about the pending arrival of her mother's new baby.

Her stepfather worked for the navy, and when the local base was shut down, he was assigned to southern California. Her mother wanted to go with him and take Jill with her. Her father wanted Jill to stay. Each offered the other reasonable visitation, but they could not agree on whether Jill should go with Mom or stay with Dad. This led to a custody evaluation. My summary and recommendations stated the following:

> In many ways, the issues in this evaluation are difficult. Jill is clearly attached to and has healthy relationships with both her mother and stepfather and her father and stepmother. Whether she stays and her mother moves, or she moves and her father stays, there are no good choices. Each has a risk of significant problems for Jill and/or one or more of the adults involved.
>
> If Jill stays with her father, I expect that she will miss her mother and will need to spend considerable nonschool time with her. In addition, she'll need help in dealing with her feelings. If mother were to stay local with Jill and be away from her husband, she will feel sad and depressed, especially because she is soon to give birth to a new baby. She is also likely to feel tremendous resentment toward Mr. L, perceiving that he forced her to separate from her family.
>
> In contrast, if Jill moves, she will clearly miss her father, stepmother, and stepsister. She will need help dealing with those losses. Mr. and Ms. L fear that Ms. Z will interfere in Jill's relationship with her stepmother (e.g., not allowing phone calls) and may start to interfere with Mr. L's contribution to Jill's schooling. Jill enjoys her time with her father and stepmother, both of whom also provide much nurturing, love, and guidance.
>
> If the move were not an issue here, I would be recommending that they continue to share parenting on a relatively equal basis. Each of the adults shows an ability to do a good job in meeting Jill's day-to-day needs, with no significant problems noted. Ms. Z and Ms. L have a history with tension in their relationship, and it appears that both have acted in ways to contribute to the problems. Finding fault between them is irrelevant at this time.

My biggest concern at the present lies with Ms. Z's apparent inability to accept Ms. L in her life, despite how it has benefited Jill. Her unwillingness to allow phone calls without Mr. L present does not serve Jill's needs, even though it might serve hers. Mr. and Ms. Z are concerned about Ms. L's "obsession" with Jill, but I see no evidence of it. Quite the contrary, I see her as someone who is motivated to care about Jill and assist in meeting her needs. Though I can certainly understand Ms. Z's reluctance to having Jill's stepmother raising her, especially because Ms. Z is available to do so, it appears that her current jealousy toward Ms. L is unwarranted.

Given Jill's general demeanor, she is likely to adjust to any plan that the adults support and make work. She appears to have a relatively easygoing temperament and seems to adapt well to changes in her life. It is likely that it will be harder for her mother or father if Jill is away from either of them. Jill will need them to manage and cope without getting angry or depressed with the outcome. Regardless of who moves, Jill will need the adults in her life to continue to be nurturing, supportive, and healthy parents. Most important, she will need them to find peace and to support her relationships with all of the other adults in her life.

No matter where Jill lives, her families will need to pay careful attention to offering her the best opportunity to maintain a healthy, ongoing relationship with the absent family and minimize her loss. She needs open access to both parents and both stepparents, and she will need an opportunity to continue growing in her relationship with her stepsister and develop a relationship with her soon-to-be-born sibling. She will need the care and support of the adults with whom she is primarily living to allow her to grow in her relationships with the other parent.

The biggest concern regarding this move is that Jill will not have easy access to *both* her father and stepmother while she is at her mother's. Ms. Z's psychological issues, as outlined above, may make it hard for her to allow Jill the necessary free and easy access. Also, if Jill moves, she will be away from other relatives and friends. The biggest advantage to moving is that she can continue to have her mother's participation in school and be with her during nonschool time rather than spending most of her time either in school or in day care while both her father and stepmother work. A further advantage to moving with her mother would be that she won't be affected by her mother's feeling that she has abandoned Jill.

In attempting to weigh the advantages and disadvantages to Jill, it is very difficult to determine what will cause her less pain, as it is likely that she will endure some pain whether she moves or her mother moves without her. After completing this evaluation, the answer of Jill's best interest remains unclear. Jill is attached to both parents and has a very good bond with her stepparents as well. She appears to have healthy attachments to extended relatives in the Bay Area. It does appear that her best interests would best be served if all of the parents remain in the same community, something that is unlikely given that Mr. Z is in the military and the base to which he has been assigned is closing. Unfortunately, the downsizing of the military has the effect of disrupting families, and Jill's life will be disrupted regardless of this court's decision.

From Jill's view, we currently have a viable and workable shared parenting arrangement. The time-share and circumstances have changed over the years, and the parents have generally worked well on her behalf. Whether she moves with her mother or mother moves without her, she loses the shared parenting arrangement. Balancing frequent and continuing contact with her father against continuing to be with her mother during the school year appears to be a social/legal issue more than a psychological one. I do not see any substantive psychological basis from which to make a recommendation. Instead, I believe that this will require a judicial decision based on the law. I offer the following recommendations, regardless of which way the court decides.

In this evaluation, I provided the court two options. I recommended that Jill should be enrolled in a year-round school, which was available in both communities. This afforded the greatest flexibility of time to be with the other parent. I then recommended that she spend 2 complete, separate weeks (1 of them during the Christmas break) with the parent whom she is with during the school year and all other nonschool vacation blocks with the other parent. I suggested that Jill travel to the other parent's home the day after school vacation starts and return 2 days before school starts to get resettled. If there were major holidays, such as Thanksgiving or Easter, not part of a vacation block of time, they should be rotated. I also recommended that Jill travel to be with the other parent at least 1 weekend per month, preferably when there are 3-day breaks from school. I also encouraged the other parent to visit Jill and participate in school or extracurricular events such as field trips, parent-teacher meetings, and athletic activities. As usual, I recommended that Jill have open phone access to all parents and stepparents. I also recommended that the adults meet together to plan each year's schedule during the spring. I suggested that this be done with the assistance of a mediator to lessen the difficulty to the adults. Finally, I suggested, if Jill were to struggle emotionally or in school, a reevaluation in about a year to understand why the problems were occurring and whether or not a change in primary custody was necessary.

As you will note from the above examples, the summary and recommendation sections of move-away reports tend to be longer than typical reports because of the complicated issues that need to be addressed.

PART II

CHAPTER 5

Issues With
High-Conflict Families

There are many families who do not fit any of the patterns of domestic violence described in Chapter 2, yet experience a high degree of conflict. Many high-conflict families may experience intermittent outbursts of anger or violence. Even when they do not exhibit chronic violent patterns, these families are so conflicted that they routinely go back to court to solve what should be relatively simple problems. They may have problems scheduling holidays and vacations; they may argue during exchanges; they cannot communicate about child-related issues or decide on day care providers; they disagree on the times and places for exchanging the children; they argue about who will attend parent-teacher conferences, arrange and pay for health care, or attend the child's extracurricular activities; and they may disagree on activities for their children.

In many ways, it appears that the life of the child must stop while the arguments between the parents continue. For many of these families, every issue becomes a potential source of conflict. Sometimes this is related to the history of the relationship and the power dynamics between the parents. Sometimes one parent will not let go of the conflict because this keeps them "together" in their relationship (albeit a destructive one).

This chapter focuses mostly on the way in which conflict is driven by each parent's respective personality traits, the lack of a system for resolving conflicts, or both. Decisions may get made by the more forceful parent when one parent "gives in" to the other. Sometimes no rational decision gets made, such as when one parent takes the child to the pediatrician and the other does the same after the exchange because he or she does not trust the other to communicate medical information. In such situations, children may see two pediatricians when one will do and no therapist when one is needed. Teachers become frustrated with the lack of cooperation toward the child's schooling. I have seen many instances in which children are enrolled in two different kindergartens because parents cannot adequately plan together for their child's education. Such parents have not learned to implement a system for communication, problem solving, and decision making. They do things the same way that they have for years. Often one parent does give in. Sadly, this may be the healthier parent. Though this chapter is designed to give an overview of the dynamics of high-conflict families and appropriate interventions, I refer readers to Johnston and Roseby's (1997) book *In the Name of the Child* for a more in-depth understanding of high-conflict parents and their impact on children.

Research on high-conflict families (Johnston, 1993, 1994; Johnston & Campbell, 1988; Johnston & Roseby, 1997) reveals a continuum of problems and a variety of factors that contribute to the problems. Some families are mildly entrenched in conflict and can benefit from guidance and structured recommendations. The more difficult of these families may seem to make little progress, even with rather extensive intervention (e.g., therapy and case management). Some parents have personality traits that exacerbate conflicts, perhaps exaggerating or being quite rigid. In the next section, I will focus on the way in which the parents' respective personality traits contribute to the degree and nature of the conflict.

THE NATURE OF PERSONALITY DISTURBANCES

Over the past 20 years, a growing body of literature has developed on personality styles, in particular, narcissistic and borderline styles. Millon (1996) focused not only on the disorders themselves but on those personality traits and features that affect relationships rather than the individual. He has grouped personality disorders into four types. Many custody evaluators observe that most high-conflict families have one or both parents who exhibit narcissistic, obsessive-compulsive, histrionic, paranoid, or borderline features. They may have parents who become rigid in their perception of the other and tend to deal with things in their extremes. Many parents are polarized, viewing themselves as all good and the other as all bad. These parents focus on the traits within the other parent that reinforce this perception, and they approach each new conflict as verification of just how difficult the other parent is. These parents experience chronic externalization of blame, possessing little insight into their own role in the conflicts. They usually have little empathy for the impact of this conflict on their children. They routinely feel self-justified, believing that their actions are best for their children. No matter how much the helping professionals try to keep the focus on the child, these parents remain focused on the conflict.

Although these parents tend to be motivated by a diverse set of emotions, I believe that most of them take this rather rigid position out of fear, often the overwhelming fear that, if they let down their defenses, they will be taken advantage of. Many parents say, "If I just give in this one time, she will always take advantage of me," or "If I give him an inch, he'll take a mile." Many parents fear being controlled by the other parent. For the more disturbed of these parents, giving in may represent a fear of annihilation or loss of self. This rigidity assures conflict. Because these families routinely go back to court, these parents are also afraid that any relaxing of their position might give the other parent an advantage in court. What gets lost in the conflict is the needs of the children. Another source of the fear is that winning or losing is so integrally tied to self-esteem. Narcissistic parents fear losing custody and control, which will lead them to feel abandoned and depressed. Borderline parents must win to contain their internal chaos and rage. Though losing might mean different things to each parent (e.g., shame, loss, abandonment, rage, etc.), the key ingredient is how *unbearable* such a loss is to each parent.

Judges and attorneys express their extreme frustration with these families. I have heard judges refer to high-conflict families as "our frequent fliers," adding that, even though they may number only 10% of the families, they require 90% of the court's resources. They might come back to court several times a year, and just when it appears that a settlement has been reached, a new issue will arise. Lacking a reasonable dispute-resolution mechanism, these parents feel justified in taking the other to court and "letting the judge settle it." Each issue is perceived as a new opportunity for victory and feared as a potential loss. These characterological personality dynamics along with each parent's righteous self-justification and fear create the high degree of conflict and the perpetuation of the court battle.

At the same time, away from the conflict, many of these parents seem concerned for their children's needs and feelings and are capable of good parenting skills. They may be nurturing and set reasonable limits with their children. They are frequently involved in their child's day-to-day activities, participate in schoolwork, and provide encouragement to their children. Many of these parents can be loving, spontaneous, and supportive to their children, even when they are cold, rigid, angry, and fearful toward the other parent. In the abstract, they understand the value of the child's relationship with the other parent, and they may even recognize that the conflict is problematic for their children. Despite this acknowledgment, it is difficult for them to relax their rigid positions and attitudes toward the other parent and extricate their child (and themselves) from the conflict.

For many high-conflict families, it seems that one parent's characterological personality dynamics get manifested in a relationship disorder with the other parent. These parents may be able to manage some of their chronic traits, including their narcissism, overreaction, rigidity, and anger, in some of their other relationships. They may be pleasant to coworkers, showing few pathological traits in their work environment. With their children, they may not personalize experiences or show signs of narcissistic injury. For these evaluations, the evaluator needs to understand if the vulnerabilities are manifested in the parent-child relationship.

In contrast, the history of the conflict, the emotions of the divorce, and the fear of letting go bring out the worst in these parents with each other. It appears that the couple's relationship has been unable to withstand the previous love, the loss of that love, and the rejection and hurt that followed. In the newly formed divorce relationship, dysfunctional personality traits flourish, but in other relationships, including with the children, healthier personality traits may abound. For the less disturbed of these parents, the pathological personality traits may surface only in the context of the conflictual relationship between the parents. Each parent's negative individual traits clash, and the conflicts continue. Left unchecked, these families return to court year after year to solve what might appear to the neutral observer to be the most minor of issues.

These families require strategies and interventions that assist them in taking care of their children and reducing their conflict. The evaluator should determine whether or not therapy or parent education is an appropriate recommendation for either or both of the parents. These may be appropriate for high-conflict parents. However, therapy and education alone are not sufficient interventions for these families. Evaluators will want to consider whether any of the following will work with a given family.

NEUTRAL DECISION MAKING (SPECIAL MASTER)

In a variety of jurisdictions, including Northern California (special masters), Maricopa County, Arizona (family court advisers), Boulder, Colorado (case managers or binding arbitrators), and New Mexico ("wise persons"), courts have begun to use attorneys and mental health practitioners as neutral decision makers to assist families in day-to-day disputes. High-conflict families frequently return to court, but the court system is incapable of handling the types or frequency of problems that these families bring. Instead, they require the assistance of a decision maker who acts on behalf of the children. This person is empowered by the family and the court to act on behalf of the children and resolve conflicts in an expeditious manner. If neither parent has control, both can relax their fear of being taken advantage of by the other. Although each parent may periodically become frustrated with the decisions of the neutral decision maker, each parent usually trusts that person more than the other parent.

An example of a recommendation for neutral decision making might be as follows:

> A special master should be appointed to assist the parties in resolving their disputes. I would recommend that this special master have decision-making authority in all day-to-day areas except for significant changes in the time-share. At a minimum, the special master needs to have authority to settle disputes in the areas of child care, after-school activities, times and location of exchanges, disputes about vacations, therapy for the child, and each parent's participation in the child's events. Both parents are discouraged from engaging in conflict within their child's earshot and will use the special master for such disputes. Both parents should refrain from calling the police, except in an emergency, without first discussing their concern with the special master. The special master needs to have the authority to alter the basic time-share if he or she deems that one parent is significantly causing problems for the child. Finally, at a minimum, the parents should meet with the special master once per month to discuss their child and the child's needs and to work toward preventing future problems from occurring.
>
> In fact, it is this examiner's opinion that the use of a special master is the single most important thing that these parents can do to help him (or her). Each needs to focus more on his or her *own* parenting and learn to be less critical of the other. If they can learn to resolve their disputes away from their child and work toward being the best parent each can be during the times he or she has their child, almost any time-share in which both parents are actively involved in their child's life will be workable and successful for their child.

When the evaluator makes a recommendation for someone to take on this role, it will be helpful to explain the benefits to the parents. Parents are usually tired of fighting and tired of the delays and costs of the court process. The evaluator can help parents recognize the benefits of a special master by talking to them about the lowered cost and the quicker decisions and assuring them that neither parent will have undue power over the other. This may help many parents accept this as an alternative mechanism for their dispute resolution.

It appears that there are three primary benefits for the use of a neutral decision maker. These are helping families more quickly resolve their differences, unclogging the courts from some of their most difficult families, and helping families with very young children manage the nuances of integrating changing developmental needs of the child into their parenting plan.

As of now, little has been published about the role of the special master in high-conflict divorce. Stahl (1995) previously described the process as one in which a professional is appointed by the court to act in a quasi-judicial manner and make day-to-day decisions for divorced families in conflict. The major task of the special master is to make decisions that help a family stay out of court and keep their children out of the middle of the conflict. Special masters need to be decisive. Just as young children often have difficulty sharing, divorced parents often have difficulty sharing their children. Although the special master needs to understand the parents' positions and feelings, it is more important for the special master to make decisions that are in the child's interest, without taking a lot of time.

A special master is faced with major decision making on a regular and consistent basis. For most mental health practitioners, quick decision making is the most difficult task of being a special master. Someone who accepts the task of special master must recognize that the child relies on the special master to make decisions on his or her behalf. When the special master keeps the focus on meeting the needs of the child, it becomes easier to make quick decisions that support and promote the child's healthy adjustment.

The role of the special master is a multifaceted one in which he or she is part detective (as parents describe their different stories, the special master tries to understand the "whole truth"), part educator (the special master helps parents learn to share their children, understand their child's developmental needs, resolve problems, and move on in their lives following the divorce), part mental health professional (the special master understands the parents' and child's feelings and attitudes), part judge (the special master makes timely decisions), and part advocate for the children (their needs are the special master's first priority). Just like the evaluator, the special master may talk with other professionals and may need to meet with the children to carry out his or her work. The task is complex, because of the ongoing conflict between the parents.

It is generally best if the special master's scope is defined by court order. Special masters may have authority to make decisions about any of the following: schedules, overnight visitation, choice of schools, extracurricular activities, troubles at transfers, holiday scheduling, parenting differences, health issues, children's therapy, and problematic behaviors on the part of one or both parents. The special master needs to understand the impact on the children before making decisions.

In my view, the work of a special master is perhaps the toughest one in the family court arena. Parents who require special masters are engaged in the most destructive conflict and tend to have limited psychological resources and coping skills and a high degree of chaos in their lives. The special master requires time-management skills that may be difficult for mental health professionals. I have heard fewer concerns when an attorney is the special master. However, special mastering requires training in child development and conflict resolution, and attorneys may have more problems with those areas of the job.

Because many of these parents are highly litigious and express their displeasure at decisions vehemently, the job requires the mental toughness of a judge and the empathy of a psychologist to withstand the pressures that some parents apply. Although this might be difficult for some, I know many special masters who find a great deal of gratification in being able to support children in these families while helping parents reduce the intensity of their conflict.

PARALLEL PARENTING

A second intervention involves parallel parenting. Psychologists describe young children who play next to each other but interact very little with each other to be in "parallel play." In the same way, parents who parent their children at different times but who have little or no direct interaction with each other are engaged in parallel parenting.

Even though much of the divorce literature focuses on coparenting, in which parents communicate and work with each other to raise their children in a cooperative fashion, high-conflict families fail miserably at this task. Each parent usually thinks his or her style is the only way to parent, and both parents are often quite critical of the other. Interactions stimulate the conflict, reducing benefits to the children.

The goals of parallel parenting are to reduce the level of conflict and make sure that the tasks of parenting are accomplished by one or both parents. It is important for parents, in conjunction with the courts, a neutral decision maker, or both, to specify which parent is responsible for various parenting tasks. Parents develop a plan that identifies how each parent will participate in the child's extracurricular activities, help with schoolwork, take care of medical needs, and so on. Plans are developed to ensure that parents communicate with each other with less conflict. Fax machines or e-mail may be used when the conflict is high. Each parent is encouraged to develop his or her separate routine and structure. With such a plan, for example, the child will not be exposed to both parents attending the same field trip and making things miserable with their conflict.

I find that the integration of these recommendations leads to the ideal intervention for many families. Though the literature suggests that high-conflict parents cannot share parenting, Johnston (1994) states that parallel parenting may work. I agree and find that it is the goal to encourage. Parents at a high level of conflict must first learn to disengage before they parent together. Parallel parenting allows them the freedom to parent separately. Working with the neutral decision maker allows them to develop the skills to coparent and use them later in raising their children, after the conflicts have settled.

To help these parents disengage and then learn to work together, it can be helpful for the neutral decision maker to meet with the parents periodically and develop a schedule of the child's activities and each parent's participation in those activities. The special master can focus on the process of parallel parenting and help parents to disengage from conflict. Together, they can develop routines for the child and help coordinate a similar routine in each household, schedule times for phone calls between children and the other parent, and assist each parent in doing those tasks that each does best. With this process, there are no winners or losers, and the child benefits from separate and parallel interaction with both parents, reducing the extent to which the child is exposed to conflict. Once a neutral decision maker is in place and the process of parallel parenting is ensured, parents can detach from each other and reduce the intensity of their conflict.

STRUCTURED RECOMMENDATIONS

A third important intervention for high-conflict families is providing structured recommendations. During the custody evaluation, evaluators have learned the routines in each household, the strengths and weaknesses of each parent, and the quality of the relationships between the child and each parent. For high-conflict families, a lack of specificity promotes parental conflict, and conflict breeds insecurity for the children. The evaluator should recommend specific and concrete plans to assist parents in fulfilling the tasks of parallel parenting and reducing the likelihood that they remain engaged in conflict. The more specific the evaluator makes the recommendations, the more he or she can help parents know the rules and help the neutral decision maker enforce the rules.

Some families have a rather vague schedule outlined in their divorce judgment stating something such as, "The children are to be with father every Wednesday overnight and every other weekend. Each parent has the opportunity for a summer vacation in each calendar year." Some are even more vague and state that "Father has reasonable rights of visitation." Though such phrases may be acceptable for many families, they will not work for high-conflict relationships. Such parents argue about the beginning and ending times of the overnight, how to define the times of the weekend, the length and times of vacations, and even how to resolve the likely occurrence that each parent desires the same vacation time. For these families, the evaluator might recommend something like the following:

> The children are to be with father from his pickup of the children at school at the end of their school day each Wednesday until he returns them to school the following Thursday morning. He will have the children every other weekend beginning at his pickup at school on Friday afternoon until his return of the children to school on Monday morning. In the event of a 3-day holiday weekend,

in which the children are off school either Friday or Monday, his time with the children will extend to include that additional day; for example, he will return the children to school on Tuesday morning following a Monday holiday. In the event there is no school on an exchange day, the father will drop off the children at mother's home at 8:30 a.m.

In addition, it is recommended that each parent can have the children for up to 14 consecutive days for a vacation in each calendar year. Such vacations can occur only during the summer school break, except as outlined in the holiday schedule below. Requests for vacation must be made by February 28 of each calendar year for the following summer, and, in the event there is a dispute over dates, father has first choice in even-numbered years and mother has first choice in odd-numbered years.

A holiday plan will need to be clear. Certainly, it will be dependent on the age of the children and the family expectations. Schools in different parts of the country are on different schedules, as well. An example of a structured holiday and vacation schedule would be as follows:

For holidays, birthdays, and school vacation, I recommend the following:
Thanksgiving break to be with father in 1999 and all odd-numbered years and with mother in all even-numbered years.
I recommend an equal split of the Christmas break from school, switching at 1:00 p.m. Christmas day. In 1999 and all odd-numbered years, I recommend that mother have the first half of the Christmas vacation. In 2000 and all even-numbered years, I recommend that mother have the second half of the Christmas vacation. The intent of this recommendation is that each parent have half of the break. In the event that the vacation does not split evenly, I recommend that it be adjusted as necessary by the special master.
I would recommend that spring break be treated as a whole, including the weekend days, with father having the children in 1999 and all odd-numbered years and mother having them in all even-numbered years.
The children should be with father on his birthday from 4:00 p.m. to 8:00 p.m. (unless it naturally falls on his time) and for the entire Father's Day weekend, and with mother on her birthday from 4:00 p.m. to 8:00 p.m. (unless it naturally falls on her time) and the entire Mother's Day weekend. In addition, I would recommend alternating the children's birthdays in the same fashion, as well.

As can be seen by this lengthy and detailed recommendation, less room exists for each parent to manipulate or feel manipulated by the other. The rules are quite clear. In the event of a dispute, it will be relatively easy for the special master to resolve. The recommendation should also include a provision that the neutral decision maker can make adjustments or modifications in the event of certain situations, such as a family emergency, a special longer vacation, the children's summer schedule, or the needs of one or more family members.

Typically, flexibility is not workable for these high-conflict families without a dispute-resolution mechanism such as a neutral decision maker, because flexibility is a breeding ground for new conflict. Parents can feel more comfortable with a structured recommendation if it can be adjusted in the event that a specific need arises. The above is only one example of the areas in which concrete and specific recommendations can be made, and it is the task of the evaluator to identify the level and sources of conflict within the family so that appropriate recommendations in all risk areas can be made.

For some families, the level of conflict does not get resolved for years. Neither parent trusts the neutral decision maker, and the use of the neutral decision maker only provides one more opportunity for engaging in conflict and battles over power and control. These families will require a very structured court order that leaves little room for dispute and potential sanctions from the court in the event that either parent violates the order. These families will have no room for flexibility, unless mutually agreed upon.

In contrast, many high-conflict parents do trust the neutral decision maker, benefit from a clear and precise order, and are encouraged by parallel parenting. They neutralize their balance of power and reduce the likelihood for conflict to erupt in front of the children. Because the neutral decision maker can make decisions (e.g., whether or not the child will participate in Little League and how each parent can participate with the child) in a timely way, the child's life is less likely to be halted or disrupted by the conflict.

In Chapter 2, I discussed domestic violence. At the beginning of this chapter, I differentiated between domestic violence families and high-conflict families. Whereas the goals for domestic violence families are to end the violence, support therapeutic interventions for batterers and victims, and normalize the relationship that the child has with each parent, the goals for the nonviolent but highly conflicted families are to reduce the level of conflict to which the child is exposed and ensure that each parent has the opportunity to do the best possible job of parenting during the time that he or she has the child. This also helps to ensure that the child's life, including his or her schooling, extracurricular activities, and peer relationships, can be predictable and occur in a healthy way.

CASE EXAMPLE: The G Family

Mr. and Ms. G had been married for 10 years. Ms. G had a daughter from a previous relationship and together they shared a 7-year-old son, Brad. The following summary and recommendations from my evaluation provide both an outline of their dynamics and the recommendations that seemed to be in their son's best interests:

In reviewing the issues in this evaluation, Mr. G views Ms. G as controlling, angry, and withholding of Brad. Evidence supports the reality that she can be controlling when she is angry, and she is often very angry at Mr. G. In looking at her, he is somewhat correct. She initially withheld Brad upon separation and has a difficult time talking with Mr. G about Brad. She does want things to go her way. However, over time, she has relaxed this rigidity, and she has added some time for Mr. G to the original stipulation (e.g., he now has Wednesday overnight). She gave him a full week with Brad when he was off work last month. There is no evidence that she wants to withhold Brad from him, as long as Mr. G, and not his girlfriend, is going to be with Brad.

At the same time, this evaluation has revealed that Mr. G lacks any insight into his own role in the problems. He appears to be feeling a terrific loss since his wife left him, and he tends to inappropriately project that his wife is depressed. He externalizes blame, as he tends to accuse her of symptoms he is experiencing. It appears that Mr. G would prefer to believe that Ms. G is fully responsible for the family's problems.

Ms. G presents a very mixed picture. She acknowledges her own role in the problems and is quick to acknowledge that the drug use that both she and her husband experienced contributed greatly to the family's difficulties. She is able to acknowledge that she is stubborn and is unwilling to work with her husband when she feels provoked and angered by him. At the same time, she points out that she left him to protect her children and give them a better quality of life than they were experiencing. She recognized that her own anger was getting out of control and feared that Mr. G was becoming intimidating to both her and Brad.

From the beginning of the evaluation, she presented a more balanced view of shared responsibility for the family problems. She portrays Mr. G as very angry. This evaluation supports her view. Much of his anger is associated with feelings of abandonment and rejection by her as well as similar feelings related to the death of his father. Though she has a tendency to feel overwhelmed and rigid when she is upset, she also has more insight into her emotions and their effect on her behavior than does Mr. G.

One of the reasons it is so easy for them to make mirroring allegations against each other is that there is a lot of similarity in their functioning. Mr. G feels rather vulnerable, angry, and depressed, and so does Ms. G. Ms. G can be rather rigid and controlling, and so can Mr. G. The primary difference is in each parent's current insight, and Ms. G appears to have more insight and desire to change, whereas Mr. G is too angry and continues to blame. Aside from that trait, their emotional similarities outweigh their differences.

As it relates to the parenting of Brad, it is this examiner's observation that both appear to be doing a generally good job. Brad is comfortable with each of them, and he is an affectionate and loving child. He truly enjoys his time with his dad and feels very close with his mother, as well. In their own ways, each spoils Brad to a certain degree. Mr. G spoils him with material things, and Ms. G spoils him with overprotection. However, the dysfunction they experience with each other appears absent in their relationships with Brad.

Finally, this couple appears to have little or no ability to communicate with each other about Brad. Joint decision making and problem solving is minimal. They have a dysfunctional and highly conflicted relationship. Both appear to be stubborn with each other, and there is a complete lack of trust between them. They appear to resemble the kind of couple that is referred to as "high conflict." They will need considerable assistance in helping them learn to disengage from each other emotionally, reduce their conflict, and engage in a process of parallel parenting until they can reach a point of being more cooperative and jointly share in the parenting of Brad. Because each is so distrustful of the other and blames the other for being controlling or resistant, it will be necessary for a neutral third party to assist them in finding solutions.

With all the above in mind, I offer the following recommendations:

1. Given the lack of both parents' follow-through on drug testing and anger management, I would recommend the short-term continuation of the current time-share schedule. Brad should continue to be with his father every Wednesday from pickup at school until return to school on Thursday morning. He should have the first, third, and fifth weekend of every month, starting with pickup from school on Friday until return to school on Monday morning. Weekends should be determined based on the Friday of the month. Thus, Brad is to be with his father during the first, third, and fifth weekend that begin with the first, third, and any fifth Friday of the month.

For holidays, birthdays, and school vacation, I would recommend the following:

The entire Thanksgiving weekend be kept as a unit, with Mr. G having the Thanksgiving break in 1999 and all odd-numbered years and Ms. G having it in even-numbered years.

An equal split of the Christmas holiday, switching at 1:00 p.m. Christmas day. In 1999 and all odd-numbered years, I recommend that Ms. G have the first half of the Christmas vacation. In 2000 and all even-numbered years, I recommend that Ms. G have the second half of the Christmas vacation. In the event that the vacation does not split evenly, I recommend that it be adjusted as necessary at the end of the vacation period, by mutual consent or direction of the special master (see below).

I would recommend that the spring break be treated as a whole, with Mr. G having Brad in all odd-numbered years and Ms. G having him in all even-numbered years.

Brad should be with Mr. G on his birthday and Father's Day and with Ms. G on her birthday and Mother's Day. In addition, I would recommend alternating Brad's birthday as well.

Finally, each parent should, at his or her option, have the opportunity to take up to 2 weeks of vacation with Brad in each calendar year. Each parent should provide at least 60 days' notice of any vacation plans.

2. I would recommend that both parents be ordered to follow through on the stipulated agreements regarding drug testing and anger-management classes.

Regarding the anger-management classes, I would recommend that they contact either Jim Smith, LCSW, or Kim Able, MFCC, to participate in an actual anger-management class. It appears that Ms. G has benefited from her therapy with Dr. Green, but I think she could benefit further from an anger-management class as well.

3. As it appears that Mr. G is struggling with boundary issues associated with the loss of the marriage, the loss of his father, and his sense of loss with Brad, it appears that he could benefit greatly from a group for men to help him grow in his awareness of these feelings and their impact on him. I would recommend that he contact Mr. Carl Horton, MFCC, to inquire about participation in a fathers' group designed to help him provide more appropriate boundaries in these areas and to help him better understand his emotions and how they affect his relationship with Brad and others. Given the psychological dynamics noted in the interviews, it is this examiner's opinion that this will be an important step in helping him deal with these issues in his life. It is hoped that it will also assist him in reducing the extent to which he relies on Brad to meet his emotional needs and increase the likelihood that the time they spend together will be more adequately meeting Brad's emotional needs.

4. Given the high level of conflict between them, it is advisable for them to agree to the use of a special master. This will assist Mr. G in accepting that Ms. G is not controlling and inappropriately making unilateral decisions. It will assist Ms. G in trying to maintain the focus on Brad and the parenting issues between them rather than on the couple's other issues. It will assist both of them in learning how to disengage from each other emotionally, reduce the level of conflict between them, and find new ways to solve problems and make parenting decisions. It is hoped that the special master can assist them in understanding the concept of parallel parenting and encouraging them to each be the best parent he or she can be during the time Brad is with each of them. It appears as if this might be the most important recommendation of all.

As this case example shows, it is not uncommon for high-conflict families to have multiple issues or mirroring allegations, such as abuse (which was unfounded in this case) or drug use (of which there was a clear history by both parents prior to separation).

CASE EXAMPLE: The K Family

In this next example, Mr. and Ms. K have numerous issues that contributed to their conflict, including allegations of domestic violence (mother alleged that father was physically abusive to both her and their daughter, Amy), significant problems in the relationship between mother and father's new girlfriend (Brenda), and distress within Amy. The following summary describes my observations in this case:

In many ways, this is a very difficult family in which to understand all of the dynamics involved. Things are so explosive, and Mr. K's and Ms. K's descriptions are so disparate that finding "truth" is very difficult. For many of their confrontations, there are few if any witnesses, rarely anyone outside the dynamics of the situation. If we look to the psychological testing to provide answers, we see that there is a mirroring quality in the ways Mr. K and Ms. K respond, in particular how they feed off each other. If we look to the children, we get glimpses that both Mr. K and Ms. K are accurate in some things and grossly inaccurate in others. In short, regarding some of the events in the past, even in their most recent past such as the bookstore incident between Ms. K and Mr. K's girlfriend (Brenda) or the alleged physical abuse from Mr. K to Amy, we are unlikely to get any real "truth." There is much that we are unlikely to know about the behaviors that have occurred between Mr. K and Ms. K, Ms. K and Brenda, and between either parent and their children.

At the same time, however, there is much that we do know. Both parents appear to be reasonably accurate in some of their concerns about the other parent. Ms. K appears accurate when she portrays Mr. K as having been relatively uninvolved with the children and relatively insensitive toward the children's feelings. It is also likely that she is accurate when she portrays him as explosive and angry, name-calling, and derogatory, especially toward her and sometimes toward Amy. His clinical findings reveal depression, anxiety, and impulsiveness that are consistent with her concerns, and both children talked about these behaviors as well.

Similarly, it appears that Mr. K is accurate in his perception of Ms. K as someone who cannot stay focused on a task or solve a problem. During this examiner's interviews, she had a difficult time staying focused on specific questions being asked. Her disorganization is one of the things that frustrates him. Similarly, he is accurate that she is extremely angry at Brenda and is having a very difficult time keeping her anger from the children. It appears that she frequently exposes the children to her anger and tells the children how terrible she thinks Brenda is. Finally, he appears to be accurate when he portrays Ms. K as controlling and rigid with scheduling and setting things up so that it is difficult for the children to have positive times and experiences with him.

It is also this examiner's observations that both Mr. K and Ms. K show limited awareness or insight into their own role in the problems between the two of them. Ms. K is a bit better, but not enough to set up reasonable boundaries in her behavior. Thus, although each is accurate in his or her perception of certain problems in the other parent, neither is able to look toward himself or herself to understand the needs of the children and the ways to reduce their conflict.

Another clear item is that the children are in distress. Amy apparently feels a strong need to take care of her mother's feelings, though she has some strong feelings of her own about her father. She struggles with her ability to get along with her parents. She acts as though it is OK to be rude and disrespectful. Timmy (their son) is quite anxious and depressed and has a hard time with behavior of both parents. Both children are feeling tremendous conflicts of loyalty, constantly being pulled toward one parent and automatically against the other. This is not healthy for either of them.

More than anything, it is clear that Mr. K and Ms. K cannot talk with each other about the children at all. Nearly every phone call between them ends up with yelling, name-calling, or hanging up the phone. The children frequently become messengers, often messengers of hostility. This is damaging to them and damaging to their relationships with both parents. For some issues, it may not matter, because Timmy's time with his dad is currently set by court order. However, working out details for Amy and making arrangements for vacations, holidays, and parental participation in the children's activities remain a significant arena for communication problems.

With the above in mind, recommendations that are clearly in the children's best interests are difficult to find. For example, though Ms. K might reduce the hostility she feels toward her ex-husband if Mr. K were to discontinue his relationship with Brenda and deal with the children on his own, he is unlikely to do this. Ending the war between Brenda and Ms. K also does not seem likely, even though it is in the children's best interests. Helping Mr. K with his anxiety and depression and helping him become more empathic toward the children would be in their best interests, as would helping Ms. K control her anger and reduce the way it negatively affects her judgment and her boundaries with the children. Having Ms. K be less controlling as it relates to Mr. K would also be in the children's best interests. Finally, helping Mr. and Ms. K develop a method and style of communicating with each other about the children would also be in their best interests. Unfortunately, these are not easy tasks to accomplish, and there is little evidence available to this examiner to suggest that either Mr. K or Ms. K is motivated to change those factors within himself or herself that contribute to the problems.

Nonetheless, recommendations need to be made, and, based on the above, I offer the following:

1. If ever there was a family that demanded a special master to solve day-to-day issues, it is this one. Through the special master, they can discuss and resolve issues around vacations, participation in the children's activities, and so on, and the special master can guide both parents toward understanding and improving the way in which each contributes to the problems at hand. It would also help ensure that the children are pulled out of the middle of the communications and are no longer put in a position of being a messenger or solving their parents' problems. In fact, without a special master, it is this examiner's perception that little will change for these children regardless of the rest of the recommendations.

2. A clear schedule must be devised in which Timmy and Amy are with their father. As long as Amy is in therapy, I see no reason that she cannot have regular periods of visitation with Mr. K. I would suggest that Timmy be with his father every other week from Wednesday after school until return to school on Monday morning. Mr. K should provide transportation to and from school for

this. Amy should be with him every other weekend from Friday after school until return to school the following Monday morning (same weekends as Timmy so the children are together). During the summer, when there is no school, the parent receiving the children should pick them up at the designated time (Wednesday or Friday at 4 p.m. and Monday mornings at 9 a.m.). This schedule should begin with Mr. K's first scheduled weekend after settlement.

Other recommendations were made for this family, but they are not being included because this example is designed to reveal the multiplicity of issues and areas that need to be addressed in such high-conflict families.

CHAPTER 6

Child Considerations in Custody Recommendations

Whether focusing on parental alienation, domestic violence, sexual abuse, relocation, or high conflict between the parents, custody evaluations are about the needs of children. The task for a child custody evaluator is to integrate the diverse data that parents present to formulate recommendations that best address the needs of the children with the ability of each parent to meet those needs.

In general, these needs will be influenced by developmental criteria, the temperament and emotional functioning of the child, the attachments of the child with each parent, the degree to which the child is both directly and indirectly affected by the parental conflict, and the child's wishes (greater weight is given as the child gets older). In families with several children, each child may have different developmental needs. It is not uncommon for siblings of different ages to have varying quality relationships with each parent. Within each child, there are competing needs, such as the need for primary attachment in infancy and the need for frequent and continuing contact with both parents. In this chapter, I will focus on developmental needs, children's reactions to parental conflict, listening to children while protecting their privacy, and competing needs between siblings and within the individual.

A DEVELOPMENTAL FRAMEWORK

Wallerstein and Kelly (1980), Goldstein, Freud, and Solnit (1984), and Hodges (1986) were among the first to comment on the differing needs that children of different ages have following a divorce. Bray (1991) refined this issue, integrating a developmental approach to understanding the child's adjustment to divorce. Bray said, "Divorce is not necessarily worse for children at certain ages; rather children at various ages tend to have different reactions and symptom patterns" (p. 423). He added, "Given developmental differences and issues, visitation and access may need to vary depending on the age of the child" (p. 424). Others (Johnston, 1995; Johnston & Roseby, 1997; Kalter, 1990; Ludolph & Viro, 1998; McKinnon & Wallerstein, 1987; Solomon & George, 1996; Whiteside, 1996) have focused on the developmental needs of children of divorce. What follows is a brief description of this research and of normative developmental tasks for children, and a discussion of how divorce affects development.

Infants and Toddlers (0-3 years)

During this stage, the foundations of basic trust and relationships are formed. In the first year of life, children develop initial attachments, a necessary precursor for the development of basic trust. By the end of the first year, receptive language skills are developing, and the infant's personality is starting to form. Once a predictable, secure relationship with a primary attachment figure has been secured, the infant begins to separate from that primary parent to form his or her own personality. This process is often referred to as *separation-individuation*. During the toddler years, children begin developing autonomy and experimenting with separation, starting to assert themselves. Their emotions are quite volatile. By age 3, if all goes well, emotions settle down, language skills are intact, and they are likely to be toilet trained. They are ready for a burst of psychological growth that will take place over the next 3 years.

Children in this age-group require predictability, consistency, and routine. When a divorce occurs during this time, there is a loss that the child cannot understand. This can be pronounced if there is a major disruption in the consistency of an existing primary attachment relationship. Symptoms may include regression, problems with feeding and sleeping, self-soothing, and irritability. Some of these children become depressed and withdrawn, especially because they cannot express their loss in words. Separation anxiety for children in this age-group can become exaggerated. If one or both parents becomes depressed, which is quite common, basic care may be diminished.

Children at this age are at risk for more serious regression or developmental delays if the basic caregiving is lacking because of depressed or disturbed parents. It is not uncommon for young, possibly immature, adults (ages 18-25) to have babies. Sometimes, the parents never lived together, or they may have separated during the first 2 years of the child's life. The developmental needs of the children may be affected by the maturity level of the parents.

The evaluator must pay attention to the quality of the attachments in the child's relationships. Rather than the idea of one psychological parent or a primary parent, recent research supports the idea that children can have a hierarchy of attachment figures, all of whom have importance for children in their postdivorce adjustment. Some children do have one primary parent who has attended to the majority of day-to-day needs. Other children may have two or three adults (two parents and a day care provider) who have attended to day-to-day needs. The task for the evaluator is to assess the nature of the child's relationship with each parent and the ability of the parents to communicate about the child. Once that is done, it is important to recommend a parenting plan reflecting the following:

- ❖ The child's relationship with a primary parent is of major importance during the first 3 years of life.

- ❖ Children up to 18 months old need stability and security in the primary attachment relationship (or relationships).

- ❖ Children can develop within normal limits when separated from the primary parent to be with the other parent. This will be affected by the extent to which each parent has been directly involved in the child's life.

- ❖ The attachments, parenting skills, and environment are important.

- ❖ Frequent, shorter visits may be ideal. Overnights may need to be limited in the first year of life if there has been one primary parent.

- ❖ The major roles of caregivers are to provide a secure base, firm support, and flexible self-control; support communication; and help with gender identity and sex role development.

- ❖ With increased capacity for memory and cognition, many children in the group from 18 to 36 months who have had one primary attachment may begin to tolerate and benefit from overnight time with the other parent.

- ❖ It may be difficult to develop a relatively equal parenting plan for children in this age-group because there may be too many transitions and disruptions to the primary attachments.

- ❖ The children who do best with relatively equal parenting plans seem to be those children who have an easy temperament and parents who are supportive of each other and exchange their child with little conflict. Children who have disorganized or anxious attachments may need one primary parent. Other key factors are similar routines in each household, relative stability of the transitions, and parents who can communicate about the child and his or her developmental, medical, and emotional needs.

❖ This communication must allow the parents to be sufficiently responsive to the child and his or her needs. These parents need to have the capacity to help each other understand the infant, work together to develop routines that are familiar to the infant, collaborate on soothing techniques, help each other as language emerges, and reassure each other in their respective parenting techniques. Such parents must be flexible in their response to the child's changing needs. Such a pattern is used in healthy, intact families, and if it is used in a separated family, the shared parenting plan will be natural for the child and his or her development.

❖ When parents are in significant high conflict, very young children appear to benefit the most from schedules that resemble their preseparation patterns of contact with each parent. Although neither parent needs to be considered the primary parent, the child needs predictability in his or her environment until the conflict can settle down.

In dealing with many families, the major task for the evaluator is to find a way to balance the child's attachments with each parent so that the child's needs for stability, predictability, peace, and security are met. The evaluator must also pay close attention to the ability of the parents to meet the child's changing moods and needs. Evaluating the emotional functioning of each parent is critical in this regard. The child's temperament is also a critical variable that needs to be understood by the evaluator. Though the rights of each parent are important during this time, the developmental needs of the child must come first. This might lead to situations that seem to one parent as being unfair.

Preschoolers (3-5 years)

During this stage, the child is developing a better ability to understand language, relationships, and feelings. Children this age are making significant progress in their cognitive skills and peer relationships. Sex role identification is developing. If the separation-individuation process has been healthy, children this age can be expected to expand their horizons, go to preschool, and establish friendships. These children are often delightful, learning to manage their feelings and being inquisitive about everything. If attachments and caregiving are secure, these children will be ready to venture off to kindergarten with good self-esteem and confidence.

On the other hand, preschoolers are at risk for fairly serious regression when attachments are anxious and they do not understand the conflicts of their parents. They may become easily confused and not understand what is occurring around them. Developmental delays and regression in toilet training, sleeping, and feeding are common. They may experience irritability and clinging behavior. Some children become depressed and withdrawn. Nightmares may become more pronounced. Self-confidence may suffer, and there can be increases in aggressive and anxious behaviors. Many of the children in this age-group worry about their parents and may try to act "perfect." They may do this out of fear, or they may be unconsciously taking care of their parents. This may be the early signs of parentified behavior, in which the children care emotionally for their parents, ignoring their own needs. A certain amount of this behavior is normal during the early stages of divorce, but when such behaviors are many or extend for more than a year, this can reflect a more serious adjustment problem for the child.

The evaluator is encouraged to see these children in home visits. This is the natural environment for the children, and it will put them at ease. A home visit will give the evaluator an opportunity to evaluate the respective attachments to mother and father. The evaluator will look for positive signs of warmth, affection, comfort, empathy, and limit setting, as well as negative signs of rigidity, detachment, hostility, or controlling interactions between the child and parent. The evaluator will also look for clues about the child's mood and adjustment with each parent. Talking to the preschool teacher(s), baby-sitter(s), and pediatrician will give the evaluator valuable information about how the divorce is affecting the child away from the home.

Once the evaluator understands the various dynamics of the family, he or she will be making recommendations consistent with the following:

- ❖ Continued focus on predictability, routine, and structure for the child needs to be maintained.

- ❖ Children ages 3 and older can certainly tolerate overnight contact with each parent.

- ❖ Discipline and routine need to be consistent in each parent's home.

- ❖ Parents will need to share information about the child and his or her eating, sleeping, toilet training, medical, and social and emotional functioning.

- ❖ Children need freedom from direct exposure to parental conflict. If the parents continue to be in conflict, parents might consider using neutral sites (e.g., school or day care) for transitions and neutral decision makers.

- ❖ Children in this age-group often benefit from longer blocks of time with each parent that enable them to be settled in routines at each home. Many of these children do not do well with frequent transitions.

- ❖ With children in this age-group, parents need to put their needs secondary to the child's. Though noncustodial parents may want longer blocks of time with their younger child, many children this age still need a primary home. This is dependent on the quality of attachments, whether parents are consistent and relatively free of conflict, and whether the child is experiencing significant vulnerability and stress.

❖ There may be situations in which each parent has some pathology or parenting flaws, *but each offers the child something the other does not.* In those cases, the evaluator will want to recommend a parenting plan that maximizes each parent's strengths while minimizing the extent to which the child is exposed to the pathology.

The major task for the evaluator is to determine the degree of vulnerability and tension in the child and the ability of the parents to coparent relatively free of conflict. For those families in which the coparenting relationship is relatively free of conflict and the children are adjusting well with relatively equal attachments with each parent, some form of joint physical custody can be workable. However, given the potential for regression and vulnerability in children this age, when the child is exposed to conflict and is feeling stressed and vulnerable, or when the routines in each parent's home are quite different, the child may need a primary home, with a growing amount of time in the other parent's home. The evaluator will want to make recommendations to encourage cooperation of the parents. However, as described in Chapter 5, when conflicts are intractable, the evaluator will want to structure the parenting plan in a way that removes the child from the conflicts and encourages parallel parenting. Just as with the younger children, the developmental needs of these children must come before the rights of each parent, even if the unfairness continues.

School-Age Children (6-12 years)

This is an age when children thrive on structure and routine. Peer relationships are growing, and they are learning to master social rules. Creativity continues to grow, and these children are adept at making up games with unique rules. Rules are important as these children focus on fairness in their lives. Socialization and being part of a group are important to children this age. They are learning to better understand and express their feelings and master cognitive and academic skills. They can be quite silly at times and still prefer to play much of the time. They are learning skills in such areas as academics, sports, music, dance, art, and so on. Self-esteem grows when they function well in school, on the playground, and in the family. It is not uncommon for children this age to have different relationships with each parent, preferring mom for some things and dad for others.

Divorce brings many challenges to children this age. Younger school-age children tend to feel the loss of the family and may experience sadness and crying, often longing for the return of the family unit. Older children in this age range may be likely to experience anger and use alignment to mobilize self-esteem. These children often feel directly responsible for the divorce, especially if they perceive that conflict focused on them. They may exhibit multiple symptoms, including tantrums, regression, sleep problems, acting out, behavioral and academic problems in school, withdrawal or aggression with peers, and depression. This is a population that believes in fairness and wants to please their parents. They feel overwhelmed by their parents' conflict and usually try to fix it, yet they are ill equipped to do so. When a parent is depressed, these children are at risk for parentified behavior in which they emotionally care for that parent.

In extreme high-conflict families, this population may present itself as asymptomatic on the surface but feel overwhelmed and vulnerable underneath. These children are at risk for emotional splitting in which one parent is "all good" and the other is "all bad." They often feel stuck by the loyalty conflicts and may become emotionally constricted, worrying about their parents. Alignments that were natural in the predivorce family become highlighted, increasing their risk of alienation. These children have difficulty maintaining a strong internalized self-image as a result of the conflict. They may become overwhelmed and disorganized, struggling with the different emotions and behaviors of each parent. The use of projective tests may help in differentiating children who may seem to be adjusting well from those who are at more significant risk emotionally (see Chapter 8.)

It is not uncommon for children to hear one parent blame the other or hear different explanations from each parent for things that they experience. For example, when one parent says, "I don't know why your mother doesn't call you when you're here. She probably doesn't care much for you," and the other parent says, "I called you three times last night, why didn't you call back? Doesn't your dad give you the messages?" this is quite confusing to children, who do not know which parent to believe. The evaluator needs to understand how the child feels and how the child processes it when the parents are derogatory to each other or if the child is placed in such confusing situations.

The evaluator should be alert to the level of confusion, emotional constriction, and vulnerability within the child. The evaluator needs to understand the child's ability to express his or her own feelings and differentiate these from the competing demands of the parents. It is important to understand how the child is managing his or her nondivorce life, such as school, extracurricular activities, and friendships. Children this age feel stress and gather fragmented pieces of information from their parents. It is important to know how they manage this stress and what assumptions they are making about fragmented details they receive from their parents.

In evaluating parents with children this age, the evaluator will be trying to understand how each parent perceives the developmental needs of the child and how he or she envisions helping with those needs. I have found that the most important traits in parents are empathy, consistency, support for the other parent, maintaining good boundaries, and being able to articulate plans for setting limits and discipline. The psychological health of each parent is also important, as it reduces the likelihood to which the child may be put in a caregiving position.

Once the evaluator understands the various dynamics of the family, he or she will be making recommendations that encompass the following concepts:

❖ A structured and consistent time-share that assures access to each parent, when indicated, needs to be implemented. Optimal parenting plans range from 35% to 65% of time with either parent (and thus a primary home) to 50-50 joint physical custody in which the child is with each parent about half the time. Although children often express a wish for equal time with their parents, this may simply be to keep things fair.

❖ Although joint physical custody may be best in a given situation, I believe it requires a degree of consistency and a willingness of the parents to resolve their conflicts away from the child. It also requires the parents to share all the tasks of parenting and help the child and each other transfer the child's things (school supplies, athletic equipment, etc.) from one house to the other without conflict.

❖ The time-share needs to promote each parent's strengths while giving each parent time alone to recover from the divorce on his or her own.

❖ Exchanges need to minimize the extent to which the child is exposed to the conflict. School or other neutral places are excellent transition places between mom's house and dad's house.

❖ The parents need a plan for conflict resolution that keeps the children out of the middle. Children should not be messengers or spies for their parents. Communication needs to be by and through the parents, with the aid of a neutral professional when required.

❖ To the extent the parents can do it, there should be a plan for coparenting. For those parents whose conflict is more extreme, a pattern of parallel parenting and detachment from each other will be optimal.

Thus, the major tasks for the evaluator are to determine the degree of emotional constriction and loyalty conflicts within the child and the ability of the parents to coparent, support the relationship with the other parent, empathize with the child and his or her feelings, and promote the child's mastery of age-appropriate skills and tasks. For those families in which the coparenting relationship is relatively free of conflict, the children have a strong attachment to each parent and are adjusting well, and both parents are relatively equal in their attachments, some form of joint physical custody is often ideal.

However, given the potential for children being caught up in the middle of the conflict and given the risk of alignment and alienation in children this age, such a plan will not always work. Instead, when the child is exposed to too much conflict, when the child is not managing his or her stress very well, when the routines in each parent's home are significantly different, or when one or both parents struggle to empathize with the child and maintain healthy parent-child boundaries, the child is likely to need a primary home, with blocks of time in the other parent's home to ensure continuity and growth of each parent-child relationship.

Adolescents (13-17 years)

The major task of the adolescent is developing greater independence and autonomy from the family. Adolescents separation-individuation process is similar to that of the 2-year-old. There can be a tendency to act with oppositional and negative behaviors. Just as with the toddler, adolescents express some resistance and rebelliousness while forming their identity. Healthy adolescents function well in school and have self-confidence and strong peer relationships. They learn to talk with their parents about life goals, and they begin to plan for driving, working, and college or vocational school. As a group, adolescents tend to be somewhat moody and reactive in their emotions. They may feel over-whelmed by pressure from their peers, use poor judgment, and be socially insecure. Their ideas, values, and goals are in a state of turmoil and may change considerably over their junior high and high school years. However, these years can be exciting ones as teens grow into productive and idealistic individuals.

However, with this considerable internal adjustment, this is a population at potential risk. This is true for adolescents of intact families as well as of families of divorce. When a divorce occurs at this age, teens worry about the loss of their family life. They tend to feel a blend of responsibility and guilt and anger for the way it has affected them. Children this age tend to be self-centered naturally, and the divorce becomes a disruption to them. They may avoid both their parents, especially if the parents are burdening them with loyalty conflicts and adult problems. When there is a pattern of high conflict, children in this age-group are at risk for persistent academic failure, depression, suicide, delinquency, promiscuity, or substance abuse. With their ability to see things more abstractly, they become much more aware of their parents' flaws. This may lead to a more rapid destruction of their idealized view of their parents, resulting in anxiety and anger. This anger may take a fairly self-righteous stance, and adolescents may resist contact with the parent whose flaws have been significantly exposed.

In interviewing adolescents, the child custody evaluator has several objectives. First, the teen must be listened to, from his or her perspective; indeed, it is *their* life, not the evaluator's or the parents'. The adolescent's maturity level needs to be evaluated, as some adolescents are rather mercenary, pitting one parent against the other in emotional (or material) blackmail. One of the primary tasks of the evaluator is to understand the degree of emotional risk that the teen is experiencing. It may be advisable to use psychological testing with adolescents if the evaluator is uncertain about the underlying psychological dynamics.

Some adolescents want little or nothing to do with one of their parents, and the evaluator must understand what that desire is about. This must be explored completely, with both the adolescent and the parents. Sometimes, it is the result of alienation by one parent; sometimes, it is the result of frustration with the conflict; sometimes, it relates to the moral indignation of the parent's divorce-related behavior; and sometimes, it is the result of legitimate frustration that has built over a long relationship of pain. When an older adolescent (15-17) is adamant about how he or she wants the parenting plan to be, it is important for the evaluator to have a significant reason whenever it is not followed. Courts do not want to set up a situation that may encourage an adolescent to rebel (any more than he or she would anyway).

At the same time, the evaluator must evaluate each parent's capacity for

- ❖ maintaining the parental role and providing structure and rules that adolescents need,

- ❖ dealing with the mood swings and emotional turmoil of the adolescent that may be aggravated by the stress of the divorce,

- ❖ supporting and understanding the adolescent's need for increasing independence and autonomy,

- ❖ avoiding the tendency to engage the child in being a confidante and seeking the teen's support for the adult issues, and

- ❖ communicating on relevant issues in the adolescent's life (e.g., school, driving, college plans, dating, working, and other activities).

Finally, the evaluator needs to understand each parent's view of their child's maturity, capacity for independence, and validity of the child's self-determined "voice."

Once the evaluator has accomplished these tasks, he or she can make recommendations that encompass the following:

- ❖ A time-share plan that incorporates a range of possibilities needs to be implemented. Many adolescents prefer one primary home, in large part to avoid confusion for their friends. Many of these teens will want weekends or evenings with the other parent. Some will prefer a balanced, 50-50 plan with their parents. Much of this will depend on the prior history of the relationships with each parent and the availability of the parents to meet their needs. At times, adolescents use one parent's home to get a break from the other. More than anything, adolescents will often want a say in the parenting plan.

❖ Adolescents may require a different schedule than siblings. If so, the evaluator will want to recommend times that the siblings can be together.

❖ A statement about the need for any possible support services such as therapy, substance-abuse counseling, tutoring, or other such needs is recommended.

❖ To the extent this is relevant, statements about the need for the parents to manage their conflicts away from the teen and maintain healthier boundaries with them are suggested. Parents should be discouraged from confiding their adult issues to their teenage children.

❖ In cases of severe high conflict, the evaluator may want to encourage the teen's autonomy and detachment from both parents. In that case, helping the adolescent find other appropriate supportive adults may also be indicated. For those teens, recommending someone to monitor and assess the ongoing risks would also be important.

Thus, the major tasks for the evaluator are to understand the feelings, wishes, and thoughts of the adolescent and integrate those with the ability of the parents to meet the needs of that adolescent. When parents are relatively consistent and when the adolescent supports it, some form of joint physical custody can be workable. However, teens and their parents may need to develop a different parenting plan when the adolescent wants a primary home. It is critical for the evaluator to understand the degree of risk to which the child is being ex- posed and whether it is the result of the conflict or the lack of adequate parenting. The evaluator will recommend a parenting plan that the child is willing to accept and that provides the necessary parental structure, reduces the child's involvement in adult issues, and keeps the child free from the conflicts of the parents.

CHILDREN'S REACTIONS TO PARENTAL CONFLICT

Certainly, the extent of children's reactions is dependent on many variables, including the following:

❖ the age of the child,

❖ the intensity and chronicity of the conflict,

❖ the degree of violence or fear of violence associated with the conflict,

❖ the degree and length of time to which the child has been exposed to all of the conflict or just fragments of it, and

❖ the psychological health of the child.

In general, a history of aggression and conflict in the family has been strongly and consistently associated with emotional, behavioral, and social problems in children. Although children from these families have more adjustment problems than normally expected, the range for individuals is broad. Kline, Johnston, and Tschann (1991) and Johnston (1994) suggest that a good parent-child relationship can buffer children from interparental conflict. Individual characteristics of the child (e.g., a more adaptable temperament or better coping skills) may help the child be more resilient to the conflict. Johnston found that "an association between joint custody/frequent access and poorer child adjustment appears to be confined to divorces that are termed 'high-conflict' " (p. 176).

Very young children may be partially protected from the negative effects of conflict because they do not fully appreciate the conflict experience, but even they are susceptible to emotional distress, somatic complaints, and regression in their development. Older preschool children may be more likely to understand the conflicts and the feelings of their parents. Their reactions may include regression, confusion, sadness, low self-esteem, and fear. They may avoid peer relationships and withdraw from their caregivers.

School-age children are much more likely to have a range of reactions, starting with guilt. Children this age often feel responsible for the conflicts of their parents. They show a greater frequency of externalizing (aggressive or delinquent) and internalizing (withdrawn or anxious) behaviors. This is a group that is highly susceptible to school problems, regression, and poor self-esteem (Johnston, Kline, & Tschann, 1989). When there is violence associated with the high conflict, boys in particular are at risk for delinquent acting out.

Adolescents who have been exposed to conflict and violence tend to be aggressive and have multiple behavior problems, including truancy, problems with authority, and revenge-seeking behaviors. They are at risk for drug abuse, promiscuity, social alienation, delinquency, and school failure. They may attach to destructive peer groups and gangs as a substitute for the family. Internalizing adolescents may feel suicidal, emotionally constricted, and numb to the pain that they feel.

Given the extent to which conflict seems to be such a predictor of postdivorce adjustment, a critical element of all child custody evaluations is the degree of conflict and the direct and indirect impact of the conflict on the child. As described in Chapter 5, recommendations should be made that reduce the extent to which parents can engage in their conflict and continue exposing the child to it.

GIVING CHILDREN A VOICE VERSUS PROTECTING THEIR PRIVACY

One of the dilemmas facing child custody evaluators relates to the issue of confidentiality within the evaluation process. Typically, when children see a therapist, the information given to a therapist can be kept confidential and, in particular, shielded from their parents and any dispute. Unfortunately, that is not the case in a child custody evaluation, in which the evaluator might have to disclose information provided by the children. The ethics of the American Psychological Association (1992) state that psychologists must discuss limits of confidentiality with their clients. In some jurisdictions, the court order appointing a child custody evaluation states that the evaluator must explain to children the limits of confidentiality in the custody evaluation process. The purpose is to be clear with the child that the information provided by him or her might be divulged to parents, potentially setting up the child for conflict with that parent. Though I have found that few younger children (under age 10) concern themselves with this issue, many preadolescents and adolescents are very aware of confidentiality issues and express concern that what is told to the evaluator might be shared with the parents.

It is important for the evaluator to explain to the child, in an age-appropriate way, when and how information can be protected. After informing children that the evaluation is not confidential, I say to the child,

> If there is anything that you want to share with me that you would rather I not tell your parents, I can leave that information out of my report or be rather vague about what I say in the report. However, if your parents continue to argue about custody, and they go to trial, it is possible that they could find out anything that you have said to me. Since that is the case, you should only share information that you would be comfortable having your parents know about.

This may not be possible when there is significant information, such as a report of abuse, that needs to be in the report. I will then inform the child that I must include such information in the report, but I will encourage the court to restrict access to that information.

At the same time, however, many children wish to have a voice in the outcome of the evaluation. Although most custody evaluators are trained not to ask children who they want to live with, it is important to provide an opportunity for the child to express his or her wishes about the custody outcome, *if the child has such wishes*. I find that this dilemma can be most easily solved by asking the child about his or her relationships with each parent and then saying to the child something such as,

> You know, one of the things about a custody evaluation is that it is about your life, not your parents', and not mine. You've told me about some of your feelings about your mother and your father, and I wonder if you've thought about how you would like to spend time with each of them. While the ultimate decision will be made by either your parents or the judge, if you have any thoughts about how you'd like to spend your time with each of your parents and if you want to share

those thoughts with me, I can use that information in making my recommendations. Just so you know, however, I don't make my recommendations based
simply on what you tell me you'd like but based on all of the issues that I think
are important in your life. As we talk, if you have any questions about that, please
let me know.

Thus, the child can be encouraged to share his or her feelings and wishes
without being put on the spot to make a decision or choose between parents.
What I generally find is that some children are quite articulate in explaining how
and why they would like to spend time with each parent, having given it much
thought. They may be comfortable with their parents knowing how they feel and
are not concerned about confidentiality. Other children avoid their feelings and
are reluctant to take a stand and be in the middle of the conflict. Not only do they
tell me that they have no preference between their parents, but they even try not
to think about how these issues affect them.

As indicated earlier in this chapter, children who experience significant
conflict between their parents tend to be hypervigilant about how things affect
their parents and very reluctant to think about how things affect themselves. It
is these children who look at me with blank stares when I express that it is about
their life and not their parents'. Even if they do not give concrete information
about their wishes, this still helps explain how the conflict is affecting them. It
is important for evaluators to remember that the content of what children say
may be less relevant than the process in which they say it, or the fact that they
may not say very much.

In my opinion, if evaluators are clear with children about the limits of
confidentiality, provide children an opportunity to express their wishes and
feelings in a neutral, nonforced way, and look for clues about the impact of the
conflict on the child, the evaluator can understand how much to protect the child
and his or her feelings or feel comfortable with sharing the child's observations
of the family dynamics with the parents and the court.

WEIGHING THE NEEDS OF A SINGLE CHILD
AGAINST THE NEEDS OF A SIBLING GROUP

One of the more complicating factors for child custody evaluators is the family
with several children across different developmental spans. There are many
reasons to keep children together and on the same schedule with their parents,
and quite often this is the most sensible choice. Siblings are a natural support
group and may be a buffer for the conflict. Young children may use older
children as a transitional object, easing their anxiety with overnight visits, for
example.

For a variety of reasons, it may be more appropriate to have children on different schedules with each of their parents. The evaluator needs to understand the individual needs of each child and integrate them as a whole into the family structure.

For example, in conducting a custody evaluation with a 6-year-old and a 15-year-old, the evaluator should recognize that each has different developmental needs. It is likely that each will have a different quality relationship with each parent. The 6-year-old may have a different need for structure in the schedule than will the 15-year-old who is beginning to develop a life more separated from his or her parents. Young school-age children often do very well in a structured schedule in which there is defined time with each parent and in which the child can gain from the strengths of each parent. In contrast, the 15-year-old may need a schedule that is looser and revolves around school, extracurricular activities, and a part-time job. Many teenagers prefer to be in one primary home, in large part so that friends know where to find them. For this situation, it may very well be appropriate to recommend different time-shares with each child, with overlaps at various points of the month.

For example, if the 6-year-old is on a schedule in which he or she is at the mother's every Monday and Tuesday, father's every Wednesday and Thursday, and then alternating weekends, while the 15-year-old is primarily at mother's and with father one night for dinner and every other weekend, it would make sense to schedule the 15-year-old to be with the father during the 6-year-old's time. This recommendation provides maximum overlap at father's and gives each parent some time alone with one child individually.

While this major age difference makes this point clearly, it is not at all uncommon for children who are even closer in age to benefit from slightly different schedules. Certainly, young children aged 2 and 5 may have a need for different schedules, especially if the 2-year-old is experiencing greater signs of separation anxiety or insecurity soon after the parental separation. Paying close attention to the different developmental needs of each child guarantees a more appropriate schedule can be found.

In addition to development, however, there can be differences in relationships. This may be because of mutually shared interests (e.g., one parent and child share an interest in athletics while the other parent and the other child share more of an interest in music) in which each child feels closer to a particular parent. Sometimes, this is the result of personality styles in which a child relates and gets along better with one parent more than the other. In this situation, the "goodness of fit" between each parent and each child is the critical issue to be understood. The evaluator may find that one parent is more attuned to the developmental functioning of an adolescent while the other parent may be more attuned to the needs and functioning of the school-age child. This might lead to a different schedule for each child.

Another reason to consider splitting children would be because of problems in the sibling relationship. When parents have been unable to manage sibling conflict, the siblings may need a period of separation from one another to allow for a period of healing. In such circumstances, it may be appropriate to have one child living primarily with mom and another primarily with dad, with some overlap on weekends or once a week for dinner. If an older child consistently acts out anger toward a younger sibling, a period of separation may be needed.

Though these examples have touched on only a few of the circumstances in which individual children may have different needs within a family, it is important for the evaluator to always pay attention to children's differing needs. Even though it usually makes sense to keep siblings together, it is always important to consider the individual developmental needs of each child, discuss them with the parents, and formulate a parenting plan that maximizes the individual needs of each child.

BALANCING THE INDIVIDUAL CHILD'S REAL NEEDS WITH THE IDEAL

Children have a variety of needs. If parents were fully committed to meeting their children's needs, they would use better conflict-resolution skills in their relationship, and they would teach those skills to their children. However, custody evaluators usually see families who do not function at that level. Custody evaluators consider a range of options in their recommendations, and it may be difficult to meet all of the children's needs. Instead, evaluators must consider the child's age and developmental needs, the emotional functioning of each parent, the respective strengths and weaknesses of each parent, the relative attachments of the child to each parent, the degree and intensity of the parental conflict, the child's emotional functioning, and the child's wishes in developing the evaluator's recommendations. The fact that parents are in two different households may make this a difficult task. One of the goals for the evaluator is to help parents meet the full range of their child's needs while living apart from each other.

For example, infants and toddlers have a need for healthy attachment relationships. This is critical for the formation of a healthy ego and separation and individuation of self. The young child who has healthy attachments can move onto preschool and other relationships in a fairly confident manner, secure that the world is a relatively safe place. If the child encounters too much stress, inconsistency, and chaos in these young years, it will be difficult for the child to manage developmental tasks.

At the same time, to foster attachments, the child needs to have frequent and continuing contact with each parent. This might result in some disruption in the child's routine. There could be a need for frequent exchanges between the parents. If there is much conflict between the parents, there may be a need for fewer exchanges, rather than frequent and continuing contact. If the attachments are insecure with one or both parents and the evaluator recommends long blocks of time with each parent, healthy attachments may not develop. Evaluators need to consider all factors when balancing the varying needs of the individual child.

Another place this frequently occurs is with relocation cases. It is impossible for a child to have frequent and continuing contact with both parents when one parent lives several hundred miles or farther from the other parent. Children may not tolerate frequent long-distance travel, either in a car or on a plane. Maintaining close ties with the faraway parent can be quite difficult. If the child is very young, the evaluator may have to sacrifice one relationship for the sake of a healthy primary attachment and the development of a healthy separation-individuation. As I indicated in Chapter 4, I believe that the child's attachment needs are more important than the need to travel to see the other parent. When weighing the various factors, I would encourage parents to find ways to help the child with his or her development and to put aside their rights until the child's attachment is secure.

I believe that evaluators should make recommendations that promote healthy child development first and the interests of the parents second. This might mean delaying a move until the child has reached the age of 5, when object constancy is intact and the attachment with both parents is secure. If a move must take place at an earlier age, I would encourage the noncustodial parent to do most of the travel to see his or her child in the *child's* environment rather than expect the child to be disrupted by frequent moves.

An evaluator may find that each parent has different strengths; for example, one parent may be very good at dealing with the structure and routine of the child's educational needs while the other parent is more emotionally bonded and attuned to the child's feelings. Developing a custody and time-sharing plan that balances all of the child's needs for emotional and academic development can be tricky.

In conclusion, I believe that the evaluator's key task is to recognize that children have a multitude of emotional, physical, relationship, developmental, and academic needs and integrate them into a hierarchy of importance. Although this will be subjective, younger children have a need for stability and security; school-age children have a need for routine, structure, and support for self-esteem; and adolescents have a need for structure and growing autonomy, along with preparing for adulthood. It is my position that evaluators must first understand the child's needs along this hierarchy and then understand each parent's ability to meet those various needs. By looking at the strengths and weaknesses of each parent and the level of conflict between the parents, evaluators can draft recommendations that meet the majority of the child's important needs while secondarily meeting the rest.

CHAPTER 7

The Components of the Evaluator's Recommendations

After collecting the data, the most difficult task may be organizing it to address the key concerns and make appropriate recommendations. It is critical for evaluators to focus on all of the major concerns raised by each parent, especially when there are allegations of issues such as domestic violence, parental alienation, or sexual abuse. The evaluator will include all the relevant data in the report and then integrate that data in such a way that the recommendations make sense and are relevant to the legal issues in the case.

A particular frustration for judges and attorneys is when an evaluation report reads as discrete pieces of data that lack synthesis or when the data do not clearly lead to the recommendations. One judge told me that he likes to read evaluation reports that read "like a good book." For this particular judge, the key is that the data are integrated so that the summary and recommendations make sense. At times, there will be contradictory pieces of data. The evaluator needs to include contradictory data and explain reasons for conclusions that may not be consistent with all data. Otherwise, it may appear as if the evaluator were biased. In general, judges like reports that

❖ are written in clear and concise English,

❖ include data relevant to the legal issues in the case,

❖ include specific recommendations that are supported by data in the body of the report and that can be easily translated into court orders,

- ❖ focus on the children's needs and what is best for their futures,

- ❖ do not include information that is not directly related to the legal questions in the case,

- ❖ do not focus excessively on the psychopathology in the parents, and

- ❖ do not use jargon or report test findings as profiles (e.g., MMPI-2 profile of 4-3 6-9).

Another key ingredient is to remember that this is a *child* custody evaluation. As such, the recommendations must be based on the needs of children rather than the wishes and hopes of parents. If the role of custody evaluators was to arbitrate, we might give something to each parent and balance their wishes. Arbitrators divide financial assets equitably for disputing families of divorce. Children cannot be divided, and their developmental needs should be paramount.

Because the evaluator's goal is to evaluate the family and the relationships within the family, he or she must focus on the strengths and weaknesses of each parent, the needs of the children, and the abilities of each parent to meet those needs. Evaluators are evaluating allegations and trying to understand the ways in which each parent's personality dynamics and the dynamics between the parents affect the needs of the children. They are trying to avoid a scenario in which one parent feels like a winner and the other feels like a loser.

If the focus is kept on the children when writing the report, evaluators will bring in the data relevant to parenting children. In their interviews, evaluators ask questions that give them considerably more information than will be included in the reports. They could write 50-page reports that detail *all* of the data, but most attorneys and judges prefer a concise report that outlines the relevant data. Organized reports that directly relate to the issues in the case, that relate to the state law, and that are in the range of 12 to 20 single-spaced pages are most appreciated.

In some families, the parents' childhood experiences may not be relevant to the recommendations and needs of the child. At other times, this information may be directly relevant. My experience suggests that parents who have their own unresolved issues from childhood are more likely to end up in a custody dispute and hope that a custody outcome will "fix" their previous experience. For example, a parent who experienced abandonment by his father at age 4 may seek to stay connected to his own 4-year-old son. Because this dynamic is so relevant to the family, this man's childhood would be described in the evaluation report. In doing so, however, the task for the evaluator is to integrate how that information, and any other information, relates to the *child* while making the recommendations on behalf of the child to the parents.

A criticism that is often levied at the use of child custody evaluations is that such evaluations exacerbate the conflict and determine a "better parent." If that simplistic goal were the only focus, evaluation reports would be written from the perspective of winning and losing, and such criticism would be appropriate. It is my view that a child custody evaluation's primary purpose is to give parents and the courts an understanding of the family's functioning and the needs of the child. By staying focused on the strengths and weaknesses of each parent and balancing each parent's respective abilities and parenting skills, evaluators can avoid a win-lose decision. By identifying sources of vulnerability and insecurity in the child and providing recommendations that strengthen the child's attachments and promote his or her development, evaluators can appropriately keep the focus on the child.

By the time a family reaches the evaluation stage, it is not uncommon for parents, their attorneys, and the court to be focused more on the allegations and wishes of each parent than on the vulnerabilities and needs of the children. The evaluator must refocus the parents onto their children's developmental needs and provide them with direction to meet those needs. Recognizing that parents truly want to raise their children in the healthiest possible way, despite the fact that they may be currently functioning at their worst, the evaluator can assist parents in avoiding blame. If evaluators refocus the problems onto helping parents meet their children's needs, they can help families reduce the conflict and the extent to which parents compete to be the "best."

I believe it is best for evaluators to identify strengths and weaknesses and outline how those strengths benefit and those weaknesses create problems for the children. An evaluator might point out how a parent's empathy is important for nurturing the child's feelings when the parent's very busy schedule and work travel make it difficult to support the child's schoolwork. With these dynamics, an evaluator might recommend that the child spend the school week with the parent who is more structured and has a healthier routine and the weekends with the parent who can relax and support the emotional life of the child. It is critical to focus on the level of conflict and the way in which each parent involves the child in the conflict. As described in Chapter 5, high-conflict families and parents who have chronic personality deficits require limited time with the children during times when their strengths can best be utilized.

I have found that one way to balance the recommendations is to stay focused on four primary areas. These are as follows:

1. Custody, time-sharing, and parenting responsibility

2. Therapeutic interventions

3. Alternative dispute-resolution mechanisms for the parents

4. Directing families to move forward

In the rest of this chapter, I will address each of these individually, providing a framework of decision making for the evaluator.

CUSTODY, TIME-SHARE, AND
PARENTING RESPONSIBILITY

In some states, which parent gets legal custody of the child is a critical issue. In others, it is usually a given that legal custody will be shared by both parents except in rare situations in which it is not in the child's best interests (e.g., upon a finding of domestic violence, as noted in Chapter 2). Because custody is a legal construct, many evaluators focus on the strengths and weaknesses of each parent as a way of supporting a custody recommendation. To make a custody recommendation, it is important for evaluators to

❖ understand the statutes and practice in their particular state,

❖ review the strengths and weaknesses of each parent,

❖ determine which parent is better equipped (or if the two parents are equally equipped) to make decisions for the child, and

❖ determine the impact on the family system if one parent is given legal custody rather than having the two parents share legal custody.

In some jurisdictions, it is uncommon to grant joint legal custody unless both parents agree to it. When a custody evaluator makes a recommendation for custody, it is important to provide data that support the recommendation. Referencing the custody law is important because the judge needs the link between the data and the law. The evaluator provides that link.

For example, the 1996 Massachusetts child custody law (209C-10; text available at http://www.state.ma.us/legis/laws/mgl/209C-10.htm) states,

> In awarding custody to one of the parents, the court shall, to the extent possible, preserve the relationship between the child and the primary caretaker parent. The court shall also consider where and with whom the child has resided within the six months immediately preceding proceedings pursuant to this chapter and whether one or both of the parents has established a personal and parental relationship with the child or has exercised parental responsibility in the best interests of the child.
>
> In awarding the parents joint custody, the court shall do so only if the parents have entered into an agreement pursuant to section eleven or the court finds that the parents have successfully exercised joint responsibility for the child prior to the commencement of proceedings pursuant to this chapter and have the ability to communicate and plan with each other concerning the child's best interests.

The evaluator who references a particular section of the law and states how the data apply to that section provides the judge with the necessary information to make a decision.

There are no clear, simple recipes for making time-share recommendations either. As outlined in previous chapters, this recommendation is likely to be dependent on several factors, including, but not limited to,

❖ the degree of conflict within the family,

❖ the presence or absence of violence or abuse,

❖ the ability and availability of the parents to meet the needs of the children,

❖ the strengths and weaknesses of each parent,

❖ the nature of the respective relationships,

❖ the feelings and wishes of the child, and

❖ the vulnerabilities and developmental needs of each child.

The task for the evaluator is to make a specific recommendation based on all of these issues. Helping each parent be realistic in his or her requests may be part of the task. I have met with many parents who want to be equal participants in their children's lives and are seeking "50-50 custody." However, these same parents might start work at 6:00 a.m. and have limited options for day care. If the evaluator determines that it is appropriate for such a parent to be equally involved in raising the children, it is important to recommend a time-share that incorporates "relatively equal" participation in the child's life yet is not disruptive to the child. This may be accomplished by arranging for the child to be with that parent two evenings per week and three of every five weekends. This avoids having the child get up at 5:30 a.m. if there are midweek overnights.

Equally competent parents of an 18-month-old child may want a week-to-week schedule. I believe that it is part of the evaluator's task to explain how that type of schedule might not fulfill the child's developmental needs for security, consistency, and stable object relations. Once that is done, the evaluator might recommend frequent contact for one parent but limited overnight time. If the evaluator has evidence that this particular child may be able to tolerate only one overnight per week (despite having an older sibling who can serve as a transitional object), the evaluator will want to explain why the child needs the routine and consistency of a primary house and the primary attachment until he or she is older. Recommending a time-share that adjusts as the child grows may ease the frustration of the noncustodial parent. Similarly, the primary parent may believe that it is best if the child sees the other parent only every other weekend. Again, it might be important for the evaluator to point out the difficulty such a schedule would create in supporting the development of a healthy parent-child relationship. The evaluator will want to encourage a time-share that meets the child's needs.

In contrast, the same child at age 3½ might do quite well with a structure in which he or she is with each parent less frequently but for longer blocks of time. By taking into account the developmental needs of the child, the level of conflict between the parents, the availability of the parents regarding the schedule, the strengths and weaknesses of each parent, and the nature of the relationships, the evaluator can develop a time-share recommendation that meets as many of the child's needs as possible. However, as outlined in Chapter 6, not all needs can be met by a given time-sharing schedule. I believe it is important to balance the most critical developmental tasks first and then integrate as many other goals as possible.

It is helpful for evaluators to help the court recognize each parent's ability to follow through on parental responsibilities. In some states, the law encourages the court to be specific on directing which parent will be responsible for particular parental responsibilities. For example, the custody and visitation statutes in Florida encourage the court to designate whether parents will share parental responsibility or one parent will have sole parental responsibility. If the parents share the responsibility, the court is encouraged to designate which parent will exercise responsibility for different aspects of child rearing.

From a psychological standpoint, the task of parenting has many demands, and not all parents are up to them. Follow-through is critical. When an evaluator identifies that one parent is better than the other at meeting the responsibilities of parenting, it is important to make recommendations that reflect this. Parents who fulfill pediatric responsibilities might be designated to make medical decisions, in consultation with the other parent. Parents who go to school conferences and help with homework will be given more of the school-related parenting tasks. This does not negate the other parent's involvement and participation with the child, but it guarantees that responsible parenting decisions can be made on behalf of the child in a timely manner. Ultimately, the evaluator needs to identify for the court whether a particular parent is more suited to follow through on these day-to-day parenting responsibilities or whether the parents should be able to manage sharing these parental responsibilities with little negative impact on the child.

THERAPEUTIC INTERVENTIONS

A second major area for recommendations is the therapeutic or other interventions for the family members. After the evaluation has been completed, the evaluator is in a very good position to identify what treatment interventions will be most useful to parents. As with the other recommendations, this will depend on the dynamics of the family and the strengths and weaknesses of each parent. Interventions will be affected by the degree of conflict between the parents and the vulnerability and functioning of the child. Some parents may require parenting classes to assist in understanding the developmental, communication, and limit-setting needs of the children. Divorce education for parents or children may be beneficial. Other parents may require a batterer's or victim treatment program if there has been a finding of domestic violence in the family. Some may need brief, focused therapeutic interventions designed to help them understand their own role in the problems while at the same time minimizing the extent to which they blame the other parent. Families who have significant problems with alienation and child alignment (as described in Chapter 1) may require more substantial therapeutic family and/or individual intervention to assist in resolving the problems.

The task of the evaluator is to be as specific as possible about these interventions and the goals to accomplish. A general statement such as "It is recommended that mother be in therapy to help resolve childhood issues and improve empathy for her children" is less useful than a more complete statement that might include the following:

> Therapy for mother is recommended to help her understand the ways in which her own childhood issues of separation from her parents have contributed to her current problems with the divorce and the encouragement of autonomy in her children. Helping her to separate her own feelings and needs from those of her children and working on the areas of empathy, impulse control, and peaceful resolution of conflict will also be components of this therapeutic work.

Similarly, for a father who is at risk for violent behavior, a recommendation such as "Father to be in therapy to help him with his impulse control" is less useful than a recommendation that states the following:

> Father to participate in a 52-week batterer's treatment program designed to help him take responsibility for his impulses, control and manage his anger, gain empathy for his victims, and reduce the extent to which he externalizes blame. In addition, psychotherapy focused on helping him to understand the way in which his childhood experiences witnessing his father beating his mother have contributed to his own feelings of vulnerability and rage may also be beneficial. In fact, the combination of a batterer's program and individual therapy might be the most useful intervention combination for him.

Such clear and precise recommendations help the court provide direction to parents and assist the therapist to whom the referral is made.

Therapeutic interventions for the children also need to be specific. The evaluator understands the child's vulnerability and the specific need for therapeutic intervention. Making a specific recommendation assists the court and the therapist in understanding the needs of the child. The evaluator will need to consider the extent to which financial resources and parental cooperation will be available. It is important to make recommendations with which parents can be reasonably expected to comply.

ALTERNATIVE DISPUTE RESOLUTION
FOR THE PARENTS

A third recommendation area involves future conflict resolution for the parents. Parents who require a child custody evaluation are typically not good at resolving conflicts by themselves, especially conflicts associated with their divorce. The evaluator needs to provide direction for future dispute resolution or else the family will be at risk for ongoing court battles and unresolved areas of difficulty.

As indicated in Chapter 5, structural recommendations can assist in conflict resolution. For example, a recommendation that says "In the event the parents cannot agree on vacation times, the father has first choice in even-numbered years and mother has first choice in odd-numbered years" reduces the likelihood that this will be a problem area in the future. By providing clear and specific recommendations for issues such as exchanges, who decides extracurricular activities for the children, and which parent might attend school field trips, the evaluator will hope to reduce the conflict.

Though the evaluator can attempt to be as specific as possible and provide as much direction as possible in areas of anticipated dispute, these families have a unique way of finding conflict where it might not otherwise exist. By understanding the reasons for the conflict and tailoring interventions to meet the needs of the child, the evaluator can support the family in developing conflict-resolution skills. These interventions are likely to exist along a continuum that includes the following:

❖ commonsense directions,

❖ mediation,

❖ nonbinding arbitration, and

❖ special master (neutral decision maker).

For the moderately low-conflict families who are seen in an evaluation, a recommendation to use common sense and periodic mediation when necessary to work on coparenting issues and resolve conflicts might be sufficient. For such families, there is no need for the more formal and intrusive interventions of arbitration and neutral decision maker. Some families can benefit from arbitration and are more likely to feel secure if it is nonbinding. This maintains the decision-making power within the family.

However, as stated in Chapter 5, high-conflict families and families with a risk of alienation, child alignment, domestic violence, frequent eruptions of conflict, and frequent court battles may need a neutral decision maker (or special master). It is best if the evaluator provides specific direction for this future neutral decision maker. An example of a concise and useful recommendation is as follows:

> I would recommend that the parents meet at least once per month with the neutral decision maker to assist in focusing on the developmental needs of the children, resolving conflicts, and talking about their children. In addition, in the event disputes arise in the areas of vacations, transportation to or from the exchanges, the time and place of exchange, child care and baby-sitting, children's extracurricular activities, health care issues, and other nondefined day-to-day routines, the neutral decision maker shall have binding authority in these areas. Legal and physical custody issues are reserved for judicial decision making only.

Refer to Chapter 5 for more information on this role.

DIRECTING FAMILIES TO MOVE FORWARD

The final recommendation area is indicated when the evaluator finds that a particular parent or child is fixated on loss and the problems of the divorce. After the evaluator has made a thorough assessment of the family, it is usually clear to the evaluator why this family is stuck and unable to process the divorce and move forward. Following a divorce, parents need to take care of their children as two separated, individual parents. If it has not already been addressed in the first three areas of recommendations, a specific statement about the nature of this impasse that provides some direction for helping the family move forward is indicated. An example of such a recommendation might be as follows:

> It is this examiner's opinion that letting go of the conflict, parallel parenting, and using a special master are the important tasks that will help these parents raise their child. Each parent needs to focus more on his or her *own* parenting and learn to be less critical of the other. Both parents should refrain from making any derogatory statements about each other to, or in front of, their child. Such behaviors reinforce their child's oppositional behavior and continue the extent to which he or she remains affected by their conflicts. If they can learn to resolve their disputes away from their child and work toward being the best parent each can be during the times he or she has the child, the parents can assist their child in his or her postdivorce adjustment.

Thus, the custody evaluator can refocus the parents onto the needs of the children, help them raise their children in a restructured divorced family, and provide clear direction to the parents on how to accomplish this goal.

DISSEMINATION OF THE REPORT

In many jurisdictions, the dissemination of the report is determined by local court rules. As communities consider this issue, the ultimate goal should be reducing the conflict. If parents have copies of the report and distribute it in the neighborhood or read sections of it to their children, conflict will probably increase. Parents must be cautioned to refrain from using information in the custody evaluation report to exacerbate their battles with each other.

Essentially, it is not enough to simply write the report and be done. As noted by Johnston and Roseby (1997),

> The practice of having the parents first learn the contents of the report from their attorneys cannot be considered constructive in any sense. Rather it reaffirms the win/lose structure of the litigation and is most likely to exacerbate the parent's sense of shame and helplessness. Giving parents the opportunity to review the report with its author provides a greater potential for diffusing the conflict and helps the parents to absorb what it has to say about the short- and long-term needs of the child. (p. 241)

I concur. I have learned that parents prefer to hear the evaluator's observations and recommendations directly from the evaluator. Judges and attorneys prefer this as well. Although this may be difficult for the evaluator, this practice serves two purposes. First, it ensures that each parent hears directly from the source about the needs of the children, the sources of the conflict, and the things that each family member must do to move forward. Second, my experience shows that this practice allows the evaluator to be understanding and supportive of both parents while encouraging them to focus on their children and learn to restructure the conflict away from the children. This meeting can help parents avoid the win-lose nature of their dispute. Because each parent typically wants what is best for the children and each wants to be a positive influence in the children's lives, this process enables the parents to begin working toward this goal at the conclusion of the evaluation. If they hear the results of the evaluation only from their attorneys in an atmosphere of litigation, the win-lose style tends to be paramount, and the needs of the children get lost.

Thus, the evaluation process needs to begin with an assumption that each parent is likely to have some postdivorce role with his or her children (except for those circumstances when it is toxic to the child). The evaluator will focus on the children's needs, both structural and developmental; each parent's strengths and weaknesses and respective parenting abilities; and each parent's capacity to meet their child's needs. The evaluator must concisely put those needs in the report. The evaluator should have a meeting with the parents at the end of the evaluation process as well.

If this thoughtful and careful process has been followed, the entire family is likely to benefit as a result of the evaluation. If the emphasis of the evaluator stays focused in these areas and avoids the win-lose context of litigation, the decisions and recommendations will benefit the children and be helpful to the parents as well.

PART III

CHAPTER 8

Use of Psychological Testing
in Custody Evaluations

Among professionals, there is controversy regarding the use of psychological testing in child custody evaluations. The view from some is that no psychological test specifically identifies parenting capacity and that psychological tests cannot differentiate parenting abilities. Others support the view that psychologists can use psychological tests and parenting inventories to develop a set of hypotheses about each parent's respective parenting ability and that the tests may help to differentiate abilities between the parents. This chapter addresses issues related to the use of psychological testing in child custody evaluations, including a description of the commonly used tests, the applicability of validity and reliability issues in custody evaluations, the benefits and risks of using psychological tests and instruments in child custody evaluations, and a suggested way to integrate the relevant test data into reports.

The decision of whether or not to use psychological tests and parenting instruments should rest solely with the child custody evaluator and should be based on the scope of the evaluation, the issues involved, and the other data available to the evaluator. It is expected that the evaluator will use multiple sources for gathering data (American Psychological Association [APA], 1994), and the decision to include data from psychological tests and instruments should rest with the evaluator. Forensic evaluations include a measure of malingering and deception, and response bias can be assessed by the use of some psychological tests. I believe it is best to include some psychological tests and parenting inventories in nearly all custody evaluations.

REVIEW OF THE LITERATURE

The American Psychological Association (1994), in its *Guidelines for Child Custody Evaluations in Divorce Proceedings,* states,

> The Standards of Educational and Psychological Testing (APA, 1985) are adhered to in the use of psychological tests and other assessment tools. . . . The psychologist interprets any data from tests, as well as any questions of data reliability and validity, cautiously and conservatively. (p. 678)

Similarly, the Association of Family and Conciliation Courts (AFCC; 1994), in its *Model Standards of Practice for Child Custody Evaluations,* states,

1. Any psychological testing is to be conducted by a licensed/certified psychologist who adheres to the ethical standards of the jurisdiction in which he or she is licensed.

2. If testing is conducted with adults or children, it shall be done with knowledge of the limits of the testing and should be viewed only within the context of the information gained from clinical interviews and other available data. Conclusions should take into account the stresses associated with the divorce and the custody dispute.

3. If psychological test data are used as a significant factor in the final recommendations, the limitations of psychological testing in this regard should be outlined in the report.

4. . . . Whatever the outcome of the testing, of primary concern to the evaluator should be the parenting skills and abilities of the individual parents. Diagnostic considerations shall be considered secondary to parenting and treatment considerations. (p. 508)

These guidelines suggest the need for evaluators to use caution and competence in the administration and interpretation of psychological tests when conducting a child custody evaluation.

At the same time, research on custody evaluation practices in the United States found that more than 90% of psychologists who perform child custody evaluations use at least some psychological tests as an integral part of their custody evaluation practices (Ackerman & Ackerman, 1996). In particular, this research revealed that 91% of psychologists used some version of the Minnesota Multiphasic Personality Inventory (MMPI) and nearly 50% used the Rorschach, intelligence testing, or both in routine child custody evaluations. A growing number of psychologists, about 33%, used the Millon Clinical Multiaxial Inventory (MCMI) as well. A smaller percentage of psychologists used other clinical instruments or parenting-related questionnaires, including instruments developed by Barry Bricklin (1995). Given this data, it appears that practitioners find psychological tests and parenting inventories to be a valuable aid in child custody evaluations.

Recently, there has been a growing body of psychological literature associated with using psychological tests in custody evaluations. Otto and Collins (1995) describe the use of the MMPI-2/MMPI-A in child custody evaluations:

> Given the rationale and basis for the Minnesota instruments, a strong case can be made for including them in some child custody evaluations. The Minnesota instruments can be used to assess the emotional functioning and adjustment of the parents, . . . and (adolescent) children. . . . To the degree that minimization or denial of problems and shortcomings is a potential concern in child custody evaluations, the Minnesota tests' validity scales may also prove of some value. (pp. 234-235)

Dyer (1997) reports concerns about using psychological tests in custody evaluations. Writing about the Millon instruments, he states,

> Many attorneys object to the use of the MCMI-II in child custody evaluations because of the statement in the manual that the instrument should not be used with normals. . . . The rationale (that the test can be used in these types of evaluations) is that if child custody litigation progresses to the point where a judge orders the litigants to submit to an evaluation, then this constitutes a significantly serious degree of interpersonal difficulty to label the evaluation as a clinical case. (p. 134)

There has been little published research on the use of the Rorschach in child custody evaluation practices, but Lee (1996), among others, has been conducting studies on the use of the Rorschach in child custody evaluations and has presented some of her findings at various conferences. She has reported that school-age children in high-conflict divorces are more vulnerable than they appear on the surface. Though this research is in the preliminary stage, it reflects a growing body of knowledge on how Rorschach data can be useful in child custody evaluations. Roseby (1995) described a rationale for using the Rorschach to evaluate areas of vulnerability in the personality development of children in high-conflict families of divorce. She stated, "The unstructured demand of the Rorschach inkblot tends to bypass defensiveness, allowing the evaluator to access aspects of the child's psychological life which may not be articulated or even acted upon except in the most subtle ways" (pp. 104-105).

She also reported that test data can be used to understand the conflict between the parents and to develop a hypothesis about the degree to which particular difficulties are situational or characterological.

TRADITIONAL PSYCHOLOGICAL TESTS

Objective Personality Tests

The two most commonly used *objective* personality tests in child custody evaluations are the MMPI-2 and the MCMI-III. Both have been extensively researched for use as personality tests, and both are apparently being used to a significant degree in child custody evaluations. Their objective status is defined by the way in which they are scored and normed, though the interpretation of test scores is still potentially affected by the subjective interpretation of the psychologist. Though the following information will be redundant to psychologists who are familiar with psychological tests, I will briefly describe each test, how it is scored, and the personality features that it measures.

The MMPI-2 is a 567-item true-or-false test. The individual reads and answers each item as it applies to him or her. Each item is loaded onto a particular scale; there are 10 main clinical and 3 main validity scales on the MMPI-2. The clinical scales measure various personality traits. The validity scales are designed to measure test-taking attitudes (i.e., truthfulness, defensiveness, fake-good, or fake-bad).

Along with the main validity and clinical scales, there are a number of supplementary scales on the MMPI-2 that also aid in the understanding of clinical and personality traits. The research on and understanding of these supplementary scales is growing, as is their interpretation in forensic work. Some of the supplementary scales are validity measures (e.g., the True Response Inconsistency Scale and the Variable Response Inconsistency Scale), and others measure additional personality traits. They are considered supplementary because they are an outgrowth of research that has been ongoing since the introduction of the original MMPI.

In general, the MMPI-2 is an instrument that provides hypotheses about personality traits that might fluctuate according to a person's stress, current life situation, or therapy. The MMPI-2 also measures characterological traits that might be consistent with chronic personality disorders. Although child custody evaluators do not make psychiatric diagnoses, the personality traits identified on the MMPI-2 are typically consistent with Axis I and Axis II personality traits found in the *DSM-IV.*

The MCMI-III measures chronic personality traits that are often seen in Axis II of the *DSM-IV.* The MCMI-III is a 175-item instrument that is taken in the same manner as the MMPI-2 and reflects the respondent's true-or-false scoring of each item. The MCMI-III also has validity and clinical scales, and the clinical scales measure characterological disturbances. Unlike the MMPI and MMPI-2, the MCMI-III is not based on norm referencing. Instead, the MCMI-III uses base rate scores as the standard score into which raw scores are translated. As stated in the test manual (1994),

> Base Rate scores define a continuum of the pervasiveness and severity of a psychological attribute against which any individual can be evaluated. Using a continuum is an acknowledgment that the difference between a clinical disorder and normal functioning, especially with personality scales, is one of degree rather than kind. (p. 26)

Base rate scores of 60 correspond to the median raw score. For all of the clinical scales, a person who scores in the range of 75 to 84 on a given scale may display some behaviors consistent with that scale. A person who scores 85 or above appears to display a more prominent degree of features. This differentiation is significant as it helps the evaluator make hypotheses and differentiate between each parent's respective abilities.

For both the MMPI-2 and MCMI-III, there is a small but growing body of research specific to child custody evaluations. The child custody evaluator should use data from psychological tests to form hypotheses about personality traits and behaviors that can be further explored through collateral interviews, direct interviews, or observations. I encourage all custody evaluators to keep abreast of future research on these instruments as it applies to child custody evaluations.

Projective Personality Tests

By definition, a projective test is one that is scored differently from objective tests, such as the MMPI-2 and the MCMI-III. The presumption that people project their personality dynamics in their stories or drawings or onto the perceptions identifies these tests as *projective*. The Rorschach, Thematic Apperception Test (TAT), and drawings are examples of projective tests. They are projective because they are presumed to reveal aspects of a person's psychological functioning by the way in which the individual approaches the task.

The Rorschach is an inkblot test in which an individual views a series of 10 cards with inkblot drawings and tells what he or she sees. It is presumed that the content of what is seen is a projection of the individual's personality dynamics, almost a "psychological fingerprint." On the TAT and other apperception tests (e.g., the Children's Apperception Test [CAT] or Family Apperception Test

[FAT]), an individual looks at a picture depicting activities and tells a story about what is happening in the picture. It is presumed that the stories are a projection of the individual's psychological dynamics.

Because the Rorschach is the projective test most commonly used and is the only one in which there is any beginning research in child custody evaluations, it is the one on which I will focus the most. In addition, the Rorschach has a systematic scoring system (Exner, 1974, 1993) that makes this *projective* test more *objective*. Use of the Exner system allows the psychologist to have a variety of scores from which interpretations can be made. The interpretation of scores and the integration of this interpretation into the child custody evaluation are still under the subjective control of the evaluator. The Rorschach measures things such as reality testing, disordered thinking, internal resources and coping skills, modulation of affect, level of depression, levels of narcissism, and other personality dynamics. The Rorschach tends to provide information across the range of Axis I and Axis II personality dynamics. Unlike the MMPI-2 and MCMI-III, the administration and scoring of the Rorschach requires a high level of training and sophistication and is dependent on the training of the psychologist. The MMPI and MCMI are not subject to this same variability because they are objectively (and frequently computer) scored and more easily interpreted.

Tests Designed Specifically for Custody Evaluations

In the last several years, two new types of instruments have been designed specifically for use in custody evaluations. The Ackerman-Schoendorf Parent Evaluation for Custody Tests (ASPECT; 1992) was designed to be an objective clinical tool to aid in the task of making child custody recommendations. The ASPECT incorporates assessment tools that many clinicians use and yields a quantitative score for each parent. The instrument includes a parent questionnaire and specific questions for parents and children, and it integrates the scores of psychological tests including the MMPI-2, Rorschach, intelligence tests for parents, drawings, and an IQ measure for children.

The ASPECT yields three scaled scores: observational (based on the parent's appearance and presentation), social (based on the parent's interactions with others, including the child), and cognitive-emotional (based on the test scores). For each parent, the ASPECT produces an overall score called the parental custody index, which is designed to be a guide in custody decisions.

The other group of tests is a variety of instruments developed by Barry Bricklin that includes the Bricklin Perceptual Scales (BPS), the Parent Awareness Skills Survey (PASS), and the Perceptions of Relationships Test (PORT). These instruments are administered to adults (PASS) or children (BPS and PORT) and are designed to help identify issues related to custody and visitation. The PASS yields scores indicating the parent's awareness of various social issues, the parent's ability to explore adequate solutions to problems, the extent to which the parent values communication with his or her child, and the extent to which the parent values acknowledging the child's feelings. The BPS is designed to measure the child's perception of the parents' competence, consistency, supportiveness, and possession of admirable traits, and the PORT is designed to assess the child's closeness with each parent. Bricklin (1995) provides a rationale for the use of these instruments in custody evaluations. Many evaluators have found them to be a useful adjunct in understanding parental competence.

However, unlike the personality tests described above, there is little research on the Bricklin scales, the ASPECT, and the PORT. In my opinion, the reported validity data of the PORT (i.e., that judges choose the same parent as the PORT 95% of the time) appear to reinforce the idea of winning or losing in court rather than identifying relative strengths and weaknesses of each parent or understanding the complex needs of children caught up in high-conflict divorces.

Though the concept of specialized instruments for child custody evaluations is exciting, I believe they should be used as adjunct information rather than definitive instruments in custody evaluations. Although the PORT may be consistent with judicial decisions 95% of the time, this does not help the evaluator discern relative strengths and weaknesses of each parent or understand the complex issues of high-conflict divorce. This does not suggest that these instruments have no value. Rather, it is my opinion that the value in these instruments is found in yielding specific data and incorporating them into the full evaluation, just as evaluators use other information gathered during the course of the custody evaluation.

Parenting Inventories

Currently, several parenting instruments are being used in child custody evaluations. The Parenting Stress Index (PSI; Abidin, 1990), originally designed as a tool in assessing parental stress related to child abuse, is used to assess stress within parents of children who are 12 years of age and under. The test measures sources of stress within six areas of the child's domain (adaptability, acceptability of child to parent, mood, demandingness, distractibility, and reinforcing the parent). High scores in the child domain are associated with parents who feel that their children display qualities that make it difficult to fulfill one's parenting role. Elevated scores suggest that characteristics of the child are major factors in the parent's overall stress. The test also measures sources of stress within seven areas of the parent's domain (depression, guilt, or unhappiness; attachment; restrictions imposed by the parental role; sense of competence; social isolation; relationship with spouse; and health). Elevated scores in these areas suggest that stress and potential dysfunction are likely to be related to dimensions of the parent's functioning.

On the Parenting Stress Index, parents answer a series of statements along a five-point Likert-type scale ranging from *strongly agree* to *strongly disagree.* The normal range of scores for all domains is within the 15th to the 80th percentile. Interpretation of scores within this range is done cautiously. A significant score of 85 or above on any of the subscales may indicate that the parent is experiencing significant stress in that area of the parent-child relationship. The evaluator should ask interview questions that corroborate or negate this and then integrate this test data with the other evaluation data when interpreting the scores.

A second parenting instrument, the Parent-Child Relationship Inventory (PCRI; Gerard, 1994), is a self-report inventory designed to measure how parents of 3- to 15-year-old children view the task of parenting and how they feel about their children. Using a four-point Likert-type scale similar to the PSI (also ranging from *strongly agree* to *strongly disagree*), the PCRI measures scales of parental support, satisfaction with parenting, involvement, communication, limit setting, autonomy, and role orientation. With a mean score of 50 and an average range of 40 to 60, the PCRI is especially useful when parents achieve a low score on any of the scales, reflecting problem areas in that scale.

In the context of child custody evaluations, the PCRI has been found useful for measuring parenting attitudes. I often find parents who score fairly high (e.g., over 60) on one or more scales. Unfortunately, the test designers did not develop a measure of defensiveness on this instrument so it is difficult to differentiate between parents who legitimately feel strong satisfaction with parenting (for example) and those who want to appear to feel satisfaction. Integrating this data with other interview test data is crucial in interpreting PCRI scores.

A lesser-known instrument, the Parent Behavior Checklist (PBC; Fox, 1994), was designed to help identify parenting strengths and needs of parents of 1- to 5-year-old children. Also using a four-point Likert-type scale (ranging from *almost always/always* to *almost never/never*), this instrument measures parent expectations and behaviors, not attitudes. The three scales of the PBC are discipline, nurturing, and expectations. I find the PBC to be particularly useful in child custody evaluations in which parents seem to have unusually high expectations, low nurturing, or potentially harsh disciplinary practices. Comparing the pattern of scores across scales can provide the evaluator with important hypotheses about the parent-child relationship, such as when the parent scores low in nurturing and high in expectations and discipline. Again, though scores may suggest problems in the parent-child relationship, they need to be confirmed from other sources.

The Achenbach Child Behavior Checklist (CBCL; 1991), though not a true parenting inventory, is a practical instrument for parents of children ages 2 to

18 that provides data on parent observation of their children's behaviors. Scores are derived in areas such as aggressive behavior, anxiety and depression, attention problems, delinquent behavior, social problems, somatic complaints, thought problems, and withdrawal. A particularly useful way to use the CBCL is to administer it to both parents and determine if they are consistent in their perceptions of their child. When there is a significant difference of scores between parents and the evaluator determines that one of the parents is more accurate than the other (based on teacher CBCL ratings, observational data, or collateral reports), the evaluator might look for other evidence that one parent is more intuitive or observant in assessing how the child is functioning.

All of these inventories are useful in that they provide some quantifiable way of understanding the parent-child relationship. Depending on the particular scores, the evaluator can make hypotheses from which to interpret and understand potential strengths and weaknesses in the parenting relationships. Though it would be inappropriate to use parenting inventories as a primary determinant of one's recommendations, they provide very useful information on the parent-child dynamics evaluated in child custody evaluations.

Tests for Children

The research by Ackerman and Ackerman (1996) suggests that children are less likely to be given psychological tests in child custody evaluations, yet when they are, evaluators may use projective tests, such as drawings, the Rorschach, or one of the apperception tests (e.g., TAT, CAT, or FAT). Evaluators also use a variety of indirect tools with children, such as dollhouse or sand-tray play or other tools used by play therapists. All of these techniques use symbolic tasks to hypothesize about or gain some understanding of the psychological dynamics of the child.

Perhaps the most widely researched of these instruments is the Rorschach, and there is some growing research on the use of the Rorschach to assess vulnerability in children of divorce. In particular, Johnston and Roseby (1997) focused on the vulnerability found in children's Rorschachs in their studies of children exposed to high-conflict divorce. Researchers who worked with Johnston and Roseby were able to use the Rorschach to assess feelings of vulnerability and inadequacy, levels of depression and disorganization, and other concerns within children of high-conflict divorce. Their data on underlying psychological dynamics are quite useful, because so many school-age children appear to be functioning well. As described earlier, and even more so with children, the use of the Rorschach requires specialized training and experience. When used appropriately, though, the Rorschach provides a wealth of information about the psychological functioning and possible psychological disturbances of children, and it may also help the evaluator be more specific in treatment recommendations.

BENEFITS OF USING TESTS

Parents who engage in high-conflict divorces, and therefore who might be more likely to require a child custody evaluation, have a potential for distortion, deception, and significant personality dysfunction (Johnston & Roseby, 1997). Psychological tests have scales that might help in understanding a parent's deception and distortion. They have scales that might help in identifying parenting deficits, such as a propensity to be violent, abuse substances, or have poor impulse control. The Rorschach can help identify perceptual accuracy, good or bad reality testing, and disordered thinking in parents. Psychological tests can assist the evaluator in understanding a parent's relationship capacity and the potential for matching the parent's abilities with the particular needs of the child.

Children rely on their parents to help them learn about the world. Parents who have a different level of perceptual accuracy and different styles in relating to the world may put children in a bind as they try to figure out what to believe. When the evaluator has data to identify such personality characteristics as a capacity for empathy, coping skills, denial and projection, perceptual accuracy, disordered thinking, emotional availability, hostility, distrust and suspiciousness, defensiveness and guardedness, and a tendency to be self-focused, he or she can assess the ability of each parent to meet the child's needs. This data may also help the evaluator understand the goodness of fit between the parenting traits displayed by each parent and the needs of the child to benefit from them.

In summary, a high-conflict divorce creates its own set of requirements for coping, and the Rorschach and other test instruments may help the evaluator understand a parent's coping ability and levels of narcissism and rage. As described in Chapter 5, many of the parents who engage in high-conflict divorce have significant, chronic personality disturbances. Though custody evaluators do not diagnose parents, understanding the nature of these disturbances assists the evaluator in understanding the extent to which the areas of disturbance interfere with parenting or coparenting issues. The benefit of using tests is that they place more information at the evaluator's disposal and provide empirical data from which to make hypotheses about and understand the complex issues described earlier in this book.

RISKS IN USING TESTS

Unfortunately, these benefits do not come without some potentially significant risks. Brodzinsky (1993) raised concern about the misuse of testing in child custody evaluations. He found that lawyers and judges often expect too much from psychological tests and may push psychologists to go beyond their limits in using these tests to help answer the ultimate question of custody. He also found that lawyers may demand "objectively needless" testing for strategic reasons. Brodzinsky feared that data from psychological tests would be misused against parents in litigation. He cited a case in which a psychologist identified the presence of a disorder simply on the basis of a computerized interpretation of the MMPI and then made unsubstantiated assumptions in his report about the effects of that disorder on parenting, now and in the future. He felt that psychologists who engage in such practices are working beyond the bounds of knowledge.

In his research, Brodzinsky found that many psychologists do not understand forensic issues, and he raised concern that psychologists tend to overtest as a result of a financial incentive. In light of the Ackerman and Ackerman (1996) research, there is some potential validity to this concern, because evaluators who use testing generally charge more for the evaluation than do evaluators who do not use psychological tests.

In describing the pitfalls that psychologists face when using psychometric instruments in child custody evaluations, Dyer (1997) reported that psychologists need to understand each test's characteristics and have their own independent ability to interpret the scores rather than rely on computer-generated reports. He noted that custody evaluations are designed to assist the court in making relative determinations of the strengths and weaknesses of each parent, and he feared the temptation to make decisions and recommendations based on which of the parties scores better on the tests. He deemed such a practice to be "inappropriate."

Roseby (1995) reported that mental health professionals experience considerable pressure to answer questions within the win-lose framework of litigation. She stated, "In this way a custody evaluation can take on the appearance of a pathology hunt which often holds the litigating divorced family to a higher standard of mental health than intact and non-litigating divorcing families" (p. 98). She suggested that a likely outcome of this process is to "unnecessarily heighten feelings of shame" (p. 99) within the parents and that this leads to an escalation of the conflict, which leaves the child vulnerable long after the litigation is over.

Talia (1997), an attorney, described concerns about the intrusive effects of testing for parents and wondered if the benefits that may be derived from testing are sufficient to outweigh that risk. She was concerned about the overgeneralization some evaluators make on the basis of test results that are more apt to focus on pathology rather than parenting strengths. She raised concern that psychological tests do not predict who will make a good parent, and they do not provide much concrete information about the parent-child relationships.

A final concern that has been raised is when an evaluator gives too much weight to any piece of data from a single test or instrument. As indicated above, the AFCC's *Model Standards of Practice for Child Custody Evaluations* (1994) states, "If psychological test data are used as a significant factor in the final recommendations, the limitations of psychological testing in this regard should be outlined in the report" (p. 508).

As indicated earlier in this book, custody evaluations are designed to assess psychological factors affecting the best interests of the child, parenting capacity of the respective parents, the needs of the child, and the functional ability of each parent to meet those needs. The issues facing a child custody evaluator are complex and require a broad-based understanding of all family dynamics before adequate recommendations can be made. In my view, *overreliance* on psychological testing is a significant risk, as evaluators, attorneys, and the courts could look for simplistic answers to these difficult questions. But I also believe that tests *do* provide invaluable data regarding psychological dynamics that relate to the strengths and weaknesses of parenting. The data provided by the multitude of tests can be a valuable tool in understanding these complex issues, as long as they are used with care.

A BALANCED APPROACH

Given the above analysis, it is my view that, if evaluators are going to use psychological tests and parenting inventories in their evaluations, it is important to consider the following:

1. Be certain that the use of testing is indicated for any particular evaluation.

2. Instruments given to one parent must be given to the other parent. If they are given to one stepparent, they should be given to both stepparents (if applicable).

3. Instruments should be used appropriately and within the bounds of validity, reliability, standardization, and administration. Tests should never be given to parents to take home.

4. Be cautious of anything that attempts to take the complexity and conceptual thinking out of custody evaluations. Computer-generated clinical reports and instruments designed to choose a "primary caretaking parent" should not be used in that fashion. As mentioned before, these instruments should be used only to develop hypotheses that the evaluator integrates with other evaluation data.

5. Do not overgeneralize from any one test or make definitive statements about a particular test that are beyond the data of the test. Avoid descriptions of "profiles" for which there is no validity (e.g., a profile of a sex offender on the MMPI-2).

6. It is unethical to use psychological tests alone as the foundation for custody recommendations. Instead, tests and inventories *can* be used as a foundation for understanding personality dynamics, as long as the evaluator integrates those

dynamics with the other data gathered in the course of the evaluation for his or her custody recommendations.

7. Evaluators should remember that they are asked by the court to offer recommendations and opinions about many different aspects of custodial determination and parenting issues (e.g., therapy, use of alternative dispute-resolution techniques, etc.). Testing can be quite useful in guiding recommendations in those areas, as well.

CHAPTER 9

Cultural Issues in Evaluations

Rosemary Vasquez, LCSW

Cultural issues may be a significant component of a child custody evaluation. Many people identify themselves along a cultural or racial continuum. How a person identifies himself or herself will be very individual to that person. The impact related to the family dynamics may be affected by that identification. In this chapter, I will provide my perspective on how this occurs and on the issues that are important for custody evaluators. The cultural identification may vary according to the individual, and it is important for the evaluator to understand the words people use in their own identification.

For example, Spanish-speaking individuals may be identified by their country of origin (Puerto Rican, Mexican, etc.). The term *Hispanic* was created for use by government agencies. Many Spanish-speaking individuals do not identify with this word, and some may prefer to be referred to as Latino. For purposes of this chapter, I will use the term *Hispanic* in reference to all Spanish-speaking cultures in the United States. In contrast, I find it is important to acknowledge that some clients choose to be identified as black and others as African American. Because assumptions about culture may influence the evaluator's relationship with the client, evaluators will need to ascertain how a client wishes to be identified. This chapter will provide my perspective on how culture might impact child custody evaluations.

THE LITERATURE

There is no research about the impact of culture in child custody evaluations. Current literature on child custody evaluations does not mention the importance of considering a family's culture or any cultural differences in a family. There are, however, articles on culture in mediation and an array of articles, books, and research on culture and mental health. There is also literature on ethnicity. Even though there is a scarcity of written material in this specific area, reading and learning about cultural differences will add to the base of knowledge that an evaluator needs. An article by Zemans (1985) emphasized the importance of considering cultural diversity in custody disputes for the judiciary:

> The task for the court, then, is both to ascertain and understand that cultural environment in which children before the court are developing. With all other factors equal, the custodial determination should be significantly influenced by the cultural, religious or social orientation of the child. (p. 67)

The book *Ethnicity and Family Therapy* (McGoldrick, Pearce, & Giordano, 1982) includes a chapter on family mediation and ethnicity. This chapter emphasizes the importance of considering the differences in certain aspects of a culture in mediation. It looks at profiles of blacks, Hispanics, Asians, and Jews in relation to their life cycle, a definition of family, and husband-wife and parent-child relations. The book has a comprehensive bibliography that can serve as a resource for the evaluator. The issues raised in the book are helpful to an evaluator when considering whether cultural perspectives are applicable to the family being evaluated.

Ethnicity and Family Therapy presents paradigms of 18 different cultures and includes three Hispanic groups from different geographic areas. Although there are many similar cultural characteristics within large minority groups (Asians, blacks, Hispanics), there can be differences within the group depending on historical circumstances, racial ancestry, and migration patterns. This book has sections on Mexican, Puerto Rican, and Cuban families that provide an opportunity to note the subcultural differences within one ethnic group.

From the literature on ethnicity and mental health, professionals are forewarned about a sense of distrust that many minorities feel toward mental health professionals. This can be an additional barrier for the evaluator. If the cultural norm of the client is to not self-disclose, information may be withheld that is important for the evaluation. If the evaluator communicates an understanding of this norm, it may facilitate more self-disclosure.

Learning about each culture and its role in custody evaluations is not the primary intent of this chapter. Culture can be a significant component in an evaluation. It is important to recognize that there is very little in the literature to give child custody evaluators specific guidance. However, the literature on culture does validate that certain aspects of a person's cultural identification may be a factor in how he or she relates to the evaluator and how his or her behavior in the family may be interpreted. This chapter focuses on the issues most pertinent to the custody evaluator, who is encouraged to read some of the references to provide a greater understanding of the issues of culture in other settings.

In "Out of the White Box," Taylor and Sanchez (1991) note that clients (who may not be "white") end up coming into white offices, dealing with white professionals, and signing many white papers. Some clients may be very aware of this; others may not. Clients' adverse feelings about working with professionals who do not share their cultural backgrounds are noted in the research (Alvarez, 1975; Miranda, 1976; McGoldrick et al., 1982). I recall a mother commenting to me about her first mediator who was not Hispanic: "Esa gringa no puede comprender nuestra cultura y nuestros valores acerca del cuido de niños que nosotros consideramos necesario." (That Anglo cannot understand our culture or our values regarding the care of children that we consider to be essential.)

Parents who disagree with evaluation conclusions and recommendations are quick to look for any basis on which to denigrate the evaluator or impugn the evaluation. Evaluators try to anticipate in what areas the parents or attorneys will try to minimize their work. Overlooking culture, when it is a significant factor, can provide an opportunity for others to question an evaluator's ability to comprehensively evaluate a family.

Issues about race and culture continue to be in the forefront today. Recent newspaper articles have focused on issues associated with President Clinton's advisory board on race. They report that there is a perceptual struggle concerning whether the disparities between whites and some ethnic and racial minorities—notably blacks and Hispanics—are the result of a lack of skills or of discrimination by whites. Biases are deeply ingrained. Learning about and experiencing other cultures can help diminish evaluators' biases about other cultures.

Evaluators are "professional experts." It is important that the differences between the evaluator's culture and the client's culture do not diminish the validity of the evaluator's conclusions. This is reflected in the American Psychological Association's guidelines for child custody evaluations (1994), which state, "The psychologist engaging in child custody evaluations is aware of how biases regarding age, gender, *race, ethnicity, national origin,* religion, sexual orientation, disability, *language, culture* and socioeconomic status may interfere with an objective evaluation and recommendations" [italics added] (p. 679).

Though evaluators cannot become experts on all cultures, they can recognize the importance of being able to understand a person's perspective on significant family issues, if that perspective is shaped, even in part, by cultural influences. Taylor and Sanchez (1991) note a number of reasons why mediators should be learning about cultural differences:

For a mediator to work effectively with such families, there must be a real understanding of these cultural themes and the level of integration and assimilation that any particular family has made. That standard approach to mediation has been to ignore family history in an attempt to create a present and future orientation to problem solving, yet with Hispanic families, it may be increasingly important to gather family history, including migration and socioeconomic standing for several generations, so as to fully understand the meaning of the presenting problems and the most likely range of outcomes. Unless we have a true understanding of the cultural background and worldview of the participants, as well as the realities they face, we will be ineffective in creating outcomes that are culturally consistent and able to withstand the economic and social pressures that will be placed on them. (p. 116)

Raiford and Little (1991) state that the "evaluator's responsibility is to provide the Court with an objective, professionally sound and honest picture of the family and its dynamics as it affects the children" (p. 1). Is it possible to give an "honest picture of the family" if culture is not considered or noted in the report? In my experience, I have found that it depends on the degree to which the parent is linked to the culture. It becomes an important part of my history taking with the parents to learn about their generational cultural ties and to ask about the cultural traditions they still maintain and the family values that may emanate from their cultural experience. Assessing the level of acculturation of family members allows evaluators to better understand the patterns of behavior among family members.

ACCULTURATION CONTINUUM

Assessing cultural significance is a part of my interview with the parents. I use the following acculturation continuum to help me with this assessment.

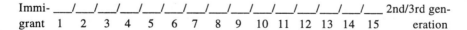

Immi- ___/___/___/___/___/___/___/___/___/___/___/___/___/___/___ 2nd/3rd gen-
grant   1   2   3   4   5   6   7   8   9   10 11 12 13 14 15   eration

At point 1 in some cultures, the following may be observed:

❖ monolingual in the language of their country of origin,

❖ strong religious ties,

❖ minimal academic education,

❖ highly educated with no professional status in the United States,

❖ large families,

❖ male as primary breadwinner and dominant in the family,

❖ mother primarily homebound,

❖ children with restricted out-of-home activity, and

❖ rigid child discipline beliefs.

At point 4, one may see

❖ mothers working,

❖ children cared for only by extended family or caretakers of their ethnic background,

❖ their first language is still primarily used in the home, and

❖ children are becoming bilingual.

At point 8, one may see

❖ children fluent in English,

❖ religious influence lessened,

❖ ties to the native country lessened,

❖ the family's social network extends beyond the native social circle,

❖ marriage may occur outside the ethnic group,

❖ mothers are driving and having more independence, and

❖ children are more involved in activities and relationships out of the home.

From points 9 to 12,

❖ families get smaller,

❖ children graduate from high school,

❖ child care is performed by someone outside the family or ethnic group,

❖ language of country of origin is spoken only by elders,

❖ child discipline is less rigid,

❖ some cultural traditions are still observed, and

❖ respect for elders changes.

To the far right of the acculturation continuum, one finds

❖ child care provided primarily by others,

❖ minimal extended family contact or living away from extended family,

❖ minimal ethnic identity,

❖ private school attendance,

❖ either new religion or no religious involvement,

❖ few or no cultural traditions observed,

❖ monolingual English, and

❖ higher education.

As part of the assessment, Casas and Keefe (1978) emphasize the importance of the strength of religious connection, socioeconomic status, level of education, and distinctions between individuals who are foreign born versus U.S. born and who are urban versus rural. Lemmon (1985) points out the importance of learning in mediation to what extent ethnicity is an issue with a particular family. He also notes that evaluators should be watchful to not assume that family members share the values that are identified with their culture.

Some of you may still ask, "Why is it important for an evaluator to assess the acculturation level of clients from other ethnic groups?" I find the answer in the conclusion of Meierding's (1992) article: "America has always been a very ethnocentric society; we assess the rest of the world's values and norms by our own standards" (p. 304). As evaluators assess others, they cannot help being influenced by their own life experiences and by how they see the world.

ETHNIC IDENTITY AND ADAPTATION

It is very important to assess the client's ethnic identity to understand if a cultural issue has significance in an evaluation. In the Association of Family and Conciliation Courts' *Model Standards of Practice for Child Custody Evaluations* (1994), the goals include "to identify the strengths, vulnerabilities, and needs of all other members of the family" (p. 504). Ethnic identity can form a base from which evaluators relate to others. People's ethnic identity may affect how they behave with family members, how they feel about significant life events, and how they perceive their environment. When evaluators interview parents, the parents typically tell them their story. From this story and the evaluator's queries, the evaluator pieces together their sense of self. Where the parents came from and how they have integrated that into their present life will add to the picture that evolves.

Generally, I find that, for ethnic minorities, there are three modes of adaptation to the dominant society. In the first, the members of an ethnic group may find it very important to be identified only as American, devaluing their own culture. Some individuals and families purposely minimize their contact with their ethnic group in an effort to appear more assimilated and to avoid the negative stigmatization that may be associated with their ethnic group. These individuals might communicate that they no longer maintain any old traditions and endeavor to convince the evaluator that they have adopted American beliefs and values. If they are denying their culture, they may not be aware of how cultural influences may seep into the way they react to or handle certain situations, particularly when they are under stress.

In the second mode, families may adapt by clinging very strongly to their cultural ways and endeavoring to immerse themselves in their ethnic community. They may feel very strongly that traditional roles in the family need to be maintained and that family members should not be tainted by the negative influences of the dominant society. Hispanic families, particularly in some parts of the United States, are able to maintain strong cultural ties because they are geographically closer to their countries of origin. Often, many individuals from the same village immigrate to one town in the United States and, thus, form a home away from home. These families might reject American ways and remain relatively uneducated. An example of this is when they are unaware of preferred parenting practices in the United States, such as the use of time-outs rather than physical discipline.

The third mode of adaptation to the dominant society involves those individuals who appear to have adapted to the American style of life but who still maintain cultural ties. These individuals are considered "bicultural." At best, they can blend the two cultures or cross over from one to the other without anxiety. For many, there is the feeling of having one foot in one culture and one foot in the other—failing to feel they belong in either. Integrating the two cultures is more of an ideal than a reality, for some. These persons, however, have a tapestry of past and present to pass onto their children. It is anticipated that evaluators will clarify what is culturally important to the parents and address that, as necessary, in the recommendations.

Casas and Keefe (1978) point out that "for ethnic minorities, including Mexican Americans, the influence of cultural variable and societal discrimination encountered in forming an identity can create a pattern of life problems which is different from that experienced by other Americans" (p. 109). This may be a factor when evaluating the parents and presenting their psychological profile to the court.

CULTURAL FACTORS IN EVALUATION

There are a number of culturally related factors that might emerge in an evaluation. The following are some of the factors of which I have been aware:

- ❖ cultural attitudes, values, and traditions toward marriage and divorce;
- ❖ spousal and gender roles and distribution of power in a marriage;
- ❖ attitudes, customs, and learned behaviors regarding the discipline of children;

❖ parent-child alignments and parent-child sleeping customs;

❖ cultural attitudes and learned behavior about the expression of emotions;

❖ the self-esteem of a minority group member relative to the dominant society; and

❖ concepts of time.

These factors may emerge in an evaluation in a number of ways.

Although I will present examples from varied cultures, it is important to note that there are both differences and similarities between ethnic groups and within ethnic groups. For one, extended families, multigenerational family networks, and extended kinship networks appear to be the norm for many ethnic minority groups. Common traditional values include respect for elders and loyalty to the family. Interdependency is valued more than independence and individualism. Autonomy, although highly valued in the Anglo culture, can be considered an attempt to alienate oneself from the cohesiveness of the cultural family group.

Cultural attitudes about marriage and divorce can underlie the manner in which one parent relates to the other parent. For example, under Muslim law, the husband can easily divorce his wife simply by stating in front of two witnesses that he wishes to divorce her (Meierding, 1992). Some Muslims, even if acculturated to U.S. culture, may still see divorce as a man's prerogative. This can influence the stance the spouses take in a divorce. For Orthodox Jews, religious law also establishes divorce as a masculine right. A get is the religious divorce that can be granted only if the husband agrees to it; if he refuses, the wife cannot remarry. Understanding this aspect of Orthodox Jewish law became an important part of an evaluation of mine in which the husband was subtly coercing the wife. He wanted her to agree to letting their son be with him for more time or he would not give her the get. He knew she wanted to remarry, and, being an Orthodox Jew, it was important for her to be granted the religious divorce. I was having difficulty understanding why the wife was presenting cogent reasons why their son should reside with her yet was considering a shared custody schedule. Shared custody did not appear to be in the child's best interests. I needed to consult with a rabbi to fully understand the significance of this law for this family and to find a way to deal with the impact it was having on the custodial arrangement.

Cultural attitudes may also affect the distribution of power in a family. Many cultures traditionally have the male at the top of the hierarchy, in a dominant role, with the wife in a subservient role. The husband is expected to provide financially for the family, and the wife is responsible for the home. First sons hold a place at the top of what is usually a hierarchical family. This power of the male in the home may include using physical force with other members of the family. These roles may or may not change as the family assimilates into the dominant culture. The evaluator needs to understand the impact of this within any given family.

Low-income African American families, on the other hand, are identified as matriarchal families because economic circumstances often lead to the male living out of the household. This instability of the male in the home often leads to situations in which different children may have different fathers in one household. Thus, we find a number of grandmothers becoming responsible for the care of the children when the mother needs to become the financial provider or enters into another relationship. African immigrants, however, might have entirely different life experiences. An African couple may come from different areas of Africa, each of which has a culture of its own.

In another case of mine, one parent came from Nigeria, the other from Malawi. The mother explained that, in her culture, it was accepted for grandparents, instead of the parents, to care for the child. In contrast, in the Malawi culture, a daughter belongs to the parents until married. If the daughter is unmarried and has a child, the child, therefore, also belongs to the grandparents. These parents were students in the United States and were an unmarried couple. When the child was born, both sets of grandparents were here. When the maternal grandparents planned to return to Africa, the mother of the child wanted to send the infant back to Africa to be cared for by her parents. To do so would have enabled her and the father of the child to complete their schooling. The father of the child was adamantly against this because it was not part of his cultural tradition to be separated from the child. The paternal grandfather insisted that it was his right to return to Africa with his grandchild. This couple had a cultural conflict as well as a child custody conflict.

As evaluators evaluate families, they learn their beliefs about child rearing. They try and discern their style of parenting. Evaluators may note the over-involvement of mothers with their children, the passivity of the wife, or her zealous assertiveness (in reaction to what had been her traditional role). It is important to put this information into the appropriate cultural context. For example, a child sleeping with the parents or a 3-year-old still nursing or drinking out of a bottle may be acceptable cultural patterns for some but not acceptable Anglo norms. Celia Falicov (1982) states, "These child-rearing practices are consonant with Mexican ideals that stress nurturance as opposed to autonomy" (p. 153). Furthermore, she says, "To judge the Mexican-American family as over involved, or overprotective, would be to conceptualize as deviant or pathological patterns that are the cultural norm and that should be respected as such" (p. 153).

How a cultural group expresses emotions is a factor that can easily be misinterpreted. In some cultures, raising one's voice, waving one's arms around when speaking, slamming doors, or making threats is considered a normal way of communicating excitement, frustration, or anger. In the Asian culture, husband-wife expressions of love and concern may be shown by caring for the other's physical needs but may appear as a separateness between the spouses. In a case of a Greek-Chinese couple, the Greek husband related that he did not hit his wife, but he would raise his voice. That caused his wife to be afraid of him. One evaluator described him as "tempestuous," though another might have described him as verbally abusive. In the chapter on Greek families in McGoldrick et al.'s (1982) book, Welts states that the Greek people are mercurial and what is constant is "the leaping spark of tension that is the only certain characteristic of Greekness" (p. 269).

Iranians have been described as emotionally expressive people regardless of gender. Both men and women show their tears, anger, and affection easily. The latter would most likely also apply to many of the Latin cultures, less so for Anglos. An evaluator's interpretation of how a parent expresses emotions may not take into consideration culturally learned behaviors.

Even in cases of alleged domestic violence, it is important to remember that many men and women were raised in a society where it is not against the law for a husband to beat his wife and where the wife is expected to endure the abuse. When a parent senses that the evaluator recognizes there may be a cultural component to the abuser's behavior, the abuser may engage less in denial and acknowledge responsibility for his actions. Culture poses barriers that abuse victims must overcome, and some abusers will use culture to justify the use of violence. Regardless of the form of the cultural influence, an evaluator needs to understand the way culture may influence the conflict-resolution patterns in a family.

A parent's self-esteem as related to the cultural experience can be another factor in an evaluation. For many minority individuals who have struggled to feel accepted by the dominant society, there is, at their core, a feeling of inferiority when they stand within the world of the dominant society. Somehow being "different" is often equated with inferiority. Those ethnic groups who have had their homeland conquered or dominated by foreigners bring with them a sense of being oppressed. Even without that, being in the United States, speaking a different language, looking different from most Anglos, and having different customs builds on the feeling of being "less than." This feeling can emerge, particularly when a person is under stress. It can appear because messages that the dominant society is superior are pervasive, even when someone has assimilated. In McGoldrick et al.'s (1982) book, Pinderhughes describes the development of a "victim system that is a product of racism, poverty, and oppression" (p. 108) that influences the African American ethnic identity. This system affects self-esteem and can help evaluators understand certain maladaptive behaviors that may emanate as a result of feeling part of this "victim system."

Finally, it is important for the evaluator to pay attention to the concept of time. As explained by Meierding (1992), people from Latin American, African,

Middle Eastern, and southern European cultures are "polychronic," which means that they process things nonlinearly and can do a number of things at one time. American, Canadian, German, and British individuals, however, are "monochronic"; they think linearly and focus on one thing at a time. When I have experienced Hispanic clients who move from one topic of discussion to another, I sometimes think in terms of their inability to focus or the possibility of their tangential thinking and wonder about their anxiety level. I often forget to consider that there may be a cultural factor involved in how they process and communicate information. It is important not to make a judgment that may minimize the individual's strengths.

CULTURAL ISSUES

A number of issues might emerge that may be linked to a person's culture. For example, in traditional Hispanic families, a husband hitting his wife has been accepted as part of his role as the authoritarian head of the family. It is not considered domestic violence. Mexico is not very progressive about women's rights. In fact, women received the right to vote only in 1953. The Mexican legislature has just passed a bill setting prison sentences for husbands who rape their wives. It has been reported that domestic violence, including beatings, rape, and psychological abuse, is on the rise but seldom reported and even more rarely punished. It can be a challenge for an evaluator to weigh the cultural influence on an abuser's behavior with the reality of how abuse affects children and the victim.

Child care can be another issue. For example, a parent may place a priority on using an alternate caretaker who comes from the same ethnic group. Doing so would provide the child more exposure to the culture and a possible opportunity to learn or practice the native language. However, there may be a cultural conflict if the caretaker is not very acculturated and maintains traditional beliefs of strict discipline practices. This person may not be aware of, or may not value, optional discipline approaches used in the United States. An assessment of the caretakers involved with the children may need to include assessing their level of acculturation.

In some Indian and Middle Eastern countries, marriages are still arranged. A conflict in values may ensue when those couples immigrate to the United States. The husband is usually the undisputed head of a family, and the extended family may be part of the household. The mother-in-law may hold a position of power above the wife. Because the husband's traditional role gives him authority over his wife and children, he is not accustomed to being questioned. In some Middle Eastern families, religious laws require the wife to be submissive to the husband. This may change after a couple has lived in the United States for a number of years. In one evaluation, I found the husband to be almost in shock that his wife was taking a stand against him. It is almost unbelievable to some of these men that they are expected to relinquish custody to their wife. This may cause them to remain in an intractable position. If an evaluator can communicate an understanding of his or her traditional culture and the conflict with Western ways, the parent might be able to accept the change that will be necessary in the postseparation family relationships.

The issue of discipline may also emerge in many cultures. Families maintaining old traditions tend to believe in strict discipline and the use of physical punishment. In an evaluation of a cross-cultural family—an Asian wife and Anglo American husband—the wife had been reported to Child Protective Services for hitting their son with a clothes hanger. She was very distressed at being required to have supervised visitations. She was a successful professional woman who had, in many ways, adapted to this culture. Yet, when her son spoke and acted disrespectfully to his grandmother, who was visiting from China, the values from her upbringing prompted her to use physical punishment. I learned about the structure of her family system in China through our interviews and came to understand the cultural conflict that she faced. As was stated in McGoldrick et al.'s book (1982), "The individual can be understood only in terms of family goals and family developmental history, adaptation and acculturation, the family sense of shame and obligation . . . and the Chinese coping styles and perceptions of problems and their solutions" (p. 529). This mother's challenge was to find a way to teach her children the values so important to her within the framework of this culture.

Another issue that often emerges in cross-cultural families involving an African American male and a non–African American female relates to the importance of a child living with the black parent. I have been told, "My child is black and needs a strong black role model in his life." If the child is male, I am told how the statistics indicate that black teens have more problems in this culture and, thereby, need a strong influence to keep them on track. How much weight can be given to this issue? Understanding that this is an important issue for black children in cross-cultural families will allow the evaluator to keep this in mind when assessing the child. A consultation on this issue may be needed to determine how important this is for the child. This may be a significant issue when considering the needs of the child and each parent's ability to meet those needs.

CASE EXAMPLE: A Hispanic Family

Mr. and Ms. A came to the United States from Guatemala. They had two children, ages 9 and 10. At the time of the evaluation, they had been separated 5 years. During the first year of the separation, the parents agreed to send the children to live in

Guatemala with their paternal grandmother. They lived there for 2 years. In the last 2 years, the children had been living with their father and grandmother. They had visitation with their mother.

When Ms. A left her husband, she went to a shelter for abused women. Mr. A had no information about her or the children for several months. After leaving the shelter, the children became ill and both needed to be hospitalized. Child Protective Services became involved because Ms. A did not have the resources to care for the children and stated that she did not have information about Mr. A. The children were placed in foster care. Mr. A, through his attorney, obtained information about the children and filed for custody. The parents then reconciled and agreed it was best to send the children to live with the father's family in Guatemala while they established themselves financially. They separated again.

Mr. A, the children, his mother, and other relatives lived together in a low-income neighborhood. Ms. A would visit with the children in the home because Mr. A feared she might abduct the children. The relationship between Ms. A and the paternal grandmother was tense. Ms. A had filed for custody of the children, and the evaluation was ordered. Mr. A wanted to return the children to Guatemala with his mother. He felt that the children were having difficulty adapting socially in a school in which the population was primarily African American. The children also were not progressing academically.

The cultural issues in this evaluation involved the alleged domestic violence, the traditional roles of the spouses, the extended family system, and the acculturation level of the family.

Evaluating alleged domestic violence in traditional Hispanic families necessitates recognizing that a husband hitting his wife has been accepted as part of his role as the authoritarian head of the family. Even though Mr. A denied hitting his wife, I considered that it might have occurred. When I interviewed the paternal grandmother, I learned that Mr. A had observed his father hit her when he was a child. Given the cultural permission of such abuse, his childhood experience, and Ms. A's descriptions of their arguments, the abuse seemed feasible. I also had to consider that Ms. A had gone to the shelter as a first step in leaving the marriage. I also interviewed a neighbor who had observed that Ms. A had been visited often by another male while Mr. A worked. The neighbor was not surprised that Ms. A had left her husband.

As the financial provider for this family, Mr. A worked very long days, 6 a.m. to 9 p.m., and Ms. A was responsible for the care of the children. Falicov (1982) points out that "the role of the mother is idealized and equated with self-denial and abnegation" (p. 141). Ms. A appeared to have difficulty fulfilling that role. Because of her experiences in her own family, she appeared to have internal conflicts regarding her mothering role. She seemed to have unmet needs from her childhood. Having been born just before her parents separated, she had not received the nurturance, attention, and loving in her own childhood that is so valued in Hispanic families. Instead, because her mother had several other children, she was sent to live with her grandmother. Although it is not unusual in her culture to be reared by extended family, her grandmother was not attentive to her emotional needs. In her marriage, she did not feel Mr. A was attentive to her. She was drawn to the attentions of another man. Her own needs may have taken precedence over what was culturally required of her as a mother. At the same time, Ms. A appeared to be very dependent. She required the assistance of many agencies to help her organize her life. After years of minimal involvement with the children, she was now determined to be a significant parent.

The role of the extended family is particularly significant for those immigrating families who cannot bring the children with them when they first immigrate. Often, it is many years before it is financially feasible to send for them. Often, arrangements for illegal entry of the children need to be made. It was not unusual that this family had decided to send the children back to Guatemala after the children had been in foster placement. Their willingness to be separated from their children was not an indicator that they did not care about their children. After dealing with Child Protective Services, both parents needed the assurance that their children would be cared for within the family system. Mr. A's decision to return the children again to Guatemala fits within the cultural norm of extending the boundaries of the nuclear family and allowing the parenting responsibility to be shared by other relatives. Mr. A's familial network in Guatemala included siblings who were professionals and who could serve as positive role models for the children.

Even though Mr. and Ms. A had lived in the United States for a number of years, their level of acculturation was not very high. Their English was limited, they spoke primarily Spanish in the home, they kept a close relationship with the Hispanic community, and they still had close ties with their native country. Mr. A felt strongly that his cultural values could be retained only if the children returned to Guatemala.

In this evaluation, the cultural factors had a significant impact on the recommendation that the children be allowed to return to Guatemala. However, many other factors were also considered. The recommendation included a period of time for Ms. A to have unsupervised time with the children to give her an opportunity to try and strengthen her relationship with them.

CASE EXAMPLE: A Chinese Family

In an evaluation of a Chinese family with a 19-month-old son, it was important to understand their traditional family system. In this family, both parents were immigrants. Mr. E was employed full-time, had a 1-hour commute, and was off one day in the middle of every week. Ms. E worked 4 days. Prior to the separation, they lived with the paternal grandparents, as is traditional. Ms. E stated that she wanted the divorce because her husband's parents mistreated her. In this family, everyone had more status than she did. The Chinese traditional family system is a vertical hierarchy. Status is determined by age, sex, generation, and birth order. The Chinese wife is usually in a subordinate position in the power structure, and a mother-in-law holds a higher position. A man's strongest bond is often with his mother rather than with his wife. Women are often denied the freedom to express or assert themselves. It is against this profile that Ms. E's situation could be understood. Ms. E appeared to be reacting to the traditional power structure of the family in asserting herself by trying to keep the child from Mr. E and his parents.

The paternal grandparents had provided the child care prior to the separation. Subsequently, Ms. E had a Chinese caretaker for the child when she worked. Mr. E believed his parents should continue to care for the child when either of them worked. Ms. E was adamantly opposed to having the grandparents care for the child. She related that her son was visibly upset and fretful after being with them. She proposed that the child be with Mr. E only a few hours per week. Mr. E was proposing the parents alternate taking care of the child one week each.

Ms. E moved to Chinatown after the separation and insisted the child was happier in a Chinese neighborhood. The Chinese community offers a sense of support for many Chinese. Ms. E may have felt that living there would provide a feeling of security for her and her son. She appeared somewhat histrionic in her reactions to the grandparents and seemed to be desperately clinging to the child. Ms. E may have hoped that the power of the Anglo legal system could combat the power of the Chinese family system and she would be allowed to keep her child with her.

The grandparents and Mr. E were observed to be very caring and attentive to the child. They acknowledged the important position the first grandson holds in a family and the value placed on having the extended family involved in raising the children. Ms. E, on the other hand, was observed to defer the care of the child to the caretaker. In China, families may have someone to help with the care of the children. Ms. E may have been following the traditional pattern of having the helper perform tasks such as feeding, changing, and so forth.

To better understand the cultural issues underlying this evaluation, the evaluator ascertained that, if this couple were in China, the infant would most likely be cared for by the father's family. The culture issue was one of many factors that were considered in this evaluation. The reality of the parents' respective work schedules, the positive caretaking by the paternal grandparents and the father, as well as other factors formed the basis for a recommendation of a shared week. The recommendation included a referral for the parents to an Asian mental health center for counseling.

CONCLUSIONS

As I conclude, let me emphasize that, if an evaluator has any question as to whether culture may be an issue, that is a good indicator that it might be. Discussing the case with a colleague may be a way of further exploring the issue. In this process of consultation, evaluators usually can clarify their ambiguities. Conferring with a colleague also invites his or her input and may help determine if it is necessary to seek a more formal consultation.

If I am questioned about my cultural expertise, I need to be wary about my reaction. When I have clients who tell me that I do not understand because I am not of their ethnic background, I try to recognize that they may have deep feelings about their ethnic values and beliefs. They may be concerned that I am unable to integrate an essential part of who they are into the evaluation. I want to honor their feelings by learning more about their culture or consulting with someone who can teach me.

There may be times when a client's cultural values and beliefs are in conflict with the evaluator's. The task of separating what fits within the framework of the particular family's background from what the evaluator considers acceptable may require involving others' input.

Clarifying issues of culture can be done in several ways. Referring to literature about ethnic groups and their family systems is one resource for evaluators. I recommend consulting with minority mental health professionals when they are available. Another resource is ethnic studies teachers or foreign language teachers. Some universities have institutes for the study of specific cultures (e.g., the Institute for the Study of African American Families, San Francisco State, San Francisco, California). Often, there are churches in the community with a large number of members from one particular ethnic group, and the clergy can serve as a resource.

In this chapter, I have attempted to provide an array of examples from different cultures. A culture that I have not mentioned does not indicate its insignificance. Every culture has its uniqueness in some way. The challenge for evaluators is to determine how that uniqueness plays a part in the task of the evaluation.

CHAPTER 10

Tackling the Terror of Testifying

One of the more difficult tasks for the evaluator occurs when a case goes to trial and he or she has to prepare for testifying in court. For many evaluators, this is a daunting task, stimulating fear, feelings of inadequacy, and insecurity. This is especially true for the relatively new evaluator who has limited court experience and has done little testifying in the past. Contemplating the experience can be terrifying, but confidence and ease can be developed.

Because the basic tools of an evaluator are interviewing, psychological testing, observation, report writing, and other such clinical skills, few evaluators are adequately trained in the art and technique of testifying. An excellent resource for forensic psychologists, *Testifying in Court* (Brodsky, 1995) provides direction for mental health professionals in the courts. However, that book is designed for forensic experts who do court-connected work in many areas, not just custody evaluations. There has been little written to teach evaluators about testifying within the context of custody evaluations. The purpose of this chapter is to focus on the experience of preparing for and giving testimony in court. It includes discussions of legal procedures and issues related to testifying. This knowledge will reduce the evaluator's anxiety about testifying and help maintain his or her professionalism.

Once a report has been completed and sent to the attorneys, it is not uncommon for parties to reach their own settlement. However, all too often, one of the parties is upset with the recommendations of the evaluator and wishes to have a judicial hearing on the matter. If a party objects to implementing the evaluator's recommendations, a trial will be necessary. In such instances, the evaluator will usually be the key, and perhaps the only, witness presenting his or her data, opinions, and recommendations to the court.

If the case is set for trial or hearing (different courts use different terms, but the procedure and results are the same), either or both attorneys may want to take the evaluator's deposition. A deposition is a formal legal procedure in which a witness gives testimony, under oath, before a court reporter. The attorney who gives notice of the deposition will question the witness first. The other attorney will follow. Each attorney has the right to make objections for the record. These are usually technical complaints about the form of the question or area of inquiry. After the deposition, the court reporter will prepare a transcript, and the evaluator will have the opportunity to review the transcript. The purpose of the review is to check that the testimony was correctly transcribed; it is not to change your testimony or try to improve your testimony by editing it. Any substantive changes made can, and probably will, be brought up by the attorney in court.

The deposition usually takes place in the attorney's office, but occasionally the attorney or evaluator may request that it occur in the evaluator's office. This gives the attorney the opportunity to see things such as what books the evaluator has in his or her office, and it takes away from the evaluator the convenient opportunity to defer turning over records or documents he or she may be uncertain about releasing ("That's in my office, and I will have to see if I can release it."). If you are asked if the deposition can take place in your office, a simple "It really won't accommodate the process" should suffice.

The purposes of depositions are to assist the attorney in preparing for trial by testing the evaluator's opinion and recommendations and the basis therefore; to see how the evaluator performs as a witness; and to pin down the evaluator's testimony. The deposition transcript may be used at trial. If the evaluator answers a question differently at trial than he or she did at deposition, the attorney may use the deposition transcript to question the evaluator about the change in testimony.

The purpose of an evaluator testifying at a trial is to assist the judge, as the trier of fact, in making his or her decisions. The job of the evaluator in testifying is the same, regardless of whether it is at a deposition or trial and regardless of who is asking the direct or cross-examining questions.

ATTORNEY ROLES

The evaluator must remember that a trial is an adversarial process in which each side is attempting to provide facts to assist the court to make a determination of custody and visitation issues. The process is a formal one, regulated by rules of civil procedure, rules of evidence, and local court rules. The petitioner of the case presents his or her side to the court, followed by the respondent. For each witness, the attorney who calls the witness asks the first questions. Before asking questions about the evaluation, the attorney will establish the witness's qualifications to testify by asking questions about his or her education and professional experience. This process is called *voir dire.* This is when the opposing attorney may attempt to challenge the witness's ability to act as an expert.

After voir dire, the first attorney asks questions that are referred to as the *direct examination.* The purposes of the direct examination at trial are to lay the foundation for putting the report in evidence, have the evaluator answer questions about the evaluation process, and support the conclusions he or she has reached. Following the direct examination is the *cross-examination,* in which the other side poses questions designed to cast doubt in the judge's mind about either the evaluation process or the conclusions. In a deposition, however, the roles are reversed: The deposing attorney is usually the one who is challenging the evaluator and the conclusions, and the cross-examining attorney is the one who supports the conclusions. In both trial and deposition, each attorney takes turns asking his or her questions. The sequence is direct examination; cross-examination; *redirect,* in which follow-up questions can be asked; and *re-cross-examination.* This process continues until questions are concluded.

During this question-and-answer process, the attorneys are to conduct themselves according to rules of evidence and local court rules. During a deposition, there is no one there to control the proceedings, so objections can be made for the record. At a deposition, the deponent must still answer the questions asked, but, before any part of a deposition is used or admitted into evidence, the judge needs to rule on all objections related to the portion offered.

During the trial, it is the judge's job to control the proceedings. When an objection is raised, judges will either sustain or overrule the objection. At the conclusion of the evaluator's testimony, the proceedings continue until both sides are finished calling witnesses and providing arguments to the court. When this process is concluded, the judge considers all the evidence and makes a decision.

For the inexperienced evaluator, testifying in court can be a terrifying process. The rest of this chapter is designed to assist the evaluator in preparing for testimony, approaching the testimony, and remaining professional. The suggestions made in this chapter are based on both my experience and training and discussions with attorneys and judges. I encourage all evaluators to pay attention to local court rules and their state's rules of evidence. Contact your local court to get the local court rules. Search the Internet (or call the state bar association) to get rules of evidence. Perhaps the best way to learn is to spend a day at the local courthouse observing other evaluators in their testimony. The suggestions in this chapter are basic tools to reduce anxiety and to help the evaluator stay in control of the testifying process.

PREPARING FOR THE TESTIMONY

Perhaps the single most important thing the evaluator can do to prepare for testimony is to write a clear, well-organized, and thorough report. It should provide sufficient information to the attorneys and the court about the evaluator's process, data, and reasons for the conclusions and recommendations. A concise, well-organized report helps the direct examination because the attorney can ask specific questions focused on the appropriate details of the report and the opposing attorney will have a harder time attacking it. As you write your report, think about whether you can support what you have said.

In contrast, when the report is brief or when it does not flow in a coherent and integrated manner, it may be difficult for either attorney to understand the rationale behind the recommendations. This is likely to invite a conference call from the attorneys, a deposition, or a trial. The strongest settlement tool an attorney can have is a well-reasoned and well-written report.

However, not even a well-done and well-written evaluation report can prevent a trial in some cases. If the two sides cannot agree on custody and visitation based on your report, one side or the other is going to request your testimony, either in support of or to question the report. Whether it is for deposition or trial, you must prepare for your testimony before it begins.

Preparation for deposition or trial begins with being thoroughly familiar with your work and your report. You will need to review your report, notes, and any materials provided to you. In some jurisdictions, the attorney who supports your report may speak with you to help prepare you for testifying. This depends on local court rules with respect to court-appointed or neutral evaluators. When an expert represents one side, the attorney always prepares the witness, and the witness may actually assist the attorney in developing questions for trial. Remember that you may be asked in deposition or trial if you talked with the other attorney or if you reviewed anything in preparation for testifying. It is a legitimate question, and it is perfectly proper to review your file and to speak with the attorney prior to testimony. You just have to know that you can be asked what was discussed. Thus, when you have a discussion with counsel, you do not want to say anything that you would not want to acknowledge having said.

Your appearance at deposition or court may be demanded by subpoena or may be arranged by an informal agreement between counsel. If it is by subpoena, the document will tell you what to bring, for example, "your complete file" or "all notes, correspondence, and any documents you reviewed along with your report." In most states, an expert witness is entitled to his or her customary fee for a deposition to be paid to the deposing attorney at the beginning of the deposition. Prior to the deposition, you should make sure that you have advised what your deposition fee is, and be clear on who will pay it and when it will be paid.

An important part of preparation is to have your file completely organized. This allows you to find things easily. Arrive a few minutes early. It makes a bad impression when you keep attorneys or the judge waiting. Bring enough copies of your curriculum vitae for each attorney and the judge, even if you think they already have it. By planning ahead, arriving on time, and having things organized, you give yourself time to relax and prepare yourself emotionally for your testimony. This will allow you to maintain control during what may be an anxious or tense experience. If you arrive late, if your file is disorganized, or you feel rushed, it will be more difficult to stay focused and calm during your testimony. Another important preparation for testimony is in your appearance. Do not dress so that your appearance invites notice. Do not wear clanking, flashy jewelry or loud ties. An evaluator should be professional and subdued in his or her appearance.

TESTIFYING PROCEDURES

Certain testimony procedures are important for the evaluator. You should speak calmly, slowly, and clearly. This ensures that the judge and attorneys hear you accurately and allows the court reporter to accurately record your testimony. Spell words that may not be familiar to the court reporter. Avoid an argumentative tone that might alienate an attorney or the judge. Do not use sarcasm or joke on the stand. By staying calm, speaking clearly and slowly, and maintaining an even voice, you will improve the credibility in your testimony.

Always allow the attorney to finish his or her question before beginning your answer. Not only is this courteous, but it allows you time to think through your answer before giving it. In speaking to attorneys and judges about testimony, one of the biggest frustrations they experience is when expert witnesses presume they know the question before it is complete, giving their answer too early.

Do not volunteer information that you have not been asked. Generally, it is best to give the narrowest answer to questions, allowing the attorneys to decide if they want you to elaborate. They will prompt you if they do. In particular, do not volunteer information that is irrelevant to the case just to impress anyone. If you say, "I've handled 25 cases with parental alienation," you are only inviting questions about your history with these cases. Usually, this will backfire. Rather than impressing the court or attorneys with yourself and your experience, impress everyone with your knowledge of the facts of the particular case.

On the other hand, if you have something that you believe is critical to the decision and you know the proponent of the report wants the information in, you might take the chance to get it into another answer or say it directly to the judge. You would do that only if you do not have an opportunity for a break during which to ask the attorney who is the proponent whether that point needs to be made.

Many judges consider it wise for the evaluator to take a few seconds after a question is asked before responding. This allows you to reflect on the answer and be more certain that you are saying what you want to say. This is true both for questions you are not sure how you want to answer and for complex questions. By pausing, looking through your notes, or reflecting on the question before you answer, you are more assured that your testimony is what you want it to be.

Another reason for pausing is related to the court process itself. One attorney may object to the form or nature of the question being asked. Pausing gives the other attorney the opportunity to object prior to the start of your answer.

When an objection is made at deposition, it is important to wait for the attorneys to complete their arguments before answering the question. At a deposition, after an objection is made, you still answer the question. If that testimony is used in court, the judge will hear the objection prior to reading the answer from a deposition. In the courtroom, it is always important to allow both attorneys to complete their arguments regarding the objection and to wait for the judge to make a ruling. You should not interrupt the judge, and you should not give an answer when the judge has sustained an objection. If a question has been asked that you want to answer, it is important to wait until you have the right opportunity. You may be able to slip in the information along with your answer to another question. If the information seems critical to you and the question is not asked, speak to the proponent of the report on a break.

It is important that your testimony remain independent and objective at all times. Though your recommendations are likely to favor one parent over the other in some areas, it is important not to become an advocate for that parent. Even when you are brought in to testify by one side, you are still a neutral evaluator working for the best interests of the child. You are the child's advocate. If you become an advocate for one parent during your testimony, the other side might question if you have lost your objectivity or become biased in your answers.

Being a neutral evaluator and being evenhanded means you are independent of either party and that you do not have a biased point of view. This is in contrast to the way you might present yourself if you were hired as a consultant for one party. As a consultant, you are not independent; you work for that party. As an independent evaluator, you have performed the evaluation process in a neutral and evenhanded manner, and you do not try to prove one side's case. You treat the parties equally in your investigation. If there were circumstances in which you did something different with respect to one party, it was for a sound, clinical reason. As long as differences in treatment of the parties were clinically justified, you will still be viewed as evenhanded and independent. As long as you remember that your task is not to determine what is best for either parent but to make a recommendation for what is in the best interests of the child, you can maintain your neutrality.

At the same time, you must be able to take a stand on issues. The only person who will be pleased with your testimony if you cannot take a stand is the person who is challenging your report. Evaluators who are too wishy-washy and seem unable to say what needs to be said, perhaps because they do not want to offend someone, frustrate attorneys and the court. The court needs evidence on which to base a decision for the best interests of the child. The evaluator is the vehicle for providing that evidence. Neutrality does not mean that you do not reveal one parent's strengths and the other parent's problems if they are relevant to his or her ability to parent and to the best interests of the child. It is not a pleasant task to talk about a person's problems and weaknesses as a parent, but that is part of your job. If it affects the best interests of the child, you must be prepared to say it.

Finally, you should occasionally look at the judge. The attorney who is questioning you is the one with whom you are having a dialogue, but an occasional turn to the judge, particularly if you are making an important point, is helpful. Do not feel intimidated if the judge appears to be scrutinizing you. The judge is trying to determine how much weight to give your testimony, and he or she needs to get a feel for you. If the judge asks you a question, answer it. Do not look at the attorney first. Remember, it is the judge who needs to know your testimony because it is the judge who makes the decisions.

STICK TO THE DATA

One of the clearest ways to ensure your independence as an expert witness is to provide answers that can be supported by your data. As evaluators, we are sometimes tempted to elaborate beyond what the data can support. In some of the tough evaluations described earlier in the book (e.g., child alignment and alienation, domestic violence, sex abuse, or relocation), you might not have enough data even at the end of a thorough evaluation to be sure about whether or not abuse has taken place, whether someone is interfering with the child's relationship with the other parent, or whether a parent should or should not move. If you have given psychological testing, there might be conflicting evidence from the tests and clinical interviews that also interfere with your level of certainty. As evaluators, we are sometimes cautious regarding our recommendations. You must refrain from speculation beyond that which the data can support.

At the same time, evaluators do make recommendations about specific items for which there may be little direct data. In those instances, you use indirect data and your understanding of developmental and divorce research to support your recommendations. For example, if you have given a recommendation for an exchange of a child at a particular time on the weekend, there is unlikely to be data that support a specific time. However, you know from the research on high-conflict families that structure and consistency reduce conflict. In addition, you know that young children need consistency and simplicity of schedules. Thus, you can testify with relative confidence even if the evaluation data might not lead directly to such a recommendation. You might not know whether someone has sexually molested his or her child even after reviewing all data. The strongest statement you might make is one of continued uncertainty.

Another area of possible concern is when the evaluator has not seen one parent and is asked in testimony to provide data about that parent. If you have seen only one parent, you cannot make definitive statements about the other parent. Rather than saying, "Mother is depressed and unable to care for the children," for example, you would say, "Father expresses concern that mother is depressed and is unable to care for the children, but I have not been able to evaluate this matter." Sometimes, as a consultant, you might not have seen some family members. You could never say, "It's in Julie's best interest to live with her mother." Instead, if you are the mother's consultant, you might say, "If the facts of the case are as described by the neutral evaluator, research would support the evaluator." It is also important to be clear that you have not seen one or more family members and that your statements are limited as a result.

Another way of sticking to the data is to admit when you do not know something, when you have been unable to find an answer to a particular question, or when you have made a mistake. Frequently, in complex custody evaluations, there will be some things that the evaluator cannot answer. In addition, psychological research is still evolving, so it may be difficult to make precise recommendations when there is limited information. Though you might make specific recommendations, you need to be cautious during testimony and express clearly what you do and do not know.

Moreover, there are times when an evaluator does not have data because he or she missed something. For example, if you did not talk to the pediatrician, you may need to explain why you did not talk to him or her. It is rare that one piece of data will sway an opinion gathered from multiple sources. However, if you realize talking to the pediatrician might have helped, admit it. If asked by the court, offer to do so. Judges are critical of evaluators who are reluctant to admit mistakes for fear of looking bad. Parents are not expected to be perfect, and when evaluators make mistakes, it is important to clarify and acknowledge them when that happens. Sometimes, inexperienced evaluators tend to become defensive and arrogant. A simple recognition that you have made a mistake would be better.

DEALING WITH HYPOTHETICALS

Attorneys often ask hypothetical questions during cross-examination, adjusting some of the facts to see if your recommendation might change. This tactic is used to question the evaluator's recommendations and to support the consideration of a different recommendation. Hypothetical questions involve situations that the cross-examining attorney will attempt to show as factual. By asking evaluators about their recommendations under hypothetical facts, the attorney is attempting to lay the foundation such that, if the court accepts the facts in the hypothetical, a different direction should be followed. Under those circumstances, it is important to answer the hypothetical questions from the standpoint of an independent evaluator. This is one of those places where it is easy for an evaluator to appear to be an advocate rather than an impartial expert. If the hypothetical facts would lead to a different recommendation, it is important to state so. This is probably the best time to pause, think through your answer, and describe out loud why your recommendation would change, if it would, with the new facts. One effective way of dealing with hypotheticals is to state clearly that the facts as presented in the hypothetical are not consistent with the facts of the case you are testifying about. Then, answer the hypothetical questions accurately.

Similarly, if you get asked a difficult, negative question about the parent you are supporting, answer it honestly. If you can, relate the question and your answer to the ability to parent. Again, avoid becoming an advocate, and be direct and clear in acknowledging weaknesses in the parent whom you are primarily supporting. If the data show that the parent is not perfect, answer the question honestly. Stick to the data and report on strengths and weaknesses of each parent. Answering questions directly and honestly assists the judge in reaching a sound conclusion. If you avoid the tough questions and minimize strengths in the parent you are recommending against and weaknesses in the parent you are supporting, it will be more difficult for the court to view you as unbiased. Then it will be more difficult for the court to use the information in your evaluation in a positive way.

REMAIN PROFESSIONAL

Being professional means being prepared. You need to be prepared for both direct and cross-examination prior to the testifying. As previously stated, you need to know everything in your file, the strengths and weaknesses of each parent, and the rationale used in reaching your conclusions. Experience may help you anticipate questions. A novice evaluator might wish to consult with a more experienced evaluator to aid in testimony preparation. Role-playing with colleagues or going to court and observing a colleague also helps. Even if you feel experienced, you must prepare for testimony in every case. Ultimately, you will want to anticipate the kinds of questions the judge might ask and the important, factual data you want to be sure and provide to the judge.

At times, a direct-examining attorney may not ask you the correct questions, and you may have data you want to give the judge. Elaborating on your answers to the direct examination may give you the chance to provide that information to the court. In some jurisdictions, it is considered appropriate to meet with the attorney who is calling you to go over your testimony ahead of time. Make certain that this does not violate local court rules prohibiting ex parte communication at all levels of the process.

Finally, as a professional, never debate the cross-examining attorney. Judges and attorneys get frustrated with evaluators who end up arguing with an attorney. Rather than argue, simply answer the attorney's questions. Do not ask questions of the attorneys. After answering a hypothetical with the statement, "Those aren't the facts in this case," answer the question as if the hypothetical facts were true. If you are annoyed by the cross-examining attorney, it is even more important to keep your answers short and succinct, focused directly on the question.

TRICK QUESTIONS

Never take questions from the cross-examining attorney personally. Remember, it is his or her job to raise a question in the judge's mind about your recommendations. Sometimes, cross-examining attorneys will ask provocative questions to try and trip the evaluator up. Sometimes, it may appear as if they are trying to blame you for your recommendations. I know of an attorney who once asked an evaluator, "Is it really your intent to deprive this child of a relationship with her mother?" Such a question can leave an evaluator feeling defensive. Sometimes, a cross-examining attorney might ask you about your experience or the number of times you have recommended for joint, sole to mother, or sole to father custody. Such questions are designed to provide an opportunity to claim bias. Answer those questions briefly, honestly, and without emotion. At other times, the attorney might ask you whether you have children or about your own marital status. You probably do not need to answer these questions. Whenever you believe the question is personal and not relevant to your professional role in the case, you can answer, "I don't believe that question is relevant to my professional role." If the attorney still wants you to answer the question, he or she will ask the judge to direct your answer. Then, do as the judge directs.

Never let your frustration interfere with professional testimony. Attorneys are trained to try and upset you. Do not give them that advantage with your testimony. They may ask "trick" questions, designed to throw you off base. For example, an attorney on cross-examination might ask a question in an incredulous tone, such as "Are you actually saying that Mrs. Smith is the best choice for primary parent?" The tone of the question suggests that there might be no reason to make that recommendation. The best way to handle this type of question is to say, simply and nondefensively, "Yes, that is my recommendation based on the information I collected during the evaluation."

Another trick is to ask a complex question that accurately reflects part of what you said while distorting part. An attorney recently asked me to read a passage from my earlier book about the developmental needs of preschool children. She wanted me to read only two paragraphs. This left out important contrary information that was in the following two paragraphs. I read the section as asked, hoping for an opportunity to state the rest. In redirect, the other attorney asked me to finish the section so that my entire opinion could be stated.

Similarly, if you are asked, "So, it's your opinion that the domestic violence allegations made by my client may not have happened as she alleged, and therefore they are unfounded," you might say that the allegations did not seem to happen exactly as she claimed, "but nowhere in my report did I say that the allegations were unfounded." Listen carefully for the entire question. Acknowledge what is true, and clarify what is false.

Sometimes, attorneys question me about something *they say I said* in my report, *but I know I did not say it.* Such a question might be, "Isn't it true that you saw no evidence of problems in the parent-child relationship when you observed my client with his child?" even when you never said this. You will not fall for this trick if you know your report exceedingly well prior to giving testimony. If such a question comes up, my response is "Could you please show me where I said that and I would be happy to respond."

Ultimately, you will maintain your professionalism when you stay neutral, calm, and self-assured. By sticking to the facts of the case, by avoiding an appearance of becoming an advocate, by refusing to debate a cross-examining attorney who provokes you, by refusing to take personally attacks on your professional or personal biases, and by answering questions directly and within the bounds of the data, you keep your professionalism intact and assure the court that there is a sound basis for your recommendations.

DOS AND DON'TS FOR TESTIFYING IN COURT

❖ Look confident and secure—be overprepared.

❖ Write a balanced, thorough report.

❖ Know your report and everything in the file.

❖ Speak calmly, slowly, and clearly—avoid argumentative tones.

❖ Avoid the splitting and polarization in the courtroom by becoming too much of an advocate for one side.

❖ However, if you are sure about something, say it unequivocally.

❖ Avoid jargon in both your reports and testimony.

❖ Avoid overexplaining or becoming too technical.

❖ Allow the attorney to finish his or her question before answering.

❖ Avoid talking when attorneys and the judge are discussing an issue, and wait when an objection is made.

❖ Stop and think before answering tough questions, and stop talking when you have finished answering the question.

❖ Refrain from speculation beyond what the data support.

❖ Give no opinions about anyone not seen as part of the evaluation.

❖ If you do not know something or if you have made an omission or mistake, admit it.

❖ If asked a hypothetical question, answer it honestly.

❖ Do not allow yourself to get emotional—do not get your feelings hurt or get angry.

❖ Remember that the judge's job is to support a fair trial and control the proceedings.

❖ The most-credible experts stay cool, honest, direct, nondefensive, balanced, neutral, and decisive.

❖ The least-credible experts get defensive; are unprepared, sarcastic, rigid, or one-sided; use jargon; and try to take control of the trial.

CHAPTER 11

Ethical Issues

There has been some direction regarding the ethical obligations of custody evaluators. The American Psychological Association (APA; 1994) has published *Guidelines for Child Custody Evaluations in Divorce Proceedings,* and the Association of Family and Conciliation Courts (AFCC; 1994) has published *Model Standards of Practice for Child Custody Evaluations.* Copies of those documents can be found in the appendix of my earlier book (Stahl, 1994a). I also wrote about ethics in a later publication that same year (1994b). Since that time, the topic has been discussed at various meetings and workshops. The Judicial Council of California (1999) has just revised the *Uniform Standards of Practice for Court Ordered Child Custody Evaluations* that evaluators are required to follow in that state. Like the guidelines and standards of the APA and AFCC, these standards focus solely on the evaluation process and apply to all child custody evaluators who conduct court-ordered evaluations in California.

Although all of these guidelines provide direction to the evaluator in the *conduct* of the evaluation, they do not help psychologists, other mental health professionals, and the courts manage a plethora of complex dilemmas.

In Contra Costa County, California, a Family Court Services task force focused on several ethical dilemmas that develop in work with family courts. These dilemmas may have a range of possible solutions, and there may be no single correct way of managing the issue. In this chapter, I will present various hypothetical situations, grouped according to topic, and provide my thoughts on each issue. I encourage the reader to use my thoughts as a guide to understanding them and to think about your own answers to these difficult issues. I also encourage communities to develop consistent local standards of ethical practice.

CONFIDENTIALITY OF SOURCES

■■ You are the evaluator preparing to contact a collateral source who has observed abuse that you suspected was ongoing but was hard to prove. Before asking for his or her input, would you inform that person that what he or she says will be available to the court? Would you be more willing not to inform if the child were an infant as opposed to an older child?

I believe that evaluators must inform all participants, including collateral sources, that information given to the evaluator is available to the court and the parents. The APA (1994) guidelines state, "Psychologists must insure that participants are aware of the limits of confidentiality" (http://www.apa.org/ethics/code.html). I believe this extends to collateral sources as well. Friends, neighbors, and relatives may ask for confidentiality. Evaluators need to inform all contacts that confidentiality cannot be assured. Also, if the evaluator suspects child abuse, the evaluator is usually obligated to inform child protection agencies of the concern.

■■ You are the evaluator who forgot to tell a teenager that what he or she said might be repeated to his or her parents and the court. The teen tells you something about a sibling that the teen definitely does not want his or her parents to know. Would you tell the teen you made a mistake and that you should have told him or her that the information was not confidential? Would you use the information anyway? Would you pretend you never heard the information but let the teen know that anything further would not be confidential?

As indicated above, it is very important to inform everyone about the limits of confidentiality as early in the process as possible, preferably at the beginning of interviews. If the evaluator fails to do so and learns critical information about one of the children, even if it is from a sibling, it is then important to inform that sibling about the limits of confidentiality.

I believe that the evaluator in this example should not use the information, unless it fell under the mandatory reporting laws of the state (e.g., child abuse laws). If the information were critical, I would ask the teen for permission to disclose it after correcting my mistake and informing him or her about the limits of the confidentiality. If the teen still refused to give permission and told me that he or she would not have given me the information if I had previously explained the limits of confidentiality, I would not use it.

■■ You are the evaluator. A family has been seeing a private mediator for eight sessions of confidential mediation. They have been unable to reach a custody decision for their 12-year-old daughter. Is it ethically appropriate for you to talk to the mediator to help in the custody evaluation? What if the mediator works for Family Court Services, is there a different ethical concern?

Local court rules might provide the solution. These rules may prohibit individual parents from releasing the mediator from confidentiality. Unless the local rules prohibit this, I believe that as long as both parents sign a release of information, the evaluator may speak with the mediator. Even though parents authorize the release, the mediator is not obligated to communicate previously confidential information to the evaluator. This would be equally true for therapists who might wish to maintain confidentiality, even if the parents authorize the release of information.

ABUSIVE CLIENTS

■■ Suppose you are a special master. You get easily frustrated and angry at one or both clients. Sometimes, the feelings border on hate and rage. How do you work with these difficult clients? How do we as special masters deal with abusive clients? How does the special master resign if he or she feels it is for the best?

Parents with serious personality disturbances in a high-conflict divorce can be extremely frustrating and difficult to work with. These clients require the evaluator's patience, firmness, and toughness. As therapists, we know that we can use our own feelings as a guide to understanding the dynamics of our client's personality. As a special master, we should do the same.

Sometimes, our feelings affect our ability to perform our job. First, I would recommend consultation to see if this helps. Consultation can give the necessary perspective to calm your feelings and allow you to resume your high-quality work. Participation in an ongoing support group can also help. Regular consultation with colleagues provides an opportunity to talk with others about your feelings. If these efforts do not work, I would resign and inform the court of my reasons for the resignation. This particular family may not be appropriate for a special master.

SECOND OPINIONS

■■ Suppose you have recommended primary physical custody to mother and limited visitation to father. At the settlement conference with the attorneys, father's attorney suggests that you were biased because of your own experiences of abuse when you were younger. He or she suggests that you misrepresented the data in your evaluation report. Father's attorney produces a report by an expert that suggests you made significant errors in your evaluation. Mother's attorney is angry because mother never knew that anyone but the court and the attorneys had access to the evaluation report and data. What ethical concerns are raised, and what should happen next?

Under what circumstances is it professional, ethical, and appropriate for the court (or the parties) to authorize a second-opinion review of a custody evaluation, and how can the court determine how much weight to give it compared with the original evaluation?

In a previous article (Stahl, 1996), I wrote that it is not uncommon for a "losing" parent to try and discredit the evaluation and suggest that the evaluator was biased or incompetent. A parent or his or her attorney may also believe that an evaluation was done poorly. There may be a legitimate reason for requesting a review or a new evaluation. Differentiating between legitimate concerns about an evaluation and unfounded complaints by the losing parent is the most difficult task facing the professional who is attempting to help the family.

If the courts are going to be able to use a second-opinion review objectively, the judge must be assured that the review process was neutral, fair, and impartial. Otherwise, the increased use of second-opinion reviews will bring the courts back to a process in which evaluators were adversarial and caught up in the polarization of the divorce.

I believe that, if there is going to be a review, it should address the procedure, whether the report follows the data, and whether the data support the recommendations. The reviewer should refrain from making recommendations for the family because he or she did not do a thorough, objective evaluation. The second-opinion reviewer must maintain a neutral, objective stance in the review, just as the original evaluator does. I believe it is best if reviews are done by court order or stipulation of the parties, after the reviewer has a release of information signed by all relevant parties. If psychological testing was used during the evaluation, the reviewer needs to be trained and licensed in a capacity to understand and interpret the raw test data.

If the review is done in this fashion, the court can consider both the evaluator's and reviewer's findings with an eye toward determining whether the evaluator erred or whether the reviewer was biased and favoring one side. This will allow the judge to manage a process in which two experts provide different information and to determine whether to be more confident with the original evaluator or the reviewer. With such a process, the judge can make decisions that are more likely to be in the child's (or children's) best interests.

Finally, I believe it is important for the reviewer to talk with the evaluator prior to rendering an opinion of any kind. The reviewer needs to know why the evaluator used procedures and made recommendations that were made. Without talking to the evaluator, it is difficult to know why the evaluator came to his or her conclusions.

PRIVILEGE

■■ Harvey and Wanda are in the middle of a very messy divorce. Their 6-year-old daughter, Chrissy, has been seeing Dr. Smith for therapy for the year that the parents have been separated. Father originally had primary custody of Chrissy pending the evaluation. The evaluator recommended joint legal custody and primary residence with father. The court adopted this plan. Mother wants records from Dr. Smith. She never met with Dr. Smith or took an interest in the therapy, until now, 1 year after therapy began. Mother wants the records given to herself or Dr. Jones, a therapist of her choice.

■■ Dr. Smith, citing privilege, objects to providing the records. She will offer both parents a summary of her findings. She believes that the child needs to be protected from both parents and wants the records kept private for Chrissy. Dr. Smith welcomes both parents' participation in the therapy, but mother refuses and just wants the records.

◆ Does mother have a right to the records? Who holds the privilege with dueling parents? Does it matter that father agrees with Dr. Smith?

◆ Should Dr. Jones get involved? Can Chrissy continue to see Dr. Smith?

Again, the answer might be found in the local court rules or judicial guidance. When there is a significant dispute over custody, the court may hold the privilege and determine who has access to Chrissy's treatment records. Unless that is the case, however, Dr. Smith will need to provide treatment records to mother. As long as mother shares legal custody, which she does, mother has a right to the records, unless the court has made a different determination.

Because the mother and father are in a dispute over who the treating therapist should be, the court may need to make an order. Without an order of the court, each parent has a right to approve or deny treatment for Chrissy. If mother informs Dr. Smith that she cannot see Chrissy, Dr. Smith must stop seeing Chrissy even if father wants Chrissy to see her. If father informs Dr. Jones that he does not want Chrissy to see him, Dr. Jones cannot see Chrissy either.

Such therapy decisions can be made only by cooperative parents or by court order. In circumstances like this, a custody evaluator would probably recommend that one parent have decision-making authority regarding therapy for the child. Because father has primary physical custody, it is likely that he would be given such authority on behalf of Chrissy, unless the court reserves it for itself or appoints a neutral decision maker.

■■ Suppose you have completed a child custody evaluation for a family in which one of the parents is in the middle of a personal injury lawsuit. You have submitted your report to the family court. You now receive a subpoena from the personal injury attorney who wants access to your psychological test data. What do you do?

This is an area in which the guidelines provide little direction. When faced with similar requests, I have sent a letter to the attorney stating that I have no release of information to provide anything. I indicate that any report that I have done would have been done for the family court, and it would be inappropriate to provide information for any other court purposes. I have indicated that any possible report would include information on parties other than the particular person involved in the personal injury complaint. I state that, though I do not want to be difficult, I would need an authorization from all parties and from the family court to provide any information about my role or my findings regarding that parent.

When I have done that in the past, I have never heard back from the other attorney. In the event that I would be pushed further for the information, I would ask for direction from the family court judge.

■■ Suppose you are a therapist working with a child in a high-conflict divorce. The court order keeps the privilege regarding the child's treatment with the judge. Your client (the child) is experiencing significant distress and you feel he or she needs hospitalization. One parent wants you to contact the hospital, but the other parent refuses. What do you do?

In such an instance, I would immediately notify the court of my concern, stating that, in my judgment, the child needs to be immediately evaluated by the hospital. If both parents cannot agree, I would encourage the court to name someone as the parent responsible for making therapy decisions so that treatment can be authorized. I would urge the court to act quickly. I may have to resign as the therapist if one of the parents refuses to work with me any longer, but the therapeutic needs of the child must come first.

EX PARTE COMMUNICATION

■■ What should you do with a child's disclosures when you feel it would be harmful to the child if it were known that the child disclosed abuse or fear of abuse? May the evaluator have ex parte contact with either of the attorneys or the judge? What if one or both parents are in pro per (i.e., acting as their own lawyer)?

This is a complicated issue. An ex parte communication is a communication between the expert and the judge without the attorneys present or with only one attorney without the other present. Such communication is generally prohibited by local court rules or rules of evidence. In some jurisdictions, this rule even prohibits the evaluator from discussing testimony with one attorney prior to a trial, even after the report is complete. Be certain of your local court rules, your state's rules of evidence, and your understanding of the court's expectations about this issue.

With concerns about abuse, the evaluator may be obligated to file a report with the local child protection agency. When an evaluator wants to inform the court of the potential risk to the child if the child's disclosures were revealed to the parents, I recommend writing a note to the court, copied to the attorneys, stating the concern and asking the court for the opportunity to share this information privately. The judge will respond, and the evaluator can follow the judge's ruling. This procedure would be the same whether there were attorneys in the case or not.

■■ May evaluators work with attorneys to prepare for trial, even with ex parte communications? Criminal witnesses plan testimony with attorneys. What about in this case?

Again, review local court rules. Sometimes, the evaluator is prohibited from working with an attorney in preparing for testimony. In such instances, there may be preparation only during depositions or joint communication between the evaluator and both attorneys. Other jurisdictions permit a neutral evaluator to assist an attorney in such preparation after the report is submitted to the court. As above, know the rules in your local jurisdiction.

I believe it is best for custody evaluators to assist families in resolving conflicts and avoid litigation. Despite everyone's best efforts, some parents still take the dispute to trial. Once the dispute reaches that level of conflict, the evaluator is in a position to support his or her findings. If neither parent hires an expert to criticize the evaluation, I would support the prohibition on an evaluator assisting only one side in preparation for trial. However, if an expert is hired by one side to try and convince the court that the evaluator made critical mistakes or erred in the evaluation, I support the position that the neutrally appointed expert should have an opportunity to work with the other side to prepare for trial. In essence, this allows the expert to prepare for testimony supportive of his or her evaluation.

DUAL RELATIONSHIPS

■■ What about dual relationships? May the mediator become the evaluator? May we perform brief nonconfidential mediation and then become the evaluator? May the evaluator become the special master, or therapist, or drug assessor? Is it appropriate to recommend an updated evaluation, and would the original evaluator do the follow-up evaluation?

The APA (1994) guidelines state, "The psychologist avoids multiple relationships," adding "if some previous relationship exists, however insignificant, it should be raised prior to accepting the appointment and discussed in order to assure each party that objectivity will not be compromised by any prior contact." They continue,

> During the course of a child custody evaluation, a psychologist does not accept any of the involved participants in the evaluation as a therapy client. Therapeutic contact with the child or involved participants following a child custody evaluation is undertaken with caution. (http://www.apa.org/ethics/code.html)

The *Uniform Standards of Practice for Court Ordered Child Custody Evaluations* (1999) in California states, "Evaluators must exercise great care to . . . avoid dual relationships and conflicts of interest" (http://www.courtinfo.ca.gov/index.htm).

In my opinion, the definition of dual role in both of these documents is too vague. Though the APA and other professional organizations do not specifically prohibit other types of dual-role relationships, I believe that caution in *any* role switch is indicated. Certainly, having any role prior to being court appointed as the neutral evaluator would seem prohibited. This would include switching from mediator to evaluator, even if the parties all agree.

I also believe that switching to a new role after the evaluation is complete should be done with extreme caution. The California Psychological Association ethics panel has determined that an evaluator may become a special master after completing the evaluation. However, I am concerned that this could present a problem. For example, a special master never knows when he or she might be called to testify as an evaluator after switching roles. Though I would encourage each evaluator to use his or her judgment in each instance and use the APA ethics or local rules as a guide, I would discourage any evaluator from switching to a different role after the evaluation is complete.

Finally, I feel it is often best if the original evaluator does a reevaluation, when needed, unless the court or the parties determine that a new evaluator should be appointed. When the evaluator is asked to become the special master and agrees to do so, the evaluator needs to inform the parents and attorneys of the consequences of the role switch. In particular, the special master would now be unable to do a reevaluation if one becomes needed.

■■ You are the evaluator in a very troublesome case. You exercise care to the best of your ability. During the evaluation, the parents seek your decision about a vacation. You explore the issue with both parents, encouraging the mother to go along with father's request. You are evaluating her level of cooperation. Mother then agrees to father's request. However, after you complete the report, mother hires an expert stating that you acted in a dual role by encouraging mother to comply with father's request. Mother files a complaint with your licensing board, citing a dual relationship. She states that you acted as a mediator during the evaluation and believes it was unethical. What can be done when an angry parent files a licensing complaint against you?

A growing concern for mental health professionals working in family court settings is the rising number of lawsuits and licensing board complaints being made against them. Of the number of cases opened by the APA for ethics violations review during a 5-year period (1990-1994), 7% to 10% concerned a custody evaluation complaint (Glassman, 1998). Angry, litigious parents threaten the well-being of mental health experts. Experts in California are granted quasi-judicial immunity when the appointment is made under Section 730 of the Evidence Code. This protects the professional from civil litigation, but there is no protection against licensing board complaints. Currently, the most common complaint against psychologists involves their work in custody evaluations. Defending yourself against such complaints can cost thousands of dollars.

It is not uncommon for professional colleagues to criticize one another's work during a custody dispute. After all, one way to win a case is to make the other side look bad. I have learned that the most effective tool to help your colleagues is to educate the court about the difference between high-quality and poor-quality work. As mental health professionals, we must work together with attorneys to reduce the degree to which colleagues are subject to unfair criticism in the courts.

It is also important for evaluators to be cautious in their criticism of their colleagues. In most communities, there are a small number of people who work with high-conflict families of divorce. Reputations in this field are potentially fragile, and it is important to support each other as much as we can. If we see colleagues whose work we question, I believe it is helpful to have a dialogue with that colleague to understand his or her work and share our concerns. If we are reviewing another colleague's work, it is important to be professional in our criticism. As noted above, I believe it is unprofessional when a psychologist acts like a hired gun, willing to be very critical of someone else's work in an unprofessional way. We should educate judges so they can differentiate between reviewers who provide useful data to the court and hired guns who unjustly criticize the evaluator. Usually, a judge can differentiate between a hired gun and a useful expert. The more we participate with attorneys and judges in interdisciplinary meetings, the more our reputation will speak for itself.

Finally, we must educate the licensing boards. I do not think that the example cited above is a dual role. Child custody evaluators are encouraged to help parents settle their disputes. As evaluators, we often make suggestions to parents for the purpose of evaluating their ability to follow through or be conciliatory. The knowledge we gain from this may effect our recommendations. If a licensing board thinks that such a practice, in the middle of a custody evaluation, constitutes a dual role, I believe that this would be a misinterpretation of the prohibition against dual roles.

"PERFECT WORLD"

■■ Is it ethical for evaluators to make recommendations for therapy, parenting classes, drug testing, special master, and other costly services when we know that the parents cannot afford them? Is it ethical not to make such recommendations when we think they are in the children's best interests?

Most evaluators believe that recommendations should be made according to the child's best interests, even when resources are limited. If an evaluator believes that such services are required, he or she should recommend them. By informing the parents and the court of these needs, they can determine how to pay for them; look for quality, low-fee providers; or prioritize them according to the available, but limited, resources.

■■ How do various professionals, all working in different capacities with the family—for example, special master, attorney for child, therapists, and so on—work together? How do we handle it when the professionals have different opinions? What might this mean about the family's "splitting" issues (the tendency to see people as either good or bad)?

This becomes a very tricky question for some families, especially when alienation and alignment are prominent. First, appropriate releases of information must be signed by the parents or authorized by the court. I would recommend that the various professionals confer on a regular basis to discuss the family. Because alienation and alignment reflect the process of psychological splitting, it is critical that the professionals working with the family avoid splitting among themselves. When differences of opinion exist, it is helpful if the professionals engage in an open discussion to establish a consensus. When this is not possible, it might be best for the dissenting professionals to develop their own conflict-resolution process, modeling this for the family. If necessary, the professionals might confer with the judge or the evaluator.

■■ Suppose you are the mediator. If a couple develops a parenting plan in mediation that you consider unhealthy for their children, do you communicate that to the family, the attorneys, or the court?

The task of the mediator is to promote conflict resolution. In child custody matters, the mediator is an expert who is promoting the best interests of the child. Families in the court system often receive scrutiny that other families never experience. With that in mind, the mediator would probably use caution in telling parents that an agreed-upon parenting plan might be detrimental. I would suggest brainstorming with the parents about the needs of the child, suggesting possible adjustments in the parenting plan that would be more likely to meet those needs.

However, regardless of my role, if I believed that an agreed-upon parenting plan would be seriously detrimental to the children, I would share my concerns with the parents and inform them that I was going to share my concerns with their attorneys and the court. The Judicial Council of California (1999) requires both public and private mediators to inform parents and the court of any such concerns. It is the judge's decision to determine whether to allow the parents to keep that parenting plan or order some modification to it. However, I would do this only in extreme situations because I believe parents should have the right to make their own decisions for their children, unless they are being physically or emotionally abusive.

■■ Should a local county set up an independent review panel of legal and mental health professionals to review allegations of ethical misconduct that come to Family Court Services or the licensing boards? Would it have any authority, and how does it obtain such authority?

I know of no local jurisdictions that have the authority to review complaints made against evaluators and other mental health professionals working in family courts. With the growing number of complaints against such professionals, special expertise is required to evaluate the merits of a case. Typically, licensing boards do not have such expertise in child custody matters. It may be difficult for a licensing board to know about the family dynamics that result in a frivolous complaint.

In my opinion, it might be best if licensing boards grant a local review panel the task of first determining whether the complaint appears frivolous. I would recommend that prominent local evaluators, attorneys, mediators, and a judge serve on the panel. Although judges are not experts at professional ethics, they have a thorough understanding of the particular family dynamics. I would encourage licensing boards to empower the review panel to make a recommendation to either drop or pursue the complaint. Members of this review panel would need to stay abreast of the research on divorce and understand the dynamics of high-conflict families.

This plan could work only if local experts were willing to participate in such review panels and if licensing boards were to grant them such authority. Though professional associations and licensing boards are usually best equipped to hear licensing complaints, an approach for custody evaluators that encourages a review panel at the local level (and that might act like a state psychological association ethics review panel) seems ideal.

CONCLUSIONS

I would like to close this chapter, and the book, by stating that child custody evaluators and others who work with high-conflict parents need ongoing training in child development, family assessment, problems of divorce, the workings of the court, and the special ethical issues this work brings. We need to network with one another to learn as much as we can about this ever-changing field. We need better research on what makes a good-enough parent and on how to evaluate that. We need to develop new instruments that help us understand the tasks of parenting and find ways to integrate them into our comprehensive evaluations.

It is our duty as professionals to learn the dynamics of divorcing families, maintain an understanding of the needs of children and the changing laws of the states in which we work, and maintain the highest ethical and professional standards if we work in this litigious area. We need to respect parents and their children, respect the process of the courts, and continue to grow in our skills. We must always work for the betterment of children, who remain the victims of divorce, until their parents can free them from the battles of parental conflict.

If we meet these standards, maintain our professional integrity, hold to our ethical principles, and write reports that encourage solutions rather than support the win-lose atmosphere of the courts, we will help families reduce the pain of divorce for their children.

References

Abidin, R. (1990). *Parenting stress index.* Charlottesville, VA: Pediatric Psychology Press.

Achenbach, T. M. (1991). *Child behavior checklist.* Burlington: University of Vermont Psychiatry Department.

Ackerman, M. (1995). *Clinician's guide to child custody evaluations.* New York: John Wiley.

Ackerman, M., & Ackerman, M. (1996). Child custody evaluation practices: A 1996 survey of psychologists. *Family Law Quarterly, 30*(3), 565-586.

Ackerman, M., & Schoendorf, K. (1992). *The Ackerman-Schoendorf Parent Evaluation for Custody Tests (ASPECT).* Los Angeles: Western Psychological Services.

Alvarez, R. (1975). *Delivery of services for Latino community mental health* [Pamphlet]. Los Angeles: University of California, Los Angeles, Spanish Speaking Mental Health Research and Development Program.

American Professional Society on the Abuse of Children. (1995). *Practice guidelines: Use of anatomical dolls in child sexual abuse assessments.* Chicago: Author.

American Psychological Association. (1992). Ethical principles of psychologists and code of conduct. *American Psychologist, 47,* 1597-1611.

American Psychological Association. (1994). *Guidelines for child custody evaluations in divorce proceedings.* Washington, DC: Author.

American Psychological Association. (1996). *Violence and the family. Report of the APA presidential task force on violence and the family.* Washington, DC: Author.

Arbuthnot, J., & Gordon, D. (1996). Does mandatory divorce education for parents work? *Family and Conciliation Courts Review, 34*(1), 60-81.

Association of Family and Conciliation Courts. (1988). *Report of the sexual abuse allegations project.* Denver: Author.

Association of Family and Conciliation Courts. (1994). *Model standards of practice for child custody evaluations.* Madison, WI: Author.

Berkow, J. (1996). "50 ways to leave your lover" or "move-away" cases circa March 1996. *Contra Costa Lawyer, 9*(5), 18-19.

Bolen, R. (1993). Kid's turn: Helping kids cope with divorce. *Family and Conciliation Courts Review, 31*(2), 249-254.

Bray, J. (1991). Psychosocial factors affecting custodial and visitation arrangements. *Behavioral Sciences and the Law, 9,* 419-437.

Bresee, P., Steams, G., Bess, B., & Packer, L. (1986). Allegations of sexual abuse in child custody and visitation disputes: A therapeutic model. *American Journal of Orthopsychiatry, 56,* 560-568.

Bricklin, B. (1995). *The custody evaluation handbook: Research-based solutions and applications.* New York: Brunner-Mazel.

Brodsky, S. (1995). *Testifying in court: Guidelines and maxims for the expert witness.* Washington, DC: American Psychological Association.

Brody v. Kroll, 45 Cal. App. 4th 1732 (1996).

Brodzinsky, D. (1993). On the use and misuse of psychological testing in child custody evaluations. *Professional Psychology: Research and Practice, 24*(2), 213-219.

Brown, S. (1979). Clinical illustrations of sexual misuse of girls. *Child Welfare, 58,* 436-442.

Bruck, M., Ceci, S. J., & Hembrooke, H. (1998). Reliability and credibility of young children's reports. *American Psychologist, 53,* 136-149.

Cartwright, G. (1993). Expanding the parameters of parental alienation syndrome. *American Journal of Family Therapy, 21*(3), 205-215.

Casas, J. M., & Keefe, S. E. (1978). *Family and mental health in the Mexican-American community* [Pamphlet]. Los Angeles: University of California, Los Angeles, Spanish Speaking Mental Health Research Center.

Cassady v. Signorelli, D.A.R. 11147 (Cal. App. 4th 1996).

Ceci, S. J., & Bruck, M. (1995). *Jeopardy in the courtroom: A scientific analysis of children's testimony.* Washington, DC: American Psychological Association.

Clawar, S., & Rivlin, B. (1991). *Children held hostage: Dealing with programmed and brainwashed children.* Chicago: American Bar Association.

de Young, M. (1981). Incest victims and offenders: Myths and realities. *Journal of Psychosocial Nursing and Mental Health Services, 19,* 37-39.

Dunne, J., & Hedrick, M. (1994). The parental alienation syndrome: An analysis of sixteen selected cases. *Journal of Divorce & Remarriage, 21*(3-4), 21-38.

Dyer, F. (1997). Application of the Millon inventories in forensic psychology. In T. Millon (Ed.), *The Millon inventories: Clinical and personality assessment* (pp. 124-139). New York: Guilford.

Exner, J. (1974). *The Rorschach: A comprehensive system.* New York: John Wiley.

Exner, J. (1993). *The Rorschach: A comprehensive system.* (2nd edition). New York: Wiley-Interscience.

Falicov, C. (1982). Mexican families. In M. McGoldrick, J. K. Pearce, & J. Giordano (Eds.), *Ethnicity and family therapy.* New York: Guilford.

Faller, K. C. (1990). *Understanding child sexual maltreatment.* Newbury Park, CA: Sage.

Faller, K. C., & DeVoe, E. (1995). Allegations of sexual abuse in divorce. *Journal of Child Sexual Abuse, 4,* 1-25.

Finkelhor, D. (1984). *Child sexual abuse: New theory and research.* New York: Free Press.

Fla. Stat. 97-242 §61 (1997).

Fox, R. (1994). *Parent behavior checklist.* Brandon, VT: Clinical Psychology.

Gardner, R. (1987). *The parental alienation syndrome & the differentiation between fabricated & genuine child sex abuse.* Creskill, NJ: Creative Therapeutics.

Gardner, R. (1992). *The parental alienation syndrome: A guide for mental health & legal professionals.* Creskill, NJ: Creative Therapeutics.

Gardner, R. (1995). *The parental alienation syndrome: A guide for mental health & legal professionals* (2nd ed.). Creskill, NJ: Creative Therapeutics.

Garrity, C., & Baris, M. (1994). *Caught in the middle: Protecting the children of high-conflict divorce.* New York: Free Press.

Gebhard, P. H., Gagnon, J. H., Pomeroy, W. B., & Christanson, C. V. (1965). *Sex offenders.* New York: Harper & Row.

Gelinas, D. J. (1983). The persisting negative effects of incest. *Psychiatry, 46,* 312-332.

Gerard, A. (1994). *Parent-child relationship inventory.* Los Angeles: Western Psychological Services.

Gil, E., & Johnson, T. C. (1993). *Sexualized children: Assessment and treatment of sexualized children and children who molest.* Walnut Creek, CA: Launch Press.

Glassman, J. (1998). Preventing and managing board complaints: The downside risk of custody evaluation. *Professional Psychology: Research and Practice, 29,* 2.

Goldstein, J., Freud, A., & Solnit, A. (1984). *Beyond the best interests of the child.* New York: Free Press.

Groth, A. N., & Hobson, W. F. (1983). The dynamics of sexual assault. In L. B. Schlesinger & E. Revitch (Eds.), *Sexual dynamics of anti-social behavior* (pp. 159-172). Springfield, IL: Charles C Thomas.

Groth, A. N., Hobson, W. F., & Gary, T. S. (1982). The child molester: Clinical observations. In J. Conte & D. Shore (Eds.), *Social work and child sexual abuse.* New York: Haworth.

Guttmacher, M. S. (1951). *Sex offenses: The problem, causes, and prevention.* New York: Norton.

Hanks, S. (1992). Translating theory into practice: A conceptual framework for clinical assessment, differential diagnosis and multimodal treatment of maritally violent individuals, couples, and families. In E. Veino (Ed.), *Intimate violence* (pp. 157-176). Washington, DC: Hemisphere.

Hanks, S. (1998, February). Presentation at a training on domestic violence issues in family law, San Ramon, CA.

Hodges, W. F. (1986). *Interventions for children of divorce: Custody, access, and psychotherapy.* New York: Wiley-Interscience.

Hoppe, C. F., & Kenney, L. (1994, August). Characteristics of custody litigants: Data from the southern California group. In *Child custody evaluations I.* Symposium conducted at the meeting of the American Psychological Association, Los Angeles, CA.

Isman, D. (1996, Fall). Gardner's witch-hunt. *UC Davis Journal of Juvenile Law & Policy,* p. 12.

Johnston, J. (1993). Children of divorce who refuse visitation. In J. H. Bray & C. Depner (Eds.), *Nonresidential parenting: New vistas for family living* (pp. 109-135). Newbury Park, CA: Sage.

Johnston, J. (1994). High-conflict divorce. *The Future of Children, 4*(1), 165-182.

Johnston, J. (1995). Children's adjustment in sole custody compared to joint custody families and principles for custody decision making. *Family and Conciliation Courts Review, 33*(4), 415-425.

Johnston, J., & Campbell, L. (1988). *Impasses of divorce: The dynamics and resolution of family conflict.* New York: Free Press.

Johnston, J., Kline, M., & Tschann, J. (1989). Ongoing postdivorce conflict in families contesting custody: Effects on children of joint custody and frequent access. *American Journal of Orthopsychiatry, 59,* 576-592.

Johnston, J., & Roseby, V. (1997). *In the name of the child.* New York: Free Press.

Jones, D., & McGraw, J. M. (1987). Reliable and fictitious accounts of sexual abuse in children. *Journal of Interpersonal Violence, 2,* 27-45.

Judicial Council of California. (1999). *Uniform standards of practice for court ordered child custody evaluations.* San Francisco: Author.

Kalter, N. (1990). *Growing up with divorce.* New York: Free Press.

Kelly, J. (1997, May). Presentation at a training on parental alienation syndrome, Corte Madera, CA.

Kline, M., Johnston, J., & Tschann, J. (1991). The long shadow of marital conflict. *Journal of Marriage & the Family, 53,* 297-309.

Koocher, G. P., Goodman, G. S., White, C. S., Friedrich, W. N., Sivan, A. B., & Reynolds, C. R. (1995). Psychological science and the use of anatomically detailed dolls in child sexual-abuse assessments. *Psychological Bulletin, 118*(2), 199-222.

Landis, J. T. (1956). Experience of 500 children with adult sexual deviation. *Psychiatric Quarterly Supplement, 30,* 91-109.

Lee, M. (1996). *The use of the Rorschach in child custody evaluations.* Paper presented at the 2nd Child Custody Symposium of the Association of Family and Conciliation Courts, Clearwater, FL.

Lemmon, J. (1985). *Family mediation practice.* New York: Free Press.

Ludolph, P., & Viro, M. (1998). *Attachment theory and research: Implications for professionals assisting families of high conflict divorce.* Paper presented at the 35th annual conference of the Association of Family and Conciliation Courts, Washington, DC.

Lund, M. (1995). A therapist's view of parental alienation syndrome. *Family and Conciliation Courts Review, 33*(3), 308-316.

MacFarlane, K., & Waterman, J. (1986). *Sexual abuse of young children.* New York: Guilford.

Marriage of Burgess, 13 Cal. 4th 1 (1996).

Mass. Gen. Law ch. 209C, §10 (1996).

Masterson, J., & Klein, R. (1989). *Psychotherapy of the disorders of the self.* New York: Brunner-Mazel.

Mauzerall, H., Young, P., & Alsaker-Burke, D. (1997). Protecting the children of high conflict divorce. *Idaho Law Review, 33*(2), 291-332.

McKinnon, R., & Wallerstein, J. (1987). Joint custody and the preschool child. *Conciliation Courts Review, 25*(2), 39-48.

McGoldrick, M., Pearce, J. K., & Giordano, J. (1982). *Ethnicity and family therapy.* New York: Guilford.

Meierding, N. (1992). The impact of cultural and religious diversity in the divorce mediation process. *Mediation Quarterly, 9*, 4.

Meiselman, K. C. (1981). *Incest: A psychological study.* San Francisco: Jossey-Bass.

Melton, G. B., Petrila, J., Poythress, N. G., & Slobogin, C. (1997). *Psychological evaluations for the courts: A handbook for mental health professionals and lawyers.* New York: Guilford.

Miller, S. (1995). Whatever happened to the "best interest" analysis in New York relocation cases? *Pace Law Review, 15*(2), 339-389.

Millon, T. (1996). *Disorders of personality: DSM-IV and beyond.* New York: Wiley-Interscience.

Millon, T., Millon, C., & Davis, R. (1994). *Millon Clinical Multiaxial Inventory-III.* Minneapolis, MN: National Computer Systems.

Miranda, M. (1976). *Psychotherapy with the Spanish-speaking: Issues in research and service delivery* [Pamphlet]. Los Angeles: University of California, Los Angeles, Spanish Speaking Mental Health Research and Development Program.

Newmark, L., Harrell, A., & Salem, P. (1994). Domestic violence and empowerment in custody and visitation cases. *Family and Conciliation Courts Review, 33*(1), 30-62.

Ney, T. (1995). Assessing allegations in child sexual abuse. In T. Ney (Ed.), *True and false allegations of child sexual abuse: Assessment and case management* (pp. 3-20). New York: Brunner-Mazel.

Otto, R., & Collins, R. (1995). Use of the MMPI-2/MMPI-A in child custody evaluations. In Y. Ben-Porath, J. Graham, G. Hall, R. Hirschman, & M. Zaragoza (Eds.), *Forensic applications of the MMPI-2* (pp. 222-252). Thousand Oaks, CA: Sage.

Pennsylvania Coalition Against Domestic Violence. (1990). *Assessing whether batterers will kill.* Pittsburgh: Author.

Peters, J. J. (1976). Children who are victims of sexual assault and the psychology of the offender. *American Journal of Psychotherapy, 30,* 398-421.

Rader, C. M. (1977). MMPI profile types of exposers, rapists, and assaulters in a court services population. *Journal of Consulting and Clinical Psychology, 45,* 61-69.

Raiford, K., & Little, M. (1991, January). *Child custody evaluation standards: A proposal.* Report to the California state chapter of the Association of Family and Conciliation Courts, Sonoma, CA.

Roseby, V. (1995). Uses of psychological testing in a child-focused approach to child custody evaluations. *Family Law Quarterly, 29,* 97-110.

Salter, A. (1988). *Treating child sex offenders and victims.* Newbury Park, CA: Sage.

Sattler, J. M. (1998). *Clinical and forensic interviewing of children and families.* San Diego, CA: Jerome M. Sattler.

Schuman, T. (1987). *Adult and adolescent child molesters: Personality traits and perceptions of their families of origin.* Unpublished doctoral dissertation, California Graduate School of Marital and Family Therapy.

Segroi, S. (1982). *Handbook of clinical intervention in child sexual abuse.* Lexington, MA: Lexington Books.

Solomon, J., & George, C. (1996). *The effect on attachment of overnight visitation in divorced and separating families.* Paper presented at the biennial meeting of the International Conference on Infant Studies, Providence, RI.

Stahl, P. (1994a). *Conducting child custody evaluations: A comprehensive guide.* Thousand Oaks, CA: Sage.

Stahl, P. (1994b). Ethical considerations. In D. Howard & P. Bushard (Eds.), *The AFCC resource guide for parenting evaluations.* Madison, WI: Association of Family and Conciliation Courts.

Stahl, P. (1995). The use of special masters in high conflict divorce. *California Psychologist, 28*(3), 29.

Stahl, P. (1996). Second opinions: An ethical and professional process for reviewing child custody evaluations. *Family and Conciliation Courts Review, 34*(3), 386-395.

Steinmetz, M. M. (1997). *Interviewing for child sexual abuse: Strategies for balancing forensic and therapeutic factors.* Notre Dame, IN: Jalice.

Summit, R. (1983). The child sexual abuse accommodation syndrome. *Child Abuse and Neglect, 7,* 177-193.

Summit, R. C., & Kryso, J. (1978). Sexual abuse of children: A clinical spectrum. *American Journal of Orthopsychiatry, 49,* 237-251.

Swanson, D. W. (1968). Adult sexual abuse of children. *Diseases of the Nervous System, 29,* 677-683.

Talia, S. (1997, October). *To test or not to test: The use of psychological testing in child custody evaluations.* Paper presented at the meeting of the Contra Costa County (California) Bar Association, San Ramon, CA.

Taylor, A., & Sanchez, E. (1991). Out of the white box. *Family and Conciliation Courts Review, 29*(2), 114-128.

Terr, L. (1990). *Too scared to cry: Psychic trauma in childhood.* New York: Harper & Row.

Tsai, M., & Waagner, N. N. (1981). Incest and molestation: Problems of childhood sexuality. *Medical Times,* 16-22.

Turkat, I. (1994). Child visitation interference in divorce. *Clinical Psychology Review, 14*(8), 737-742.

Waldron, K., & Joanis, D. (1996). Understanding and collaboratively treating parental alienation syndrome. *American Journal of Family Law, 10*(3), 121-133.

Wallerstein, J., & Blakeslee, S. (1989). *Second chances.* Boston: Houghton Mifflin.

Wallerstein, J., & Kelly, J. (1980). *Surviving the breakup: How children and parents cope with divorce.* New York: Basic Books.

Wallerstein, J., & Tanke, T. (1996). To move or not to move: Psychological & legal considerations in the relocation of children following divorce. *Family Law Quarterly, 30*(2), 305-332.

Ward, P., & Harvey, J. C. (1993, March). Family wars: The alienation of children. *New Hampshire Bar Journal,* 30-40.

Whiteside, M. (1996). An integrative review of the literature pertinent to custody for children five years of age and younger. *AFCC California Newsletter, 7*(1), 24-25.

Wood, C. (1994, June). The parental alienation syndrome: A dangerous aura of reliability. *Loyola of Los Angeles Law Review, 27,* 1367-1415.

Zemans, F. H. (1985, May). *The issue of cultural diversity in custody disputes.* Association of Family and Conciliation Courts conference materials, Vancouver, BC.

Name Index

Abidin, R., 145
Achenbach, T. M., 146
Ackerman, M., xi, 26, 140, 144, 147, 149
Alsaker-Burke, D., 7
Alvarez, R., 155
American Professional Society on the Abuse
    of Children, 61
American Psychological Association, 121,
    139, 140, 155, 181, 182, 188
Arbuthnot, J., 16
Association of Family and Conciliation
    Courts, 45, 140, 150, 158, 181

Baris, M., 5, 7
Berkow, J., 70, 72, 73, 75, 77
Bess, B., 66
Blakeslee, S., 46
Bolen, R., 39
Bray, J., 110
Bresee, P., 66, 68
Bricklin, B., xi, 141, 144, 145
Brodsky, S., 169
Brodzinsky, D., 148, 149
Brown, S., 48
Bruck, M., 52, 54, 55, 60, 61

Campbell, L., 3, 5, 94
Cartwright, G., 5
Casas, J. M., 158, 159

Ceci, S. J., 52, 54, 60, 61
Christanson, C. V., 45
Clawar, S., 5
Collins, R., 141

de Young, M., 48
DeVoe, E., 45
Dunne, J., 5
Dyer, F., 141, 149

Exner, J., 144

Falicov, C., 161, 165
Faller, K. C., 45, 48, 59, 67
Finkelhor, D., 51
Fox, R., 146
Freud, A., 109

Gagnon, J. H., 45
Gardner, R., 1, 2, 4, 5, 7, 18
Garrity, C., 5, 7
Gary, T. S., 48
Gebhard, P. H., 45
Gelinas, D. J., 48
George, C., 110
Gerard, A., 146
Gil, E., 53

Subject Index

About the Author

Philip M. Stahl, Ph.D., is a psychologist in private practice in Dublin, California. He has been a frequent presenter at meetings of the Association of Family and Conciliation Courts (AFCC), American Psychological Association, California Psychological Association, and American Orthopsychiatric Association, and at the local interdisciplinary meetings in Contra Costa County, California. As a provider of continuing education for psychologists, LCSWs, and MFCCs in California, he has conducted trainings for child custody evaluators. He has also helped to train evaluators in Las Vegas, Baltimore, and Hartford. He is an active member of the AFCC and is the chair of AFCC's Child Custody Evaluation Committee. He is also on the board of the California chapter of AFCC.

Dr. Stahl has participated on task forces and committees that promulgated local standards for custody evaluations and helped to establish a program of low-fee custody evaluations by private practitioners. He is on a newly formed interdisciplinary committee that is drafting standards and guidelines for special masters in Contra Costa County, California. He is the author of *Conducting Child Custody Evaluations: A Comprehensive Guide* (Sage, 1994) and has written an article on ethics in AFCC's *Resource Guide for Custody Evaluators* (1995) and an article on second-opinion reviews in custody evaluations (*Family and Conciliation Courts Review,* June 1996).

About the Contributors

Theresa M. Schuman, Ph.D., is a psychologist in private practice in Concord, California. She has worked in the field of general and forensic mental health for 25 years. She specializes in various aspects of child abuse, including assessment and psychotherapy with child and adult survivors, offenders, and families. Her interests include the use of psychological testing in court evaluations, expert witness testimony, and issues of child custody and divorce. She also serves as a special master with high-conflict families of divorce.

Rosemary Vasquez, LCSW, has been a bilingual/bicultural mediator with Alameda County, California, Family Court Services since 1983. In her private practice, she has performed child custody evaluations, served as a special master, and worked with children, individuals, and families. Previously, she was the minority services coordinator for Marin County Mental Health Services, and she has been a trainer and consultant on issues of cultural awareness and diversity for corporations. She presently serves on the board of directors of the Association of Family and Conciliation Courts.